Designers' Shakespeare

Theatre Design involves everything seen on stage: not only scenery but costumes, wigs, make-up, properties, lighting, sound, even the shape and material of the stage itself. *Designers' Shakespeare* presents and analyses the work of a half-dozen leading practitioners of this specialist art. By focusing specifically on their Shakespearean work, it also offers a fresh, exciting perspective on some of the best-known drama of all time.

Shakespeare's plays offer an unusual range of opportunities to designers. As they were written for a theatre which gave no opportunity for scenic support or embellishment, designers are freed from any compulsion to imitate original practices. This has resulted in the extraordinarily diverse range of works presented in this volume, which considers among others the work of Josef Svoboda, Karl-Ernst Herrmann, Ming Cho Lee, Alison Chitty, Robert Wilson, Societas Raffaello Sanzio, Filter Theatre, Catherine Zuber, John Bury, Christopher Morley, Ralph Koltai and Sean Kenny.

Designers' Shakespeare joins *The Routledge Companion to Actors' Shakespeare* and *The Routledge Companion to Directors' Shakespeare* as essential reading for lovers of Shakespeare from theatre-goers and students to directors and theatre designers.

John Russell Brown directed plays in England, the USA and around the world. He was an Associate Director of the Royal National Theatre for fifteen years and chaired the Drama Panel of the Arts Council of Great Britain. He authored numerous works on Shakespeare and contemporary theatre, including *New Sites for Shakespeare* (Routledge, 1999) and was editor of *The Routledge Companion to Actors' Shakespeare* (2011) and *The Routledge Companion to Directors' Shakespeare* (2010).

Stephen Di Benedetto is currently Chair and Associate of Theatre in the Department of Theatre Arts at the University of Miami. He is Associate Editor (Drama) for *ASAP/Journal*, Associate Editor for *Scene*, and Treasurer of the Association for the Study of the Arts of the Present. He authored *The Provocation of the Senses in Performance* (Routledge, 2010) and *An Introduction to Theatre Design* (Routledge 2012).

Designers' Shakespeare

Edited by John Russell Brown and
Stephen Di Benedetto

LONDON AND NEW YORK

First published 2016
by Routledge
2 Park Square, Milton Park, Abingdon, Oxon OX14 4RN

and by Routledge
711 Third Avenue, New York, NY 10017

Routledge is an imprint of the Taylor & Francis Group, an informa business

© 2016 John Russell Brown and Stephen Di Benedetto for editorial material
and selection; individual chapters, the contributors

The right of the editors to be identified as the authors of the editorial
material, and of the contributors for their individual chapters, has been
asserted in accordance with sections 77 and 78 of the Copyright, Designs
and Patents Act 1988.

All rights reserved. No part of this book may be reprinted or reproduced or
utilised in any form or by any electronic, mechanical, or other means, now
known or hereafter invented, including photocopying and recording, or in any
information storage or retrieval system, without permission in writing from
the publishers.

Trademark notice: Product or corporate names may be trademarks or
registered trademarks, and are used only for identification and explanation
without intent to infringe.

British Library Cataloguing-in-Publication Data
A catalogue record for this book is available from the British Library

Library of Congress Cataloguing-in-Publication Data
Names: Brown, John Russell, editor. | Di Benedetto, Stephen, editor.
Title: Designers' Shakespeare / John Russell Brown and Stephen Di Benedetto
[editors].
Description: Milton Park, Abingdon, Oxon ; New York : Routledge, 2016. |
Includes index.
Identifiers: LCCN 2015042144| ISBN 9780415618007 (hardback) | ISBN
9781315850139 (ebook)
Subjects: LCSH: Shakespeare, William, 1564-1616—Dramatic production. |
Shakespeare, William, 1564-1616—Stage history—20th century. |
Theaters—Stage-setting and scenery—History—20th century. |
Costume—History.
Classification: LCC PR3091 .D45 2016 | DDC 792.9/5—dc23
LC record available at http://lccn.loc.gov/2015042144

ISBN: 978-0-415-61800-7 (hbk)
ISBN: 978-0-415-52507-7 (pbk)
ISBN: 978-1-315-85013-9 (ebk)

Typeset in Bembo
by FiSH Books Ltd, Enfield

In memory of John Russell Brown, teacher, scholar, theatre maker and friend.

Contents

List of figures	*ix*
List of contributors	*xii*
Acknowledgements	*xvii*
Preface	*xviii*

1 Looking at contemporary design practice and Shakespeare   1
STEPHEN DI BENEDETTO

2 "Here is my space": Josef Svoboda's Shakespearean imagination   12
CHRISTIAN M. BILLING

3 Scenography at the Royal Shakespeare Company 1963–1968: towards an empty space   38
LIAM DOONA

4 Karl-Ernst Herrmann: unfolding Shakespeare's space   54
KLAUS VAN DEN BERG

5 Ming Cho Lee   81
ARNOLD ARONSON

6 Alison Chitty – the public sketch   102
HILARY BAXTER

7 Robert Wilson   118
MARIA SHEVTSOVA

viii Contents

8 **The form of (her) intent: Catherine Zuber's costume design for Nicholas Hytner's *Twelfth Night* (1998)** 137

BRANDIN BARÓN-NUSBAUM

9 **Designing sound for Shakespeare: connecting past and present** 152

ADRIAN CURTIN

10 **BEYOND LANGUAGE: performing "true-meant design;" "that risky and dangerous negotiation between a doing... and a thing done"** 170

DORITA HANNAH

Afterword 195
Index 198

Figures

2.1	Model box showing disposition of reflective screens for *Hamlet* (Prague, 1959)	15
2.2	Composite image: model box for *A Midsummer Night's Dream* (Prague, 1963), showing (i) disposition of leaf shapes on floor and hung from flies, and (ii) the scene in performance, showing the effects of projection onto these surfaces	19
2.3	Svoboda's model box for *Romeo and Juliet* (Prague, 1963), showing the floating balcony, two side-trucking walls and an ascending/ descending front wall	21
2.4	Rendering for *King Lear* (Budapest, 1964), showing immense rectangular boxes attached to the theatre's flying system – used as both architectural mass and light sources	23
2.5	Model box for *Hamlet* (Brussels, 1965), showing disposition of mirror and apparent existence of reflected surfaces	24
2.6	Model box for *Macbeth* (Milan, 1966), showing lighting effects on back wall and juxtapositional effect against trucking and flying downstage architectonic elements	26
2.7	Model box for *Macbeth* (Prague, 1969), showing scaffold stage and three-sided set, with clustered boxes, acting as architectonic elements and projection screens (influenced by Polyecran)	28
2.8	Photograph of the Epic Theatre-inspired *Henry V* (Prague, 1971)	31
2.9	Production photograph of *Hamlet* (Prague, 1982), showing the revealed flight of monumental steps	33
4.1	*Peer Gynt*, production photograph showing the exhibition space and nineteenth-century visual consciousness, (Berlin, 1971)	61
4.2	*Shakespeare's Memory*, production photograph showing Herrmann's landscape of Elizabethan spaces (Berlin, 1976)	63
4.3	*Shakespeare's Memory*, production photograph showing Herrmann's rendering of the effects of perspective in a 3-D space (Berlin, 1976)	64
4.4	*Shakespeare's Memory*, production photograph showing the stern of an Elizabethan ship (Berlin, 1976)	64

x Figures

4.5	*As You Like It*, production photograph showing Herrmann's rendering of the Elizabethan court as an image of modernity (Berlin, 1977)	67
4.6	*As You Like It*, production photograph showing Orlando (Michael König) and Charles (Günter Nordhoff) and the audience surrounding the platform for the wrestling match (Berlin, 1977)	69
4.7	*As You Like It*, production photograph showing Herrmann's rendering of the forest of Arden as modern panorama (Berlin, 1977)	70
4.8	*As You Like It*, production photograph showing Jutta Lampe (Rosalind) near the lake (Berlin, 1977)	72
4.9	*As You Like It*, production photograph showing the arrival of a processional wagon in Arden (Berlin, 1977)	74
4.10	*Othello*, production photograph showing Othello (Gert Voss) and Iago (Ignaz Kirchner) inside the boxing ring with piano at centre (Vienna, 1990)	76
5.1	*Merchant of Venice*, sketch, New York Shakespeare Festival, 1962	85
5.2	*Richard III,* model, New York Shakespeare Festival, 1966	88
5.3	*Measure for Measure,* ½″ model, New York Shakespeare Festival, 1966	89
5.4	*Hamlet,* ½″ model, New York Shakespeare Festival, 1972	90
5.5	*Two Gentlemen of Verona*, model, New York Shakespeare Festival, 1971	91
5.6	*Much Ado About Nothing*, model, New York Shakespeare Festival, 1972	92
5.7	King Lear, model, Repertory Theatre of Lincoln Center, 1968	94
5.8	*Henry IV, Part 1*, Mark Taper Forum, 1971	95
5.9	*Romeo and Juliet*, ½″ model, Actors Theatre of Louisville, 1994	97
5.10	*Macbeth*, model, directed by Joe Dowling, Shakespeare Theatre Company, 1995	99
5.11	*King John*, directed by Michael Kahn, Shakespeare Theatre, 1999	99
6.1	Storyboard drawings for Julius Caesar by Alison Chitty, 1980	104
6.2	*Julius Caesar*, designed by Alison Chitty, Riverside Studios, 1980	106
6.3	*Antony and Cleopatra*, costume Design for Cleopatra played by Dame Judi Dench, Royal National Theatre, 1987	112
7.1	*The Winter's Tale*, Berliner Ensemble	122
7.2	*Hamlet*, Berliner Ensemble	128
7.3	*Shakespeare's Sonnets, Sonnet 148*, Berliner Ensemble	132
7.4	*Shakespeare's Sonnets, Sonnet 23 – Nozzle*, Berliner Ensemble	133
7.5	*Shakespeare's Sonnets, Sonnet 66*, Berliner Ensemble	134
7.6	*Shakespeare's Sonnets, Sonnet 66,* Berliner Ensemble	135
7.7	*Shakespeare's Sonnets, Final Scene*, Berliner Ensemble	135
8.1	*Twelfth Night*, final rendering for Antonio, Vivian Beaumont Theater, 1998	142
8.2	*Twelfth Night*, Author's sketchbook rendering of Viola as Cesario (Helen Hunt), (Act V, Scene 1), Vivian Beaumont Theater, 1998	143
8.3	*Twelfth Night*, final rendering for Olivia (Act I, Scene 5), Vivian Beaumont Theater, 1998	144

8.4	*Twelfth Night*, final rendering for Olivia (Act III), Vivian Beaumont Theater, 1998	145
8.5	*Twelfth Night*, author's sketchbook rendering of Olivia (Kyra Sedgewick) (Act III, Scene 1), Vivian Beaumont Theater, 1998	146
8.6	*Twelfth Night*, final rendering for Orsino (Act 1, Scene 1), Vivian Beaumont Theater, 1998	147
8.7	*Twelfth Night*, author's sketchbook rendering of Orsino (Paul Rudd) (Act I), Vivian Beaumont Theater, 1998	148
8.8	*Twelfth Night*, final rendering for entrance costume of Malvolio, Vivian Beaumont Theater, 1998	149
9.1	*A Midsummer Night's Dream*, Ferdy Roberts as Puck initiating the sound of the forest, Filter Theatre, Royal Exchange Theatre	162
10.1	*Giulio Cesare*, Dalmazio Masini as Marco Antonio, Societas Raffaello Sanzio	182
10.2	*Roman Tragedies*, Toneelgroep Amsterdam	184
10.3	*Roman Tragedies*, Toneelgroep Amsterdam	184
10.4	*Roman Tragedies*, Toneelgroep Amsterdam	186
10.5	*Roman Tragedies*, Toneelgroep Amsterdam	187
10.6	*Roman Tragedies*, Toneelgroep Amsterdam	187
10.7	*Roman Tragedies*, Toneelgroep Amsterdam	188
10.8	*Roman Tragedies*, Toneelgroep Amsterdam	188
10.9	*Sleep No More*, Punchdrunk and Emursive	190
10.10	*Sleep No More*, Punchdrunk and Emursive	190

Contributors

Arnold Aronson is a theatre historian and has taught at Columbia University since 1991. He is the author of *Ming Cho Lee: A Life in Design* (2014); *Looking into the Abyss: Essays on Scenography* (2005*); American Avant-Garde Theatre: A History* (2001); *Architect of Dreams: The Theatrical Vision of Joseph Urban* (2001); *American Set Design* (1985); and *The History and Theory of Environmental Scenography* (1981), as well as chapters in several anthologies. He edited *The Disappearing Stage: Reflections on the 2011 Prague Quadrennial* (2012) and *Exhibition on the Stage: Reflections on the 2007 Prague Quadrennial* (2008). In 2007 he served as the first non-Czech General Commissioner of the Prague Quadrennial of Stage Design and Theatre Architecture. Aronson served as the editor of *Theatre Design & Technology* from 1978 to 1988 and is currently co-editor of the journal *Theatre & Performance Design* (Routledge). His articles have appeared in *The Cambridge History of American Theatre, Cambridge Guide to World Theatre, The Drama Review, American Theatre, Theatre Forum, Theatre Research International*, and *The New York Times Book Review*, among many others. Aronson has chaired theatre departments at Columbia, Hunter College and the University of Michigan and has also taught at Cornell University and the University of Virginia.

Brandin Barón-Nusbaum is an Associate Professor of Design at the University of California, Santa Cruz. There, he currently teaches studio design and design history to undergraduates of the Theatre Arts and ART Departments, as well as graduate level students of the Digital Arts and New Media (DANM) MFA programme. His chapter on Mariano Fortuny's innovations in scenic and lighting design was published in *Palgrave's Theatre, Performance and Analogue Technology: Historical Interfaces and Intermedialities* (Palgrave Studies in Performance and Technology, 2013), edited by Kara Reilly. As "Brandin Barón", he has designed costumes for productions at Asolo Repertory Theatre, American Conservatory Theater, the Aurora Theatre (Berkeley), The Apollo Theater (Chicago), La Jolla Playhouse, Marin Theater Company, The Magic Theatre (San Francisco), The Public Theater/New York Shakespeare Festival, San Diego Repertory Theatre, San Jose Repertory Theatre, Shakespeare Santa Cruz, and Theatreworks (Palo

Alto). He received a MFA in Design from the University of California, San Diego, and took part in the NEA/TCG Career Development Program for Designers and Directors.

Hilary Baxter is a Designer/Visual Artist /Researcher in Theatre Design with considerable experience of costume design for theatre, film and television. She has taught BA costume and theatre design students for twenty years, as well as acting as an external examiner and PhD examiner in costume. Her costume research has been funded by the AHRC and the British Academy. She was the Principal Investigator for The Oral History of British Theatre Design, part of the National Life Stories Collection at The British Library. Her current visual practice is centred on museum collections in London including the National Gallery, Sir John Soane's museum, the National Maritime Museum and soon to include the Foundling Hospital. Baxter's professional design credits include: Theatre Design: *Dr Faustus* (RSC The Other Place 1997) *The Good Sisters* (Crucible Theatre, Sheffield 1992) *The Mistress* (World Premiere in Rome 1990 directed by Arnold Wesker); Costume Design: *School of Change* and *All Suffering soon to End* (Jennet Thomas, Matts Gallery 2012/ 10) *The Lost Vegas Series* (Riverside Studios 1998) Torquatto Tasso (Edinburgh Festival 1994); Costume Supervision: *'Red Dwarf' T.V. Series 8* (BBC2/Grant Naylor Prods 1998), *The School for Wives* (Royal National Theatre 1986). Her research interests are focused on costume, theatre design and costume in public performance, including the influences and working practices embedded in the processes currently used by professional practitioners. Her published work includes a chapter on 'Masquerade, pride, drag, love and marriage' for *Masquerade* (ed. Bell: Macmillan 2015). She has research interests in systems of attribution, peer review and judgements of quality that are applied to costume design practice. In practice-based research she seeks ways to bring together costume design inspired narratives with performers, costume construction, direction and public performance, most notably at the Banqueting House in Whitehall (Soane Banquet 2010).

Christian M. Billing is Senior Lecturer in Drama and Theatre Practice at the University of Hull. He studied Drama, Theatre Studies and Greek Civilisation at the Universities of Kent, London, Leeds and Warwick; and first joined the permanent academic staff of the School of Drama, Music and Screen at the University of Hull in 2001 – after eleven years working professionally in film and theatre, as well as teaching dramatic literature and theatre practice at various universities in the United Kingdom and the United States of America. He is author of *Masculinity, Corporality and the English Stage 1580 – 1635* (Ashgate, 2008); co-editor of *Czech Puppets in Global Contexts* (Masaryk University Press, 2015); *Rehearsing Shakespeare: Alternative Strategies in Process and Performance* (Johns Hopkins University Press, 2012) and *Czech Stage Art and Stage Design* (Masaryk University Press); and author of numerous book chapters and journal articles in relation to the theory and practice of scenography; transnational and intercultural theatre and performance; current professional rehearsal and performance practices for historically-distanced playtexts; and gender studies, particularly in relation to early modern English and ancient Athenian drama and society.

Adrian Curtin is a Lecturer in the Drama Department at the University of Exeter. He is the author of *Avant-Garde Theatre Sound: Staging Sonic Modernity* (New York: Palgrave Macmillan, 2014). He has written journal articles and book chapters on theatre sound, musical performance, and modernism. He is a recipient of a Presidential Fellowship from Northwestern University and the 2010 winner of the New Scholar's Prize, awarded by the International Federation of Theatre Research.

Stephen Di Benedetto is currently the Chairman of the Department of Theatre Arts and an Associate Professor of Theatre History at the University of Miami. Additionally, he is the Treasurer of the Association of the Study of Arts in the Present (ASAP), an Associate Editor of *Scene (Intellect)*, an *Associate Editor of ASAP/Journal* (Johns Hopkins University Press), and Series Editor with Joslin McKinney and Scott Palmer of *Performance and Design* for Bloomsbury Methuen. Di Benedetto's books include *The Provocation of the Senses in Contemporary Theatre* (Routledge, 2010) and *An Introduction to Theatre Design* (Routledge, 2012). Dr Di Benedetto has held teaching positions at the University of Houston; the Drama Studies Centre, University College Dublin, National University of Ireland; and DePaul University. Among his other professional affiliations he was a convener of the Scenography Working Group of the International Federation for Theatre Research, an artist board member of DiverseWorks Art House in Houston, a theatre critic for *Houston Free Press* and *Irish Theatre Magazine*. He has worked as a dramaturg in such places as Infernal Bridegroom Productions and the Connecticut Repertory Theatre, and was formerly Book Review Editor (North America), for *Theatre Research International*.

Liam Doona is a freelance theatre designer and Head of the Department of Design and Visual Arts at Dun Laoghaire Institute of Art, Design and Technology. Graduating from Nottingham Trent University in 1986 he worked extensively in the UK both as a practising designer and academic before relocating to Ireland in 2006 to take up the post of Head of Art and Design at IADT. At IADT he co-authored Ireland's first suite of honours degrees in design for stage and screen, incorporating production design, make-up design and costume design. He is an Expert Panellist (Art, Design and Drama) for the Higher Education Training and Awards Council (HETAC Ireland) and a highly experienced external examiner, currently at University of the Arts Bournemouth in the UK and AVA (The Academy of Visual Arts), Ljubjlana, Slovenia. Doona was a founding member of the Association of Courses in Theatre Design and LEAD (Learning /Education/Art/Design). Alongside his educational work he has maintained a practice as a set and costume designer which enabled him to work for a number of leading touring theatre companies and theatres in Britain and Ireland. His work was included in the Collaborators' Exhibition at the Victoria and Albert Museum London. He writes for *The Blue Pages – The Journal of the Society of British Theatre Designers*, and his work can be seen in "2D 3D" (2002) and "Collaborators"(2007), the quadrennial reviews of British stage design published by SBTD. His Study of American designer Jo Mielziner is included In *A Reader in Scenography* (Routledge)

Dorita Hannah is a performance designer and theatre architect and is Research Professor of Interdisciplinary Architecture, Art and Design at the University of Tasmania (Australia) and Adjunct Professor of Stage and Space at Aalto University (Finland). Her creative work, teaching and research focus on the intersection between performance and space. She publishes on practices that negotiate the visual, spatial and performing arts, while collaborating with artists, designers and cultural organizations to co-conceive, design and direct events, installations, exhibits, objects and constructed environments. Hannah also focuses on postgraduate research centred on public space, performance practices and socio-political design, principally through the concept of "event-space": demonstrating that the built environment housing an event is itself an event and an integral driver of experience. Dr Hannah is an active contributor to the Prague Quadrennial (PQ) and World Stage Design (WSD), while sitting on several editorial and executive boards; including PSi (Performance Studies inter-national), OISTAT (International Organization of Scenographers, Theatre Architects & Technicians) and Performance Paradigm. Her publications include *Performance Design, An Anthology on Trans-disciplinary Design Performativity*, as well as the guest editorship of journals with themed issues on performance/archi-tecture and sceno–Architecture. Dr Hannah has gained international awards for her design and research, including gold and silver for costume and set design at WSD 2009. She is currently Theory Curator for PQ 2015 and Research Curator for WSD 2017, and is completing a book for publication by Routledge Press titled *Event-Space: Theatre Architecture and the Historical Avant-Garde.*

Maria Shevtsova holds the Chair in the Department of Theatre and Performance at Goldsmiths, University of London, having previously held chairs at the University of Lancaster (Founding Chair of Theatre Studies) and the University of Connecticut. She is Dr honoris causa of the University of Craiova. Shevtsova is the author of more than 130 articles and chapters in collected volumes, including *Directors' Shakespeare* (2008) and *Actors' Shakespeare* (2011), both edited by John Russell Brown. Her books include *Dodin and The Maly Drama Theatre: Process to Performance* (2004), *Fifty Key Theatre Directors* (2005, co-ed), *Jean Genet: Performance and Politics* (2006, co-ed), *Robert Wilson* (2007), *Directors/Directing: Conversations on Theatre* (2009, co-authored) *Sociology of Theatre and Performance* (2009), which assembles three decades of her pioneering work in a field she has established, and *The Cambridge Introduction to Theatre Directing* (2013, co-authored). Her publications have been translated into eleven languages, most recently Robert Wilson into *Mandarin* (2013), *Dodin and the Maly Drama Theatre into Russian* (2014), and *The Cambridge Introduction to Theatre Directing* into Serbian (2016). Since 2002, she has been co-editor of *New Theatre Quarterly* and is part of the editorial team of *Critical Stages*, the online journal of the International Association of Theatre Critics. She in on the editorial boards of various international journals, notably *Stanislavski Studies*. She has been a Guest Professor at a number of major institutions in Europe, among them the St Petersburg State Academy of Theatre Arts and the Grotowski Institute in Wroclaw, and was a Fellow of the International Research Centre 'Interweaving Performance Cultures' at the Freie Universität, Berlin in 2012 and 2013. Shevtsova is programme consultant for the Craiova International Shakespeare Festival and the Gyula Shakespeare Festival in Hungary.

Klaus van den Berg is an independent scholar. His most recent work examines scenography in performance, the role of spectacle in our society, the interlacing of urban landscapes and performance venues, and the image as a central issue in critical theory. He is currently working on a book project entitled *Image Space: Walter Benjamin and Cultural Performance* that rereads philosopher and cultural critic Walter Benjamin as a performance theorist. His essays have been included in books on Strindberg, Wagner, Tabori, Libeskind, Benjamin, Gotscheff, Thalheimer, and Frisch and his essays have been published in *Theatre Research International*, *Theatre Survey*, *TheatreForum*, *Contemporary Theatre Review*, *Theatre Journal*, *Brecht Yearbook*, *Monatshefte*, and *Bühnentechnische Rundschau*. He is also a professional dramaturg specializing in translations and stage adaptations, His most recent work, a translation and adaptation of Schiller's eighteenth-century classic *The Robbers*, was produced professionally at the Asolo Conservatory in Sarasota in February 2012.

Acknowledgements

This collection was originally proposed by John Russell Brown as the logical extension of his collections charting how actors and directors make sense of Shakespeare's plays. John's prodding got the ball rolling and his guidance made it possible to convince such fine scholars to contribute. From the time he started the process to now he retired and recently passed away. Throughout the whole process his kindness and gentle urging kept the project alive. I need to thank each of the authors with in this piece for their patience over the years as I tended to the material. They have been waiting a long time to share their work with the public. Thank you Talia Rogers, Ben Piggott, Harriet Affleck and Kate Edwards for all the work on your end. Without assistance from Somar Van Lahn, who sorted out correspondence, permissions and other details I would not have ever finished this book. Professor Brown's insights and scholarship are missed.

Preface

Years ago John Russell Brown approached me about creating a collection that would carry on his sequence of Routledge Companion to Shakespeare volumes highlighting the work of theatre makers. Brown's love of Shakespeare and the English Renaissance was inescapable, revealing itself in his teaching, publishing and independent directing projects. He taught that alongside the poetry and beauty of the plots the plays were dramatic texts meant to be spoken and embodied, revealing their multi-faceted complexity in performance. To ignore the spoken qualities of the words and the ever shifting visual pictures of the plays only reveals a small fraction of why Shakespeare is the greatest English dramatist. To that end he sought to find ways to instigate discussion of the plays in performance by showing literary critics the ways in which theatre makers interpret, understand, and bring to life each of the plays. His publishing merging two fields of inquiry helped theatre makers see Shakespearean texts not only as platforms for monumental acting, but also as vessels for making tangible subtle political and social readings of the propensity of humankind to find meaning in action. He hoped the volume would work similarly to the Actors' Shakespeare and Directors' Shakespeare showing what master artists make with Shakespeare's texts. While this book transformed over time to a collection showcasing tactics of design and tools of design as seen through contemporary Shakespearean practice Brown's central aim of showing what designers see and make manifest in Shakespeare as a tool for seeing Shakespearean performance anew is retained.

Designers work collaboratively with other designers and with directors to bring a play to life. It is difficult to speak of a single designer's vision of a production as the visual world is a manifestation of negotiated choices in service to the immediate and practical need to bring the play to life by the opening night. Each of the contributing authors has given focus to the work of a particular designer on a particular production never forgetting the co-creators who worked to conceive, create and fine-tune the elements of design to work with the vision of a director and the interpretations of the actors. Design is not a linguistic form governed by description. It is a visual expression guided by the masterful use of the elements and principles of design to create practical environments and visual signifiers that give context to the actions and characterizations being carried out on stage. At once aesthetically intriguing and hugely utilitarian, these design make visible that which exists beyond the words of the dramatist, beyond the culture of the play in a realm where the fictional becomes manifest in the present for a live audience.

While some remember and can recite Shakespeare's verses, my memory is filled with images from productions that I had the pleasure to experience. Whether it is the sound of Gloucester's eye popping as it hit the wall of the set, the bloody hand-kerchief raised above Othello's head, or Mark Anthony's funeral oration intoned by an actor with a tracheotomy, it is the rich world created by designers in tandem with an actor that hovers in my mind like ghosts. I'm in love with these sounds and images that I carry with me. I hope that the following chapters give you a glimpse into how designers work to create these images and reveal what the visual can teach us about Shakespeare.

Stephen Di Benedetto, Coral Gables

Chapter 1

Looking at contemporary design practice and Shakespeare

Stephen Di Benedetto

A discussion of Shakespeare and design is productive to foreground methods of contemporary design practice used to construct the worlds of widely known dramatic texts. From the perspective theatre of scholars who study Shakespeare in performance, contemporary design practice provides sufficiently different insights from the study of contemporary acting or directing practice. In comparison with the rest of the production team designers are relatively free from the tyranny of historical production practices. That English Renaissance practices did not rely on visual spectacle has allowed practitioners to experiment with the visual aspects of performance as new technologies were introduced and tastes changed. Shakespeare has offered designers a fertile ground to experiment with representational styles. Historically, at the start of the twentieth century Adolphe Appia and Edward Gordon Craig broke the hold of realist staging practices when they began to construct abstract, evocative settings and designers were freed to play with means of creating the visual worlds of the characters in each of the plays. This volume explores the process of design practice as seen through Shakespearean staging. By looking at what designers see in Shakespeare and what they make of the worlds he imagines we can begin to see how designers make manifest interpretations of plays in distinctive ways different from their peer directors and actors. This look askance of how Shakespeare's plays are made to mean can offer novel insight into those plays.

There have only been a few studies that look at Shakespeare through the lens of design practice. The most systematic is Denis Kennedy's seminal *Looking at Shakespeare: A Visual History of Twentieth-Century Performance,* which traces the historical lineage of production styles from the turn of the twentieth century and is the key text for understanding the various historical approaches to designers towards the staging of Shakespearean text.[1] As taste and convention may dictate the ways in which we expect to view Shakespeare, designers have been instrumental in shifting audience perception of what the potentials are for Shakespearean performance. Without watershed productions such as Peter Brook's *Midsummer Night's Dream* we might still be expecting to see period costumes and Renaissance frippery as the visual language of the text. Kennedy's text places design practice within hegemonic theatrical history connecting changing aesthetics to directorial and acting styles. His text is organized from the perspective of the influences of nineteenth-century design practice upon twentieth-century design practice followed by an examination of each of the seminal design theories, which influenced major practices in the twentieth century. He looked at the scenographic revolution, the styles of politics, the heavily decorated realistic school later moving to the styles that led to increasing abstraction. This analysis of design practice foregrounds the ways in which design practice mirrors developments in acting, directing and dramaturgy.

While *Designers' Shakespeare* follows in the footsteps of John Russell Brown's edited collections of the *Routledge Companion to Directors' Shakespeare* and the *Routledge Companion to Actors' Shakespeare*, its central focus is on the ways that designers work to create the visual elements of production as a means to support or embellish a directorial concept.[2] The aims of this volume are twofold: on the one hand, an examination of Shakespeare and design allows accessibility for a large readership into issues and concepts of designers' work; and on the other, it reveals how a visual sensibility can yield richer readings of the seminal work of Shakespeare. The traditions of design guide the aesthetics and practice of interpreting Shakespeare's plays in performance as much as the conceptions of directors. Design practice is both collaborative in nature and choices executed in performance are a complex negotiation between the differing aesthetics and styles of a team of artists working in tandem with a director to realize an interpretation of a play for a particular time and place. Trying to give a taste of the differing aesthetics that shape the production elements, the subjects chosen are from designers or teams of designers who have had a particular influence on Shakespearian aesthetics in a variety of cultural traditions. Each is indicative of the strategies employed at revealing readings or interpretations of the scripts as conceived by the director or the design team.

A comprehensive examination of seminal productions where design is central from the late nineteenth century to today is prohibitively long. The design of this volume is to share images associated with different productions to show how Shakespeare is revealed through production elements. To be able to share these illustrations we chose to limit the scope of the volume allowing for a taste of how designers can offer alternative readings of Shakespearian texts, how their aesthetic can tease out environmental and contextual elements and can offer insight in to the visual and spatial organization of the world depicted within each of the plays. The designer's manner of interpretation and articulation is different from that of a writer, actor or director. Visual principles of design and composition evoke in a manner akin to poetry and thereby offer poetic analysis of the texts. The resulting designs assist the text and the bodies of the actors on the stage to bring to life the play for audiences to understand and experience the world of the plays. Visual and spatial analyses of Shakespeare's texts yield useful anchors to support traditional literary and historiographic studies. These frameworks situated within the practical considerations of stagecraft allow us to distill abstract themes into pragmatic representation used to bolster performance interpretations and assist in real-time communication of moment-to-moment transformations of meaning.

Shakespeare's words are spoken by bodies in space—more than naked corporeal entities or voices emerging in the dark space of our imaginations they are located in a fictive space in time in concurrence with the audience's shared experience of the duration of the performance. As such, audiences use their senses to make sense of what they see and hear within the confines of the theatre. But as with other fashions of interpretation the analysis of the mechanics and traditions of stagecraft enables us to say new things with the plays of Shakespeare. The following essays describe the practices of a few designers whose work has been influential in the articulation of a Shakespearean visual aesthetic. They represent a plurality of voices of set, costumes, lighting, and sound designers. Their voices are not created in isolation but as part of a creative team whose opinions and aesthetics influence each other's choices in the building of a performance, in the creation of a stage image. In concert with a director these creative artists craft a world for these characters to inhabit which provides audiences with the necessary signifiers to understand and consider the Shakespearean text. Their work shapes our experience of Shakespeare and subtly guides us through an interpretive journey, visually and sensuously offering our understanding of the shared experience unfolding in front of us.

Just as an editor's choice of a semi-colon or word with an edition of a play subtly affect Shakespeare's verse and the arguments of the play, a designer's palette or choice of texture creates subtle nuances in the potential meanings generated during performance. Design work is not fixed. A single image does not evoke an entire play. Pictures unfold and change over the course of a play and only in performance is an image whole, pregnant with potential meaning. It is not as a single-image moment capturing action but a flow. How that flow is constructed and executed is the artist's doing and can provide insights in to what designers see in Shakespeare, what they feel is important to make clear to audiences and what is important to add detail to make it intelligible. Their choices have something to show us as literary or performance analysis.

Theatre Design involves everything seen on stage, more than scenery but also costumes, wigs, makeup, furniture, properties, the shape and material of the stage itself, lighting and sound. "Scenography" or "Performance Design" would be used in the title were they in more general use beyond specialists within theatre and did not include the actors' on-stage contribution and every directorial decision. Stage design is much about collaboration and so preliminary sketches are sometimes reproduced as well as finished renderings to convey the influence of the other members of the design team and director. Theatre design is a more comprehensive term than "set design" and is used in this book as appropriate to each designer studied and each author's particular interests and experience. Traditions outside of mainstream theatres are incorporated thereby representing the latest trends in design practice. Examples include a few scenographers who also work as directors and tend, responsibly and/or imaginatively, to re-write Shakespeare.

Contemporary visions of Shakespeare

This volume moves through time from the early twentieth-century to twenty-first-century practices. Chapters present case studies on single designers and also on teams of designers situated in a single company or at a single theatre. Rooted in practices that challenge the prevailing trends that were current in the late nineteenth century the designers here experiment with styles influenced by avant-garde experiments with space and place, which value imagination and abstraction over realistic or emblematic depiction. Opening the volume is Christian M. Billing's "'Here is My Space': Josef Svoboda's Shakespearean Imagination", which places Svoboda's practice within the context of his total oeuvre and influence as designer. He explores the ways in which Svoboda's aesthetic shaped performance and influenced alternative readings of various Shakespearean productions. Here the designer's vision almost controls the visual and performative possibilities of the Shakespearean text. The visual language opens up multiple layers revealing a meta-discourse and commentary on the action of the play. He situates Svoboda's aesthetic against the background of the social and cultural upheavals in Czechoslovakian culture of the time and traces his practice back to Craig. Svoboda, coming from an architectural background conceived of space and later the use of screens as a means to create an environment to house the action of the Shakespearean plays performed. His experimental techniques were instrumental in opening up the visual metaphors seen in the works. He unpacks major stepping-stones through significant Shakespearean productions that are emblematic of Svoboda's dynamic architectonic designs. Through Svoboda's interpretations of Shakespeare's plays we learn about recurring approaches the designer employs in his construction of stage space.

Tracing the lineage of Svoboda's influence, the volume moves to England with a look at how Peter Brook worked with a range of designers preoccupied with finding appropriate techniques to foreground the political messages that influenced his work at the RSC in the 1960s. Liam Doona's "Scenography at The Royal Shakespeare Company 1963–1968; Towards an Empty Space" looks at Shakespeare design practice from the larger prospective of the collaborations at a particular influential theatre over a period of time with different directors and designers. This allows us to see the ways in which a particular influential theatre made its mark on the visual languages of presentation with the UK and the legacy of the designer's influence on facilitating interesting readings of Shakespearean texts. Central to the discussion is the network of collaboration that parses out meaning and interpretation as choices are made to build the visual world of a production. In performance interpretation is negotiated through the articulation of choice— what each choice does to the ways in which action is read and understood from the spectators within a particular location and culture amidst a unique political climate. Doona's discussion of the aesthetics brought by designers to the visions of directors reveals the notion of political and social reading of Shakespearean performance. Productions are viewed through the lens of the aspects brought out of the texts as influenced

Looking at contemporary design practice 5

by the period politics of its creators and its audiences. What is seen of Shakespeare is seen through the lens of its contemporaneous audiences. Likewise the lineage and networks are shown to be transmitted through teams of collaborators and legacies of teachers sharing with subsequent generations the modes and styles of expression that take on a signature style of a particular time and place. This lens helps understand the networks of theatre makers and the ways in which differing collaborative teams affect the ways in which meaning is drawn from Shakespeare's texts.

Moving to Germany Klaus Vandenberg's "Karl-Ernst Herrmann: Unfolding Shakespeare's Space" places the Herrmann within the perspective of post-war culture. He defines Herrmann's contribution to Shakespeare design in Germany as one grounded in an image space that leaves open an unfolding space enabling contemporary interpretations of the classic texts. Using Walter Benjamin's notion of an 'image space' as a theoretical lens Vandenberg analyses Herrmann's design aesthetic as a material manifestation of the philosopher's ideas. He explains "His idea was to eliminate the theatre of illusion and replace it with a stage that performed as a visual field in which location and image lay open similar to a display case in which actors shared deliberate gestures." For example, he uses *As You Like It* to demonstrate how image space carries with it the potential for deep analysis. Herrmann's view of the forest of Arden as something darker and more nefarious than traditional depictions had been up to that point is revealed in his conception of the spatial organization of the setting. Each spatial element references the past as well as reframes the present in the space. The designer's hand provides tools with which the directors and actors can exploit the space in their own interpretations and choices. Vandenberg's analysis serves both to discuss design as a mode of philosophical and aesthetic commentary as well as a practical mechanism for creating stage space where the actions and settings are organized in a way to make clear the progression of locations. The arrangement and organization of the settings become an analytical mechanism for understanding the social and political worlds of Shakespeare's plays.

Next, the discussion shifts to North America and an examination of contemporary American strategies for staging Shakespeare in non-traditional spaces. Arnold Aronson's contribution on 'Ming Cho Lee' places Lee's work in the context of the traditions he challenged that were in place in the United States from the mid-eighteenth century. Aronson shows how Lee's work is a deliberate response to the prevalent scenographic trends of the early twentieth century such as those of Robert Edmond Jones and Orson Welles. He shows Lee's departure from these illusionistic traditions freed the stage space from naturalistic considerations and instead favored an open staging that fits more holistically with outdoor spaces and spaces influenced by American attempts to rediscover theatre architecture based on reconstructions of the Globe Theatre. Aronson, whose seminal work on Lee examines his entire career to date, charts here Lee's development and style specifically through Shakespeare. He shows how Lee approached the open theatre space combined with the abstraction of a Brechtian inspired theatricality, which moved

6   Stephen Di Benedetto

productions that he was involved in away from representation to a spare abstraction that aids spectators in their analysis of the action and the organization and utility of the stage space. With each production we see how this aesthetic grew and how he became more adept at providing an open space to support directorial metaphors for production. Lee's influence goes beyond his physical designs but also his position like many of the designers featured in this volume as a teacher at the preeminent design school in the country.

Likewise Alison Chitty's work has had a similar impact in the United Kingdom as Ming Cho Lee's has in the United States, both as a designer and as a teacher. Hilary Baxter, a practicing costume designer, similarly analyses Chitty's work from a pragmatic perspective focusing on the design process and the ways in which choices affect audience analysis. Her chapter "Alison Chitty – The Public Sketch" charts the ways in which Chitty's Shakespearean productions are emblematic of her manner of theatre production and her insights of the ways in which design provides concrete interpretation of dramatic action. Her methods of storyboarding are integral to her for working out and interpreting dramatic actions. By drawing the characters within their physical environment she creates a tool for seeing the effect of design choices on an audiences' perception of the characters and she is able to understand Shakespeare's text from a material perspective that reveals the social, political and personal embodiment of the presented characters and actions. This allows her to contemplate the transmission of a director's vision. Does a set help or hinder action? Do costumes reveal mood and underlying personal or political status? Do these moods color our perceptions of the words and action performed within the other aspects of performance? For example, Baxter discusses the way that color choices or rakes of stage affect the audience's perception of the action. Through the use of interview extracts she unpacks the ways that designers use practice to understand the works that they are presenting, and the effectiveness of the design principles and practices to make clear a director's view of the actions. Whether it is a color choice of a setting or the cut of cloth used to shape the silhouette of the character the choices reveal Shakespeare. Design choices also make sense of the Renaissance texts for a contemporary audience. While the archaic language is accessible to language the design elements help make the language, the action, the emotions intelligible to the audience and give them a means to enter into the world and ideas presented in the action of the play. Chitty crafts how the audience looks at Shakespeare and also looks at the world of each play. She sets a frame of vision. In contrast to the elaborate language her designs are economical and spare leaving room for the audience to see the other elaborate modes performance. The different performances described take place in different locations and show the role of design in crafting reception of the piece in different environments. There is not a ubiquitous style or approach because each location is unique and demands different means to communicate. Unlike the action and words in a textual analysis, the space, bodies, materials all shift an audience's experience and understanding of the production.

An international figure such as Robert Wilson has had a broad impact across traditions and as such continues to influence contemporary design aesthetics. Maria

Shevtsova's "Robert Wilson" explores the blurred line where Wilson creates as a designer and a director simultaneously. As a scenographer Wilson is an auteur collaborating with set, costume and sound designers to create the living design of his works. He commonly oversees a team of designers collaborating together to build his interpretations. Shevstova places his aesthetics within the influencers of his technique. While minimalist in look, she connects his work to the Bauhaus and constructivism of the 1930s both in concept and in its blurring of the line of director/designer supremacy. Shevstova then traces those influences alongside his American influences of the late 1960s in a black mountain college with John Cage, Merce Cunningham and Robert Rauschenberg. She approaches his work from the concept of Wilson as an architect, who starts the conception of a production from its architecture and sees his aesthetic as a hybrid mixed media designer. Wilson treats Shakespeare as he does all other writers, starting instead from a spatial interpretation rather than verbal approach. His storyboarding, or visual book approach, allows him to begin with the spatial form moving audiences through experiences of the plays. Tracing his process from storyboard, to collaboration and then on to staging she then concentrates her discussion on his use of light as an articulation of the emotions of the production. Lighting is at once the mechanism for organizing the architectonic space as well as the emotional underpinning of the event. Light propels the action forward. Through close reading of his visual dramaturgy she analyses the subtle influences of a designer's aesthetic upon a director's practice. Design is "not bound by semantic meaning" and design is an oblique mirror into the core of a play's essence not constrained by words and action. Wilson's approach to visual dramaturgy has influenced a generation of theatre makers to create scenographically driven narratives through the principles and elements of composition within design.

The next contribution considers a designer who works in regional American theatre, and is typical of contemporaneous practice of her peers, who relies heavily on storyboarding as a means of exploring potential visual interpretations of play texts. Brandin Barón-Nusbaum, from the perspective of a working costume designer, traces the production practices of noted American designer Catherine Zuber. "The Form of (her) Intent: Catherine Zuber's Costume Design for Nicholas Hytner's *Twelfth Night* (1998)" explores questions of the manner in which designers collaborate with directors to develop the visual context of performance and reveals the ways that designers strip down images to create visual analogies to the unseen social and political metaphors that underpin the action of the play and contextualizes the performances of the actors. Zuber's collaborative process reveals the ways in which a designer's vision can challenge a director's vision and add layers and complexity to his or her interpretation of the Shakespearean text. Using a case study he describes the ways in which a design shapes a reading of a text. Barón-Nusbaum shows how Shakespeare's texts are littered with clothing and other visual metaphors and this linguistic motif provides an armature for a costume designer to build upon when crafting the visual language of the costumes within the play. By starting here the designer begins to see how to communicate and resonate with the explicitly defined visual characteristics that were used as a means to build the action and characterization within the play.

Barón approaches the topic of designers working in Shakespeare from the perspective of fashion, art and clothing; How does the role of costume, dress and adornment play out in everyday life and then find meaning in the context of designed aesthetic experience. This lens of the clothing helps us see Shakespeare as a repository of material imagery, a master of using physical metaphors of what we know through everyday living that can be accessed as a means of understanding the action and characters placed in motion by Shakespeare's writing. Designers seek simplicity cutting away visual embellishments and material embellishments to allow space for the words, crafted through embellishment and advocating an economy of image that when read, felt and experienced become larger than the semantics of their grammar. Much of the twentieth century has been a reaction against the cluttered Victorian verisimilitude and period costumes in favor a spare, pared down version of the word where Shakespeare's language can be heard amongst an abstracted repetition of a visual metaphor of the sinister contexts of the court. Rather than following an eighteenth- or nineteenth-century vision of the opulence of court and the glamor of its inhabitants, designers make use of visual notation as a means of revealing the political and social forces that underpin the action of the drama. By making manifest these contact points, spectators are given access to the articulation of that which is behind the words and the characters. Audiences are allowed to see the unseen forces, the moods and the morality of what is happening. They are being shown behind the layer of artifice. By using visual representation we are given access behind the curtain of the propaganda. Thus the settings and costumes can become political or social commentary. The action can be read in relation to contemporary notions of social order and corruption. The plays can become metaphors for our everyday experiences that may be behind the old-fashioned politics of the court.

From here the book shifts focus to more collaborative and free adaptations of Shakespeare's work with two case studies created from the perspective of performance design. Performance design is a mode of production where the designers take a more active and central role in conceiving the interpalation and composition of the production. Here the line between director, scenographer and craftsman is at its most blurred. By looking at these contemporary practices we are able to see how digital sound and other technologies are opening up the design potentials of Shakespearean performance. Focus is drawn away from the centrality of words and pushed to aural abstraction and visually as a means of communicating the complexities of the Shakespeare's plays. Elizabethan language is transliterated into twenty-first-century modes of communication. While textual scholars will no doubt question the veracity of such claims, performance practice has always necessitated adaptation and innovation as a means of seeking the most effective and efficient modes of creating live exchanges bringing to life interpretations of plays for contemporary audiences. Novel approaches can often generate insight into well-traversed interpretations.

Looking at contemporary design practice 9

Any discussion of contemporary design practice necessitates a discussion of the role of sound in the creation of the world of any play. Alongside set, costume and lighting designers are now sound and projection designers who work with the latest technologies experimenting with approaches to harness the capabilities of the media to create richer environments for the actors to inhabit. Adrian Curtin's "Designing Sound for Shakespeare: connecting past and present" brings the aural world separate from the actor's words to the forefront. He explores the role of sound as used historically and then posits that with the advent of technology in the 1980s sound has become more essential in the design of theatre. Audiences have begun to expect designed soundscapes underscoring the action of plays much in the way that cinema and television use underscoring on a regular basis. An increasingly sophisticated audience requires multiple tracks of stimulation in their experience even of classics. While he does explore the historical use and response to sound design, he explores how Filter Theatre experiments with what sound can reveal in performance when applied to Shakespearean production. Curtin makes use of anthropological studies of sound culture as a means to consider the role of sound in performance. These recent trends in sound studies try to recapture what the experience of sound would have been like in the context of the experience of living at other times. By trying to model what events sounded like and how they took on meaning as a result of the types of aural experiences those living in past centuries had in everyday life, these anthropologists are trying to approximate how experience may have been interpreted in those conditions. By applying this lens we can begin to see how we can craft experience to be imbued with particular meanings. To understand this process we can begin to see the multiple layers that sound adds to our interpretation of Shakespeare in performance. Furthermore it can reveal how Shakespearean performance exploits aurality as a further means of helping audiences grasp the content and potential meanings of the play. Curtin unpacks the techniques sound designers use to respond and interpret aural worlds in ways that make sense to the ways in which the theatre has traditionally incorporated sound within live practice. While discussing new technologies and techniques it becomes apparent the subtle interpretations that designers are able to tease out with the additional attention to the sonic worlds suggested by the plays. Like light, sound is able to evoke emotional responses through an ever-present soundscape that propels the action. The potentials of sound to add layers of meaning to the text enrich the designed environment.

What happens when Shakespeare's dramaturgy is considered from the perspective of the designed environment before language and character is considered? Scholar and Performance Designer Dorita Hannah challenges the text-centric adherence to Shakespearean dramaturgy and instead challenges readers to consider Shakespearean performance from a position where text is but one of the modes of evoking the production. In "BEYOND LANGUAGE: performing "true-meant design ..." "... that risky and dangerous negotiation between a doing ... and a thing done" she uses a range of internationally known performance of Shakespeare from companies whose work defies easy categorization in terms of hierarchy of production practice. Most of the companies that she describes are driven by visual or visceral dramaturgy. These eclectic examples with sprawling influence across the globe reimagine Shakespearean worlds as experiences. Challenging the notion that Shakespearean performance needs to be rooted in language Hannah explores the notion of reimagining Shakespeare from a pre-linguistic perspective. She argues that theatre is an experience and the role of performance design is to craft experiences of productions. It is about making designs visceral. She uses the work of Societas Rafeallo Sanzio, Punch Drunk, Nigel Charmuck, Robert Wilson, *Periférico De Objectos* and other companies and practitioners who shatter the linguistic narratives in favor of visual representations that use crafted experiences driven by design practice to communicate to audiences.

Hannah works from the prospective of performance design where the traditional hierarchies of theatre production are broken down. As she says, "Design liberated from the burden of Shakespearean language comes a sensory script for critiquing our contemporary times." By breaking down the hierarchies and recognizing the multiple strands of communication used to create a performance, the means of bringing an experience to life is highlighted. She asks us to free ourselves from the dominance of written language and to see language as a part of the tapestry of performance embodied in actors moving through designed environments, clothed and lit as a means to bring to life that which is beyond the words themselves. Performance design makes material the social, political, and the emotional as played out through time. The words are no more or less important than the bodies performing actions and speaking the poetry. Beyond language communication across cultures becomes possible and allows us to view the classic text from multiple perspectives revealing facets unseen before. The different contemporary cultures we experience today are no more or less accessible that of the English Renaissance. Freeing ourselves of this and allowing that which we see and hear with an experience can add nuance to our cognitive understanding of the ideas, images and actions represented in Shakespearean or any performance.

Most difficult from the perspective of design scholarship is that discussions of Shakespeare typically begin with his language, characters and plots and not the context in which actors playing characters perform actions and intone words. *Designer's Shakespeare* begins with the ways in which a designer's work reveals something different about the Shakespearean text. The power of Shakespeare in my experience is less in the poetry and the language and more in the experience of the action and the flow and rhythms in the spoken dialogue. Shakespeare is alive in the experience of the moments between the characters in the midst of the plot and action. It is not that I am concerned with the way Shakespeare looks in a given time but more in the ways that the images, color, sounds and smells of the experience are embedded within my memories of experiencing Shakespeare at various times in my life. From the long faded memories of *Othello* at Yale rep in the 1980s where Othello in Elizabethan garb kneels with handkerchief outstretched beseeching God, to the passions of the Renaissance Theatre Company's early 1990s *King Lear* where Gloucester's eye is plucked out and splattered, or a Royal Shakespeare

Company's version of *Richard II* at the Barbican in the mid-1990s where the theatre itself remains in my mind, Shakespeare has been an ever-present influence on my life. Yet I remember few of his words, few of his plots or character names. The words all blur and the images are what remain my experiences of the events and productions. While the concepts in these performances are guided by the work of monumental directors who have shepherded and conceived the productions, the visual worlds and the forgotten designers are the life of Shakespeare that inhabits my memory. I do not remember the designers but I do remember their sets, costumes, lights, sounds and experiences. These nameless influences are far from nameless and often are the most influential designers working in the theatre today. Their work and their choices have shifted the way that audiences expect to see the worlds of Shakespeare. Their visions have crafted ways of producing and of collaborating and have forever changed the notion of Shakespearean performance as a never changing constant over the centuries. Shakespeare means different things and is experienced differently in each epoch. What is that spark that the visual producers add to the words, poetry and literary meaning that are latent in the words of each script?

Shakespeare while occupying spaces in discussions of poetry, drama and theatre lives in a realm where performance is integral to understanding how the plays work. They are works made to be performed and brought to life in a theatre in front of spectators embodied by actors dressed and inhabiting constructed worlds. The facets of understanding Shakespeare in performance enrich the study of the language and meter of the stories presented in dialogue form. Seen from the angle of design practice, how can views of the visual and material provide fresh insight into the practices of an Elizabethan master? Understanding the ways in which designers approach a text and find material solutions for creating the settings, costumes, lighting and sounds of a production brings the unarticulated visual possibilities embedded within the verse to the forefront. Designers see, feel and interpret words as a tool to make manifest the worlds the characters inhabit and make intelligible how these worlds comment upon or support the action that transpires on stage. Their designs are another pathway into discovering the rich possibilities of Shakespeare's plays, so pregnant with meaning and so useful to any age in exploring what it means to be human in a social and political world.

Notes

1   Dennis Kennedy. 1993. *Looking at Shakespeare: A Visual History of Twentieth-century Performance*. Cambridge: Cambridge University Press.
2   John Russell Brown and Kevin Ewert. 2012. *The Routledge Companion to Actors' Shakespeare*. London: Routledge; John Russell Brown. 2008. *The Routledge Companion to Directors' Shakespeare*. London: Routledge.

Chapter 2

"Here is my space"
Josef Svoboda's Shakespearean imagination

Christian M. Billing

The Czech scenographer Josef Svoboda was born in 1920 and died in 2002. He was principal designer for the Czech National Theatre from 1948 to 1992 and came to world renown in 1958, when he created with his long-term collaborator, the director Alfréd Radok, the *Laterna Magika* for Expo 58 in Brussels. This development brought live stage action together with pre-shot, edited film in a new type of intermedial performance incorporating dance, spoken drama, music and interactive and immersive scenography. Technological experimentation of this sort was typical of Svoboda; his persistent investigations with materials led to many novel and impressive inventions – from projection onto, and illumination through, nylon chords (thereby making projection surfaces and apparent stage masses through which actors could move), through the deployment of small to stage-wide mirrors (used to reflect light, and displace items of set and stage action in multiple dimensions), to the massive, kinetic and architectonic designs that characterise much of his approach to Classical Greek drama, Wagnerian opera and Shakespearean tragedy. His technical expertise was born of an early apprenticeship to his father, a cabinetmaker, from formal studies in architecture and art at Prague's School of Industrial and Fine Arts, and a lifetime in the theatre. A qualified architect, Svoboda returned late in his career to teaching architecture, whilst also practising stage design in the major theatres of the world.

Svoboda's scenographic work spans a time of great turbulence and upheaval for the Czechoslovak nation. The effects of this turmoil can be clearly seen in his design work. During his lifetime, the two modern nation states that now occupy the geographical, political and cultural terrain of the former Czechoslovakia were not stable and defined territories; but rather were variously incorporated into a variety of disparate cultural and political figurations. Culturally and linguistically Slovak and Czech territories were, in the generation of Svoboda's parents, ruled as part of the Austro-Hungarian Empire. Some culturally and linguistically Czech lands were seen by their neighbours as German territories, and the areas that were brought together as one nation in the post-World War I project of a united Czechoslovakia, just two years before Svoboda's birth, were all too quickly invaded by Nazi Germany. Subsequently, for most of the post-World War II period, they were either occupied by Soviet forces or run as a satellite state of the former

Eastern Bloc. Towards the end of Svoboda's life, but temporarily once again, the united Czechoslovakia achieved independence from Communist control in 1990; but the constituent nations of the Czechoslovak amalgam separated in the 'Velvet Divorce' of 1993, in order to form two new nations: the Czech Republic and Slovakia. Finally, both countries joined an expanded European Union just two years after Svoboda's death. Such a turbulent cultural and political history can be used by scholars of art history, scenography and Shakespeare in performance as an informative case-study of the ways in which scenographic art, expressed through Shakespeare in particular, can be used as a vehicle for speaking to changing concepts of self, nation and identity. The forms and shapes of Svoboda's scenography for Shakespeare therefore not only appeal to us from aesthetic, artistic and technical perspectives, but also from social and geo-political ones.

Beginnings, the yolk of social realism

Josef Svoboda first created a stage setting for a production of Shakespeare at the Divadlo J. K. Tyla (Plzeň) in Prague in 1952. This collaboration on *Veselé paničky windsorské* (*The Merry Wives of Windsor*) with the director Zdeněk Hofbauer is frequently overlooked, because it pays so little resemblance to the later monumental and architectonic work for which Svoboda became internationally renowned. Nor does it in any way explore the scenographic possibilities of new materials – which became Svoboda's other great stock in trade. Yet, in the development of Svoboda's career and artistic output, and also in the progress of scenographic approaches to Shakespeare in Europe during the twentieth century, the design is in its own way significant as a point of departure. The project, a realist exercise in illusionistic Shakespeare which clearly follows the models of the Duke of Saxe-Meiningen and the nineteenth-century pictorialists, offers both interior and exterior domestic settings in a grand Tudor style, as well as two external pastoral locales. One features an open playing space bordered on two sides with a medium height angled wall, receding towards a pastoral backdrop upstage. The other is the arch of a huge stone bridge, or viaduct, through which one can again see a pastoral painted backdrop, this time of tall trees and other realistic undergrowth. The design is meticulously executed. Svoboda's model box in particular shows significant attention to architectural detail, ingenious use of the theatre's revolve and thoughtful consideration of how the number of realisable settings could be increased with minimal additions, such as the theatre's flying border, in order to create apparently new spaces. The design is not, however, anything other than a good example of Soviet-inspired Social Realist scenery – the art form obligatory in Czechoslovakia in the immediate post-war period.

Of greater interest, although still in this vein, is Svoboda's production of *Kupec benátský* (*The Merchant of Venice*), at the *Národní (Tylovo) divadlo* (now the Estates Theatre) (Prague) in December 1954, directed by František Salzer. This production was, in many ways, another exercise in Social Realist illusionistic scenic decoration. Within three large arches (occupying the space inside the theatre's own proscenium frame and static for all scenes), Svoboda created a series of changing two-dimensional locales to be framed by his own arches, placed in front of a changing series of upstage scenic backdrops. The ensemble design for each setting was intended to evoke the locale of the eighteen scenes required in Erik Adolf Saudek's translation of the play. The overall decorative scheme is of interest because it shows Svoboda beginning to acknowledge, and work with, the architecture of his theatre buildings – particularly in this case with the internal arches of his set juxtaposing themselves against the somewhat grander arch of the Estate Theatre's proscenium, thereby hinting at the metatheatricality of Shakespeare's text. The set is noteworthy for two additional reasons: (i) the Christian religious symbolism of its overarching triptych-like arrangement, conceived of as picture frames within which scenes were played out – an aspect that shows Svoboda already beginning to think in less literal and more metaphorical terms, particularly given the ways that Shakespeare's text frames its characters within the Christian doctrinal mentalities of Renaissance Venice; and (ii) in the quality of the painted backdrops flown in behind the triptych arches. These monumental canvasses show a pastoral setting for Belmont that might have been taken directly from Serlio (another playful metatheatrical reference); various views of Venice, including some astonishing false perspective work in the ghetto scenes; an interesting triple juxtaposition/compression of the Rialto bridge impossibly sandwiched between the Campanile di San Marco and the Column of Saint Theodore; and, most inspirational of all: a full stage backdrop that is a re-working of Tintoretto's *Il Paradiso* from the Great Council Hall of the Palazzo Ducale. For those in the know, with this canvas Svoboda visually transformed the National Theatre, Prague into the seat of absolute Venetian authority. Used for the trial scene, this gargantuan art-historical, cultural and political reference created quite some stage for a little Portia to occupy. Even in these constrained exercises in Socialist Realist representation, then, Svoboda was seen to demonstrate both technical skill and grand artistic vision.

European main stages: radical experimentation

Svoboda's first significant breakthrough with an alternative mode of scenic representation came in designs for a November 1959 *Hamlet* at the Národní divadlo (Prague), in collaboration with the director Jaromír Pleskot. The translation was by Zdeněk Urbánek and, together with Pleskot's direction, the language of the text worked towards a notion of the play as an exercise in slow, thoughtful deliberation. The extreme repression of the cold-war Soviet system was by the late 1950s beginning to thaw, slightly (even if it had not yet quite resolved itself to a dew), and Radovan Lukavský performed a Hamlet (seen by many as the greatest of his generation) as a profoundly philosophical, rational and thoughtful individual – a man who observed events and commented pensively upon them as a representative not only of the audience, but of the whole Czech people. Lukavský saw around him, reflected not only metaphorically in the actions of those in power, but literally in the distorted reflections of Svoboda's scenography, the monumental oppression and

Josef Svoboda's Shakespearean imagination 15

warping of reality to which his whole nation had been subjected. Hamlet first appeared on stage from the auditorium, watched events, recounted his interpretations of what had transpired to the audience, and then decided to take logical, reasoned and entirely justifiable action against those responsible. To match this reading of the play as an examination of the individual pitted against a repressive state, Svododa conceived of a stage that was essentially a monumental flight of stairs, broken into three principal sections: a forestage, made up of a run of short-depth steps running across the entire width of the proscenium; behind these, a central acting space, made up of four, equally wide, but much larger-depth steps, capable of accommodating several actors each; and then a final run of narrow-depth steps leading up to one last large-depth towering platform. Onto this gigantic wall-to-wall staircase of varying depth but equal height and width steps, Svoboda placed a series of tall (approximately 2.5m by 9m) screens that could be moved along the horizontal plane of the stage at six parallel points. The first five sets of screens consisted of just two panels each; but the last set was composed of six, which could be disposed so as to make a slightly offset, seemingly impenetrable back wall to the set. The screens were covered in a shiny black plastic capable of reflecting any light that was shone directly onto its surface (thus becoming mirror like), but also of becoming sinister, monolithic architectonic masses of blackness, when illuminated from the side or behind.

Figure 2.1 Model box showing disposition of reflective screens for *Hamlet* (Prague, 1959)

Source: Image from the private collection of Josef Svoboda © Šárka Hejnová, reproduced with permission

16   Christian M. Billing

Svoboda thus created the idea of a repressive hierarchy that diminished the individual through its oppressive architectural force. Ascension to the heights of power (represented by his massive staircase) was frequently blocked. Whilst the steps were completely static, the screens were arranged in twenty-one different configurations throughout the course of the production. Illuminated with a variety of front, side and back lighting, the combination of stark architectonic blocks created the emotional atmosphere of an open, courtly reception room, which was at the same time the bleak claustrophobia of Denmark as prison. The plastic design was new and bold, distorting as it reflected and underlined the manipulations of truth and appearance that exist in Shakespeare's play; but it also cleverly incorporated and re-worked two of the great Shakespearean designs of the early twentieth century: the steps of Emil Pirchan's design for Leopold Jessner's 1920 production of *Richard* III (a production riddled with references to fascist dictatorship in the eve of the Second World War), and the tall screens of Edward Gordon Craig's production of *Hamlet* for the Moscow Art Theatre in 1911–12 (the production that claimed the play for the Slavic people as they began their eighty year struggle to escape the oppression first of the Tsars and then of failed-Communist dictators). A significant amount had happened in theatre's technological terms since either of these earlier productions, however; and through his use of new materials and a world-class theatre workshop, Svoboda largely avoided his predecessors' pitfalls (squeaky, noisy steps and large and over-toppling screens respectively). The thin plastic used to skin Svoboda's screens, for example, was only a fraction of the weight of the canvass used by Craig. It was therefore relatively easy to lower the centre of gravity of his towering structures. Restricting their movement to only a horizontal plane (and designing screens that were much wider than they were deep) also meant that that the chances of toppling as a result of inertia were also virtually eliminated. On a national level, the production was revolutionary because it returned Czech theatre to the kind of avant-garde scenic experimentation that had characterised the inter-war years, and, in particular, it picked up the design baton offered by a *Hamlet* designed by Vlastislav Hofman for Karel Hugo Hilar in 1926, which had also used tall screens, in silver-grey, and had combined these forms with other prisms and large items of furniture mounted on platforms.

The model box photographs that survive in Svoboda's private archive for the 1959 design are the first of the designer's Shakespeare works that show a holistic and methodological approach to scenographic process because by this phase of his career, Svoboda was using sophisticated lighting systems in his studio to compose individual scenes and experiment with their illumination in 1:25 scale maquettes. The many photographs for the 1959 *Hamlet* show extensive tests with both reflective and light-absorbing materials for the screens, as well as their form and disposition. Crucially, all of this experimentation with material happened within model-boxes that were lit so as to reproduce real theatrical lighting effects. From these extremely well worked out beginnings, Svoboda took his final design to the craftsmen in the workshops of the *Národní divadlo*, Prague, with whom he was at this stage of his career establishing an excellent working relationship. As a designer who was proud to have been trained as an architect, rather than having come to design uniquely through the *école des beaux arts* route, Svoboda from the very start of his career had been adept at providing detailed working drawings that showed exactly how each of his scenic elements was to be constructed. As he worked with the set construction team at the Czech National Theatre, his ability to understand the materials with which he worked grew, as did his desire to experiment with them. Although the standard joke/accusation levelled against Svoboda's design for the 1959 *Hamlet* is that it used up the entire annual allocation of wood given to the theatre as part of the Eastern-Bloc command economy within which it worked, in reality the really interesting aspect of this staging is its use of reflective plastic film. It is through this material that the production created its sense of claustrophobia and facilitated the introspection of Lukavský's Hamlet, and it was a material through which the production developed its most significant metaphor: the un-packing and exploration of Hamlet's advice to the players concerning the role of theatre (III.ii.) in which the mirror is developed as a complex, although sometimes distorting and oblique surface on which, through which, and with which we reflect upon the world as it is, as well as our place within it.

After *Hamlet,* Svoboda again worked with Pleskot for a January 1963 production of *Večer tříkrálový* (*Twelfth Night*) at the *Národní (Tylovo) divadlo* (Prague). In this production he saw the need for great fluidity of movement, both because the play is a comedy, and also because it is structured in a series of shorter scenes that often comment ironically on what has just happened. Svoboda therefore created a sparse stage that was built out over the theatre's orchestra pit for extra depth and was entirely open except for a receding back 'wall' composed of an inverted V made up of two large straight-line runs of pliable chords extending vertically from the stage floor to the theatre's fly tower above, arranged as a dense backdrop capable of taking rich colour from a number of strongly gelled stage lights. In front of this receding 'wall' were located on the stage floor a simple series of small, diamond-shaped platforms, which in perspective looked from the auditorium like little floating squares. Some were trucked onstage and others were lifted up and out of the stage floor – as with the one that became Malvolio's prison, in which the actor appeared from within its support bars, acting through a head-high opening from the stage-basement below whilst his tormentors stood on the low platform above.

Shakespeare's play is an intensely watery one, beginning with a shipwreck, having much aqueous imagery and creating a metaphorical environment in which 'the rain it raineth every day' (V.i.). Svoboda's design caught this symbolic aspect of the text by evoking an ocean of open stage space in which little island platforms were used as nodes of solo and small group performance. Thus the ways in which characters fail to come together and/or understand each other in this play were visually augmented. It seems that Svoboda's guiding principle was the exchange between Viola and Olivia: "I am not what I am. / I would you were as I would have you be" (III.i), with its revelation of the existential isolation and miscomprehension that is inherent in any human relationship, and must be overcome; as the metaphysical poet, John Donne put it: "No man is an island, Entire of itself, Every

18   Christian M. Billing

man is a piece of the continent, A part of the main". Svoboda's ground plan shows eleven such diamond-shaped islands to be used at different parts of the action with their use broken down into a scenic analysis that justifies the requirement for, and interconnectedness of each. Reviewers commented on the paucity of stage properties, and the use of limited objects with symbolic, allusive potential.

Whilst seeking to maintain both the fluidity of space and the instantaneous transformation of locale that is essential to Shakespearean comedy, Svoboda wanted further to add to the metaphorical quality of his imagined Illyria by hanging many chords from the flies, this time of varying lengths and dropping down in seemingly random clusters throughout the entire stage space (sometimes even reaching below actors' head height). Onto this three-dimensional network of chords he placed different shapes, composed of modern-looking materials and suited to the metaphorical mood of the relevant scene. Sometimes they were geometrical shapes, composed of curves and rectangles; at other times, runs of falling balls, of increasing and decreasing size, looking like droplets of water running down a string. The production was praised for its constant shifting of colours, for its fluidity, and also for the perfect balancing of lyrical comedy with the profoundly analytical lens provided by Otomar Krejča's Malvolio – who had numerous moments of intimacy with the audience, and whose ambition was seen as entirely understandable by critics writing in a regime that ideologically subjugated the citizen to the state and individual motivation to centralised authority.

Five months later in June 1963, a production of *Sen noci svatojánské* (*A Midsummer Night's Dream*) directed by Václav Špidla opened at the *Národní (Tylovo) divadlo* (Prague). For this play, Svoboda did something that characterised his working method as a scenographer. He took an idea initiated in a previous production and experimented further with it formally, taking it to a new level of artistic interpretation, whilst combining it with other new elements. This time, his experimentation took the V shaped form of his slatted, pliable-chord back wall for *Twelfth Night*, turned it on its side and made it into a curve. The result was what has come to be known as Svoboda's *Fabion* – a half parabola taking the stage floor smoothly up into the back wall of the set. This time, the device was composed of hundreds of slats, which due to their horizontal disposition were now of necessity made from rigid extruded steel. These receding and rising slats were collectively capable of providing great contrast when lit; but also, because of their orientation, they brought a significant sense of horizontality to the set. Additionally, on the stage floor of this huge parabola, four sections were cut out in the shape of giant leaves and these shapes achieved significant further visual definition as a result of the fact that their slats, otherwise identical to those of the parabola, were laid at different angles from those of the regularly horizontal floor. As the action proceeded, the 'leaves' achieved further distinction by rising up and out of the stage floor, adding a further sense of definition that augmented their oversized, magical effect. Above the slatted-leaf floor platforms (each large enough to accommodate several actors) were hung numerous similarly enormous leaves from the flies. These un-slatted, solid objects were capable of taking theatrical colour from lights and defined shapes from gobos, but also acted as projection screens onto which images of leaves, and abstract patterns evocative of the vein structure of actual foliage were shone. Svoboda's working drawings for these shapes reveal that their structural integrity was derived from pipe steel, welded into the vein structure of real leaves. In this metaphorical evocation of a forest, built from modern materials, but following nature's patterns, actors appeared like little beings, lost in a realm of nature that

Figure 2.2 Composite image: model box for *A Midsummer Night's Dream* (Prague, 1963), showing disposition of leaf shapes on floor and hung from flies (top), and the scene in performance, showing the effects of projection onto these surfaces (bottom)

Source: Images from the private collection of Josef Svoboda © Šárka Hejnová, reproduced with permission

20   Christian M. Billing

was both magical and overwhelming. Faries and humans sat or stood on the leaves like tiny creatures perched precariously on immense lily pads. Athens was differentiated from the forest by the fact that the floor leaves were not raised out of the stage for the civic landscape (thereby making a flat stage floor) and, rather than huge leaves flown in, as they were in the forest, geometrical forms were lowered instead. Svoboda thus established in this production one of the general tenets of his Shakespearean design: that architectonic, rectilinear and geometric shapes are primarily tragic, or oppressive; whereas curves, natural shapes and the colours of wildlife are primarily comic and pastoral.

Along with his 1959 *Hamlet*, the October 1963 *Romeo a Julie* (*Romeo and Juliet*) created with the actor-turned-director Otomar Krejča is perhaps the Shakespearean scenography for which Svoboda is best known. The production was an immense success in Czechoslovakia, became the subject of an internationally recognised documentary by Radúz Činčera, was itself filmed, and was subsequently revived (albeit in a slightly simplified scenographic version) for performances at the *Conjunto Dramático Nacional, Teatro Mella*, Havana (May 1964) and the *Bühnen der Stadt*, Cologne (May 1969). For this production, Svoboda took further the kinetic, architectonic principle that he had developed for Shakespearean tragedy in his 1959 Prague *Hamlet*. In that play, he had restricted all movable elements to a horizontal plane; now he designed an architectonic set composed of numerous components that moved in all three physical dimensions throughout the course of a fourth, temporal one. Built in an austere white, and deliberately evoking the architecture of an Italian Renaissance city, the set disposed its segmented elements in twenty-one different configurations that created both open spaces, and confined, claustrophobic enclaves. The design was based on mobile units that rose and fell from the stage floor, trucked forwards and backwards from upstage to downstage, or trucked from stage-left or stage-right to centre. Each unit had a different function, representing: arched loggia, flights of steps, stark high walls, the colonnaded balcony on which Juliet stands for II.ii, or a romantic fountain that later became the lovers' bed, then tomb. A sign of its pre-Prague Spring cultural and political moment, Krejča wanted his production to be about tolerance and modernity. Svoboda achieved this atmosphere through a set capable of establishing the presence of a believable Renaissance Verona and then slowly absenting itself from the stage as the various elements that had created it disappeared in order to create more timeless, open spaces in which actors could move and speak the newly translated text of Josef Topol.

A distinctly hybrid modern-yet-period feel was achieved through a combination of translation, direction and the casting of popular figures from youth culture. Svoboda contributed to this scenography that used alternately closed and then open spaces to evoke an oppressive mood, and then the hopes, emotions and relationships of youth escaping it, rather than simply providing pictorial or literal settings. The production thus spoke very powerfully to two moments in history at the same time: an imagined Italian Renaissance and a Czech modernity in which youth was daring for the first time in a generation to escape its surroundings and

Josef Svoboda's Shakespearean imagination 21

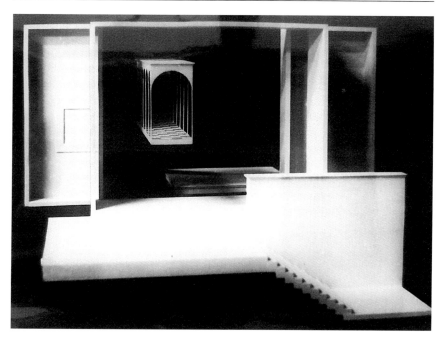

Figure 2.3 Svoboda's model box for *Romeo and Juliet* (Prague, 1963), showing the floating balcony, two side-trucking walls and an ascending/descending front wall

Source: Image from the private collection of Josef Svoboda © Šárka Hejnová, reproduced with permission

question the inflexible and dogmatic approaches of their elders and oppressors. Such duality was particularly resonant in the context of Czechoslovakian social and political history during the mid-1960s and in many ways the impossible optimism of this moment of cultural history was summed up by the scenic device for which the production was best known, the 'floating' balcony on which Marie Tomášová stood and spoke to Jan Tříska's Romeo in II.ii. Appearing to hover in space, over three metres in the air, the gravitationally impossible balcony was achieved by a platform cleverly cantilevered onto a moving truck that propelled it forward, but remained unseen by audiences. The unseen rear section of the truck was weighted to provide the physical moments necessary to counterbalance the floating balcony in front; it also contained a flight of seventeen steps that were required as access for Tomášová and any other actor who was needed on the platform. Svoboda's preparation of elements such as these in a model box environment was intense, and his archival photographs show a wooden maquette that not only has a series of complicated backstops marked up for each position to which an element of the set moved, but also a specially designed, geared mechanical system with drive shafts for smoothly propelling the model through its twenty-one scene changes. The fluidity of the ambition is seen in Činčera's documentary, which captures the designer

22   Christian M. Billing

and his electrically powered model going through its paces. The designer and director wished such transitions to be entirely fluid, demonstrating Svoboda's firm conviction that theatre is never static, but kinetic; scene changes were, in fact, clunky at best, and needed to be underscored by the music of Jan Klusák to avoid audience impatience.

Further architectonic mobility is in evidence in Svoboda's May 1964 production of *Lear király* (*King Lear*), directed by Endre Márton at the *Nemzeti Színház*, Budapest. In this production Svoboda further developed his bold architectonic method, albeit working in a theatre that was slightly less sophisticated than the National in Prague with regards to both trucking and trap work. In Budapest, Svoboda achieved scenographic mobility by means of a clever utilisation of the theatre's flying system and he designed thirteen immense, but hollow, right-angled parallelepipeds, the majority perfectly rectangular, but one single form having its base cut across at 45 degrees. These rectilinear, three-dimensional objects were raised and lowered horizontally using fixed positions along the receding parallel bars of the theatre's flying system. During various moments of the play, different combinations of floating blocks would occupy the frame of the proscenium, taking up positions that varied from actually touching the stage floor to being just visible at the upper limit of the proscenium arch. To this ingeniously adaptable system, Svoboda added two further elements: (i) the exterior surfaces of the parallelepipeds were lightly textured and of a mid-grey colour, meaning that they could take light and thereby alter their apparent form and texture, and (ii) they also contained theatrical lanterns, which meant that they could double as immense down-lighting boxes. Svoboda quickly realised that *Lear* is a play in which significant metaphorical darkness is occasionally pierced by moments of shining light (sometimes for the good, as at Dover cliffs, or in the 'gilded butterflies' speech of V.iii, but oftentimes unremittingly harsh, as in the III.vii. blinding of Gloucester). He also saw that this play (unique amongst the tragedies for having a double plot) requires many quick changes of clearly defined space. In order to move from interiors to exteriors, or warmth to isolation and coldness, Svoboda combined architectural mass with rapid changes in lighting states. His setting for *Lear* was seen to evoke harshness, isolation and the ability not only of man, but of nature to turn against humanity: 'As flies to wanton boys, are we to the gods. / They kill us for their sport' (IV.i.). His design accordingly both emulated and built on the 'theatre of cruelty' approach to the play that was simultaneously being explored by Peter Brook at the Royal Shakespeare Company (seen on a world tour the previous year). But more than this, Svoboda's floating parallelepipeds, hanging ominously above the heads of his protagonists, threatened at any moment to fall out of space and crush them, like insects under the metaphorical thumbs of dispassionate human forces that observed them coldly, ready to snuff out any rebellion, tear apart efforts at human love, or destroy any hope of salvation. Designed for performance in a Hungary that had only eight years previously experienced the harsh military response of Soviet armed forces against the Hungarian Revolution, 1956, the metaphor needed no explanation.

The last of Svoboda's great mobile architectonic tragedies was a production of

Josef Svoboda's Shakespearean imagination 23

Figure 2.4 Rendering for *King Lear* (Budapest, 1964), showing immense rectangular boxes attached to the theatre's flying system – used as both architectural mass and light sources

Source: Image from the private collection of Josef Svoboda © Šárka Hejnová, reproduced with permission

Hamlet staged in January 1965 at the *Théâtre National de Belgique* (Brussels), directed by Otomar Krejča. Convinced of the scenographic success of their sliding-block based, trucking, raising and lowering production of *Romeo and Juliet*, the creative team were keen to take up where they had left off, but now with a more heavyweight tragedy. In Brussels, Svoboda recognised and attempted to correct the technical limitations of transition speed that had plagued critical responses and audience reactions to the 1963 *Romeo and Juliet*, and deliberately limited the movement of his new *Hamlet* set (described by one critic as a 'construction game') to lateral movement only in the upstage/downstage horizontal plane. Ingeniously, however, as a result of an immense mirror that Svoboda placed behind the upstage setting line of the set, leaning forwards, above and over the entire set at an angle of 45 degrees, any movement downstage by the architectonic blocks of which the set was composed also created the illusion of simultaneous movement in an apparent vertical wall situated in a reflected virtual reality *above* the set. This combination of virtual vertical and actual horizontal components was further played upon through the deployment of strong directional lighting that could either pick out, or hide in shadow, relevant elements of the design. Thus in the image below (a photograph taken by Svoboda of his model box, as part of his experimentation with its architectonic arrangement and lighting), the real unit A1 leads to the apparent appearance of A2 (as with B1, C1, D1 and B2, C2, D2 respectively); whereas unit E has its corresponding reflection denied by a lack of lighting. The design was unique and new. It led to significant praise for the production's ability to create an atmosphere redolent of oppression so prevalent in Central and Eastern European readings of the play. In particular, critics praised the ability of the set to produce hidden recesses and niches from which the play's frequent eavesdropping and surveillance can take place. The ability to create niches for eavesdroppers was ironic given that Svoboda was himself an informant to the Communist authorities; but this fact was not at that time known by his artistic collaborators. In a developmental sense, the overarching composition can be seen to build towards the juxtapositional and controlled elemental work on illumination and tight framing that followed two years later in Svoboda's work on Polyecran technology (for Expo 67 in Montreal). Svoboda's subsequent use of Polyecran ('many screens') projections allowed for the rapid manipulation of images within small screens that formed the sub-units of a larger projection whole. Through juxtaposition of such images, narrative or subliminal effects could be produced. The whole system relied on drawing audience attention towards certain illuminated areas of rigidly defined space and away from others, which moved into

Figure 2.5 Model box for *Hamlet* (Brussels, 1965), showing disposition of mirror and apparent existence of reflected surfaces

Source: Image from the private collection of Josef Svoboda © Šárka Hejnová, reproduced with permission

darkness. The Brussels *Hamlet*, likewise used light and rigidly defined boxes into which actors could be fitted to manipulate the ways in which they could be perceived by audiences and this technique was deployed alongside more conventional movement and blocking on the forestage.

The following year, in October 1966, Svoboda designed *Macbeth* for the *Teatro San Babila* (Milan) and the acclaimed Italian director Tino Buazzelli. Work on the Brussels *Hamlet* seemed to have opened up for Svoboda the importance of the rear plane in his Shakespeare designs: a backdrop that now, far from being the illustrative scenery of his first Shakespearean designs, was an affective canvas for the combination of space, objects and light in abstractions that could be both metaphorically evocative, whilst also throwing forward kinetically, as a sort of animated relief, the architectonic and dramatic action taking place in front of it. In Milan, Svoboda designed a back wall that had the impression of scrunched up and then lightly unfolded and spread-out paper. This he achieved by placing material over twisted wire frames. The rear of the stage accordingly had a crumpled appearance of semi-random lines (most of which, however, were deliberately roughly horizontal, vertical or at 45 degrees to each other). No line in this backdrop was regular, and no two lines were exactly parallel. The effect was therefore a strikingly natural one, resembling the bark of an aged hardwood tree, or its spreading branches depending on how it was lit. Svoboda was a designer fascinated with the individual components of his sets and amassed, over the course of his career, literally thousands of photographic slides and prints that document themes, such as 'water', 'fire', 'trees' and so on, or particular objects 'armour', or 'medieval gates'. The many photographs of the Milan *Macbeth* that survive in Svoboda's archive show repeated experimentations with lighting onto this back wall, as the designer explored ways in which directional lighting could create numerous effects of sharp contrast, hinting at the representation of myriad objects either spoken of in, or evoked by the play.

In front of this enormous backdrop, Svoboda placed architectonic objects that deployed the techniques of his Budapest *Lear* (i.e. flying rectilinear objects), and both of his *Hamlets* (i.e. trucking and sliding rectilinear panels). The result of the tripartite combination was extraordinary in its plasticity: assemblages of architectural elements with little shadow play on the wall behind creating a space evocative of a medieval Scottish castle; removing some of the architectonic elements and lighting the back wall from the front evokes a heath, complete with what looks like wispy haze; top-lighting the back wall and placing long thin blocks in front of it creates the branches and tree trunks of an overbearing forest. The effect of the combination of these three elements was thus both metaphorical (creating mood and ambience for the play's dark acts) and also strangely pictorial at times (through the emergence of clearly recognisable shapes, like castles and trees). With such a tool-kit at his disposition, Svoboda could achieve the rapid changes of location that are required by this play, and the palpable sense that evil forces can melt away and transform one's perceived reality with another one, entirely different and unexpected. Shakespeare's mood for this play, from its opening in the disquieting trochaic tetrameter rhythm of the witches, rests on the idea that the world is not what it seems, that the forces of evil not only know your name, but that they're coming to get you. The Milan *Macbeth* thus achieved, through an almost total synthesis of manipulable scenic elements, a scenographic fluidity that the previously architectonic tragedies had not always managed, and with it Shakespeare's emotional mood for the play. An immense success in Milan, the production was interestingly followed in Svoboda's Shakespearean oeuvre by another production exploring the same text, but in which he abandoned his mobile architectonic principles entirely. Perhaps once they had been perfected, he became tired of them.

June 1969 saw Svoboda again team up with Jaromír Pleskot on a staging of *Macbeth* at the *Národní (Tylovo) divadlo* in Prague. The Prague *Macbeth* design is striking as a departure from all previous sets Svoboda had undertaken for Shakespeare. Keeping architectonic elements now only as a background, arranged in a static pattern on the back and two side walls, the design emphasised not the expression of mood through architecture, but rather the act of playing itself. In front of solid back and side walls (that were simply a variant of a standard box set, but made up of various geometric squares and rectangles assembled in relief),

Figure 2.6 Model box for *Macbeth* (Milan, 1966), showing lighting effects on back wall and juxtapositional effect against trucking and flying downstage architectonic elements

Source: Image from the private collection of Josef Svoboda © Šárka Hejnová, reproduced with permission

Svoboda simply placed a medieval looking scaffold stage, built of rough hewn timber, with three modest sets of open steps leading up to it: one from downstage, one from stage-left, one from stage-right. This platform (which was more like an execution scaffold than a market-square, low-slung medieval pageant stage, but which alluded to both) was the location for most of the action of the play. It was left sparse and open for the witches, who draped themselves over it and moved on and around it in lithe, sensual ways, lying on its floor, or sliding up and over its pillars and edges (in Svoboda's archival records, the witches are taken in long-exposure photographs, so that they appear like wisps of moving smoke). For the evocation of a courtly castle, on the other hand, a curtain rail of approximately seven metres was flown in, complete with ornate finials, from which bar opulent crimson-red curtains hung, drawn up to the sides so as to create an almost ironically metatheatrical frame around the pageant stage on which Shakespeare's drama of blood and ambition was being played out. The production also used numerous projections, whose unidirectional and firmly framed quality on the squares of the backdrop wall was clearly influenced by the tightly-focused changing images projected into the sectional Polyecran screens that Svoboda had two years previously produced for the Montreal Expo 67. The negatives for these projections are preserved in Svoboda's archive and consist of images of medieval knights in armour, children wearing crowns (the descendants of Banquo?); and one highly disturbing image of a baby with its eyes clenched tight shut, its face streaked with fresh blood pouring from an open head wound. Svoboda had been exploring the juxtapositional potential of combining projections with live theatre and performance since his development of the *Laterna Magika* with Alfréd Radok in the late 1950s and, although in this case the images are not kinetic ones, the ways in which they are intended to juxtapose themselves against the action, or even illustrate linguistic allusions within the play, are powerful. This is particularly true with the image of the blood-stained baby's head, which is perhaps the most radical image of all because it speaks not to an event, but to the metaphorical evocation of evil that is created by Shakespeare in the slaughter of innocents within the play – moments such as the butchering of Macduff's children, or the act of barbaric, psychologically chilling, sui-infanticide and is evoked by Lady Macbeth, with the words:

> I have given suck, and know
> How tender 'tis to love the babe that milks me:
> I would, while it was smiling in my face,
> Have pluck'd my nipple from his boneless gums,
> And dash'd the brains out, had I so sworn as you
> Have done to this.
>
> (I.vii)

In Shakespeare's text, such images are created in the mind's eye; they happen offstage, or in the darkness of night; they are reported. In Svoboda's design, they were flashed onstage in the cold light of day.

28 Christian M. Billing

Figure 2.7 Model box for *Macbeth* (Prague, 1969), showing scaffold stage and three-sided set, with clustered boxes, acting as architectonic elements and projection screens (influenced by Polyecran)

Source: Image from the private collection of Josef Svoboda © Šárka Hejnová, reproduced with permission

Further radical experimentation came in Svoboda's unrealised 1969 design for *Antony and Cleopatra*, originally destined for production in the *Schillertheater* (Berlin), to be directed by Fritz Kortner. Designs for this production demonstrate a combination of Svoboda's developing operatic style (the designer was to work increasingly on the great operatic stages of the world during the 1970s and 1980s) and experimentation with an extremely adventurous use of a tilting and revolving stage. The design is based on a circular platform; double hinged approximately two-thirds of the way across. The largest two-thirds of this disc contain within it an elliptical, but irregular, sloped walkway that is itself hinged in two; the smaller third is composed of a set of monumental stairs, evocative of Svoboda's 1959 *Hamlet*, or the even grander staircase of his 1963 *Oedipus Tyrannos*. These Classical, architectural steps diminish in their horizontal length as the geometrical chords along which they are composed decrease in length, approaching the revolve's perimeter. When the platform rises in the middle and tilts upwards, as a result of the overarching, rising arc of the circle, these steps resemble the hull of a ship (which configuration is added to with a figurative prow, full sails and oars that stick out from the steps' individual risers). At other times, smaller scenic units (such as architectural blocks, columns, flights of stairs or large human statues), all dressed as stone, are trucked in place, obscuring the rising curves at the edges of the stairs so as to hint at more extensive, monumental steps belonging to the civic buildings of Rome and Alexandria. As with so many of Svoboda's later designs, the environment is both metaphorical and literal. The curved walkway of the larger section of the revolve (reminiscent of the laminated glass pathway of Svoboda's 1959 design for *The Excursions of Mr Brouček to the Moon*) creates a perfectly abstract environment for actors to explore as an empty space; whereas the opposing sector can be used to create a tangible representation of the Mediterranean, its barges and buildings, in the first century BC.

In June 1970 Svododa designed *Jak se vám líbí* (*As You Like It*) for the *Národní (Tylovo) divadlo* (Prague), in a production directed by Jaromír Pleskot. The set was, like his Milan *Macbeth*, a combination of plastic and architectonic elements merged with sculptural and abstract projections. These included: multiple Romanesque masks, overlaid patterns of leaves, and other more stylised images – all techniques that had been explored in Svoboda's two *Macbeths*, but were now taken towards a different, lighter and more colourful realisation within the genre of comedy. The design worked on a principle of layering. At the rear of the stage was a large cyclorama made from a translucent pliable plastic that took projections extremely well (a material known as Studio Folio, that Svoboda had discovered and used extensively during the 1960s, and which was a substance that he particularly liked because it looked dark grey from the front, but became explosively colourful when projected onto from the rear); in the next downstage plane the set contained nine large panels of irregularly meshed wire screens, overlaid with material in exactly the same manner as the back wall for the Milan *Macbeth*. These nine crumpled, floating screens also took projections and, as in the Milan *Macbeth*, were capable of evoking the required forest (albeit with a less necromantic sense of theatrical 'magic'). Finally, the downstage acting area was composed of a floor of five large, over-layered, diamond-shaped platforms that created a kind of low-terraced, imperial staircase moving upwards and away from the audience. Each platform stage of this 'staircase' provided ample space for a scene to take place, although usually all platforms were used in combination. As well as providing a significant, open and rhythmic standing/walking/moving space for actors, these platforms doubled as seating blocks, on which actors could perch, play a lute, or eavesdrop on others. The back platforms also had enough height for actors to use them as tables, sitting behind them to eat and listen to Duke Senior or Jaques' discourse about the merits and demerits of pastoral living. The set was thus largely static, but achieved a multipurpose, poetic and metaphorical effect through projection and lighting effects; the

30   Christian M. Billing

aesthetic changes made to it, necessary to provide the changing emotional contexts of court and forest, were made almost uniquely through lighting states and different sorts of projection. The design was thus significant in the development of Svoboda's Shakespearean scenography because it was much less mobile than any set previously attempted by the designer for Shakespeare. Perhaps it is no coincidence, then, that reviewers commented on the rapid, clear-cut changes of tempo that the production achieved, rather than the laborious nature of scene changes that had to be covered by specially composed incidental music. The production was favourably compared to the celebrated 1937 version by Jiří Frejka, which had achieved its success largely as a result of the innovative scenography of Svoboda's teacher, František Tröster.[1]

Intimate Shakespeare: returns and re-workings

Svoboda's design for *Jindřich V* (*Henry V*) in February 1971 at the *Národní (Tylovo) divadlo* (Prague), directed by Miroslav Macháček, is of interest for several reasons: (i) because it is the only Shakespearean history play that Svoboda designed in his entire career;[2] (ii) because its sparse utilitarian design is unlike anything Svoboda produced in his Shakespearean scenography or elsewhere; and (iii) because one fact is a direct product of the other. Despite his already-proven ability to create enormous, monumental scenography, or to utilise complex structures to achieve plasticity and fluidity in his designs; or, indeed, Svoboda's role in the development of projection technology as a major instrument in the toolkits of late twentieth-century theatre designers, Svoboda also often looked for what he termed *divadlo nula'* [theatre zero]: the minimum amount of paraphernalia to achieve the maximum theatrical effect. Nowhere was this approach more so than in his design for *Henry V*. The set consisted of a bare stage with a curved cyclorama above it, beginning eight feet above the stage and rising a further seven metres into the air (but not quite reaching the flies or having its top masked by the proscenium arch). The height above the stage floor of the cyclorama facilitated entrances and exits and, in particular, quick and dynamic movement from the back and wings of the theatre towards a primary downstage acting area. Onto this expansive curve Svoboda projected for the most part a very simple pattern: a close-up of the warp and weft of coarse, hessian-like fabric. Below this immense, simple screen, the stage held: a clothes rail of costumes, a variety of stage properties (including a regal throne and several less grandiose chairs), and other theatrical paraphernalia used during the show. The actors came on stage in everyday clothing and, both at the beginning of the play and throughout its course (as a result of much use of doubling), they changed into alternative costumes in front of the theatre's spectators. Sometimes these costumes were no more than scraps of clothing, to denote particular parts. The exception to this rule was Luděk Munzar, who had a full costume and played only one part: King Henry V. The production was very well received and was praised for its metatheatrical inventiveness. Both Svoboda and Macháček had recognised in the play the fact that history is itself a series of narratives about narratives, and decided to emphasise the ways in which individuals write and act out their own parts in the performance of overarching international politics. The fact that the play (and the history it manipulated) was virtually unknown to a Czech audience was also seen by most critics as a significant advantage, allowing the potential jingoism of a potentially patriotic English text to be un-packed, debunked and critiqued. Svoboda's scenography was praised as perfect for such and interpretation of such a play. His obvious debt to Caspar Neher (and the scenographic aesthetic of mid-twentieth century Brechtian Epic Theatre as practised by the Berliner Ensemble) was, however, not openly acknowledged by the production's Czech reviewers. Despite their sincere appreciation of the apparent humour of giving Fluellen and MacMorris Slovakian and German accents, it seemed that they could neither see nor hear the other German voices speaking in the piece's direction and design.

Figure 2.8 Photograph of the Epic Theatre-inspired *Henry V* (Prague, 1971)

Source: Image from the private collection of Josef Svoboda © Šárka Hejnová, reproduced with permission

32   Christian M. Billing

In April 1982 Svoboda returned once again to *Hamlet* in a production at the *Národní (Smetanovo) divadlo* (Prague). The director was Miroslav Macháček, who had played Macbeth in Pleskot's 1969 production. This *Hamlet*, however, was Shakespeare for a different age, and was created for a Czechoslovakia that was now still in the hard grip of the period of so-called 'Normalisation'.[3] Increasingly confident with the metatheatrical and self-referential elements of his staging, Svoboda deliberately worked with the architecture of the National Theatre, and in particular made significant use of its opulent gilt proscenium arch and side boxes in his design. Building a large forestage out from the normal setting line of the theatre's apron (and well over the orchestra pit), Svoboda created what was, in effect, a reverse thrust configuration. This open playing space, receding backwards into the theatre from the front of the pit, was bordered on two sides and at the rear by two low but long steps that led up to a medium-width acting platform. At the back, there were two further steps running the entire width of the stage, again leading up to another medium-width platform, which was itself backed by an enormous black curtain. In effect, the playing area of the theatre had been shifted forward by approximately one-third, right into the audience. The effect was augmented by a lowering of the theatre's golden safety curtain (which coincided spatially with the front line of the first raised acting platform and was moved to several different vertical positions during the course of the action). Additionally, the theatre's plush red front curtains were gathered around the extremities of its equally golden proscenium arch.

Thus Svoboda created a design that was monumentally metatheatrical – and within this openly acknowledged National Theatre frame, he playfully composed a sort of palimpsest of his own Shakespearean designs, his own personal meta-theatre mirroring that of the play. When the players acted *The Murder of Gonzago*, for example, their performance was framed by the same style of red drapes, curtain pole and finials that had been used by Svoboda in his 1969 Pleskot-directed *Macbeth*. Set within the National's own red curtains, the crimson drapes onstage made a frame within a frame that commented ironically on the acts of spectatorship in which all present were engaged. Consciously therefore, as the lead actor of Pleskot's 1969 *Macbeth* was recycled as the theatrical director of this 1982 *Hamlet*, so the set on which Macháček had acted subtly appeared as the setting for another tragedy's most metatheatrical moments. Astute members of the audience were in tune with these intertextual references, but Svoboda kept his general stage trickery minimal. Little moved, flew or trucked in what was seen as an austere production. To avoid even excessive use of stage properties, parts of the inverted thrust of low steps and acting platforms were turned at different times into chairs, a throne and even Ophelia's grave. Svoboda deliberately kept his one *coup de théâtre* for the closing moments of the play: as the sword fighting of V.ii. reached its conclusion, the dying Claudius fell back onto, and pulled down, the long black drapes hanging at the upper end of a virtually bare stage. Suddenly, in the glare of strong open white lights, appeared a flight of twenty monumental steps, running the entire width of the stage, and mounting to a height of nearly five metres above the low main stage.

Backlit, and dramatically dwarfing the action on which the entire piece had played out, these steps recreated the cold and hostile metaphorical ambience of Svoboda's first *Hamlet* at the National, some twenty-three years previously. From the top of this architectonic statement of hidden power and authority (which had always been there and was now revealed almost as an accident to spectators in the closing seconds of the play), Fortinbras, the Norwegian Prince, descended. Described by one critic as the embodied beginning of a new era for the state of Denmark, he ordered four captains to bear away the dead prince. The seeming corpse of František Němec's Hamlet, carried upwards, his head towards the audience, was the closing image of the production: 'Good night, sweet prince, And flights of angels sing thee to thy rest!' (V.ii). Macháček's production was thus one of the very few stagings of the play that has achieved such a dramatic and stately exit for the deceased Dane. The moment was reminiscent of the slow pomp of the extended, ascending, funeral tracking shot that concludes Laurence Olivier's 1948 film production, but the Czech production's hope for redemption and yearning for the emergence of heroic leadership unknowingly presaged the fall of communism and the first democratic presidency of Václav Havel just seven years later.

Figure 2.9 Production photograph of *Hamlet* (Prague, 1982), showing the revealed flight of monumental steps

Source: Image from the private collection of Josef Svoboda © Šárka Hejnová, reproduced with permission

34   Christian M. Billing

In April 1987 Svododa returned to *Twelfth Night* in a production for the *Hochschule für Musik und darstellende Kunst, Max Reinhardt Seminar* (Vienna), directed by the academic theatre director Nikolaus Windisch-Spoerk. In the years following his first design for the play (1963), Svoboda had perfected the system of projecting onto string chords that he had first sought to utilise for the comedy in 1963 (a technical achievement largely arrived at in his production of *Tristan und Isolde* at Bayreuth in 1974). With this chord-projection technology mastered, Svoboda now developed radically the idea that he had first had for the play in Prague a quarter of a century previously and, working within the proscenium stage of the only extant Baroque theatre in Vienna (a gorgeous structure first opened in 1747, remodelled in high-Rococo style in 1767, and in which both Haydn and Mozart conducted), Svoboda placed a series of receding projection panels, each seven-and-a-quarter metres high and made up of multiple nylon and cotton chords (five millimetres in diameter and located with centres four centimetres apart). These string 'screens' were arranged in six receding rows, with either three or four screens to each row. There were gaps between screens so that actors could walk between them, but the location of these spaces was offset in each row so as to create as an ensemble a 'forest of strings' effect when seen through the proscenium arch. These chords were never fully illuminated and were most often lit with projected images from angles at the sides, creating a projection surface of incredible three-dimensional depth. Svoboda's ground plans for the set contain flow-chart drawings, showing the ways in which he anticipated actors would move in and around his maze-like forest. Thus performers appeared both within the projections and in dialogue with other actors who were located on the theatre's forestage, or also on a set of steps that Svoboda constructed leading from the stage into the theatre's auditorium so as to break the isolation of actors from audiences. This single, difficult to achieve, but extraordinarily simple scenic technique dominated the production. Aqueous visual metaphors again abounded, and the most enchanting images show the chords taking projections that make it look as if it is raining on stage.

The last Shakespeare production Svoboda designed opened in May 1991 at the *Raamtheater op 't Zuid* (Antwerp), directed by Walter Tillemans. This staging, of *Driekoningenavond* (*Twelfth Night*), arose in equal measure from Svoboda's admiration for the youth and vitality of the Belgian director with whom he collaborated, and also his respect for (and sense of joy derived from) the architecture of the space in which they worked. The Raamtheater is an intensely intimate space, converted from one of Antwerp's old historical buildings, but with the intention of recreating a galleried Elizabethan-style theatre. In fact, the effect is more like a French Neoclassical tennis court conversion. The theatre has a rectangular stage floor with wooden floorboards; rising from the level of the stage is a steeply raked set of stalls seats and around this space on all four sides are metal-worked, terraced galleries, rising to two levels above the theatre floor. The galleries are more airy than conventional theatre boxes because only elegant metal pillars with classically influenced ironwork capitals separate each section of them. Svoboda fell in love with this tiny space, which he came to only by chance at the invitation of Nikolaus

Windisch-Spoerk; he worked in it several times towards the end of his life. Each of his designs for the space, although radically different, was realised through the principle that this theatre could not be an environment for technical trickery, but rather was a space within which any design should carefully and respectfully exploit the architectural qualities of a wonderful, enclosed and yet light and airy performance environment: in short, the scenography of found space, or site specific theatre. Accordingly, Svoboda's set for this production of *Twelfth Night*, and his last Shakespeare design, was apparently very simple. On and above the bare wooden boards of the stage he himself spent three days hanging hundreds of translucent, silver-white, pearl-like balloons. Some clustered on the floor like the spawn of an absent aquatic beast, others floating in mid-air, like frothing bubbles ascending; or, perhaps, lost pearls falling downwards through water. Reviews of the production commented on the beauty of the balloons as they were pierced by directional theatrical lighting, of the playfulness of the design, and of the way in which it complimented Tillemans' fresh, vibrant cultivation of Shakespeare's imaginative language, his re-working of everything until it was clean and smooth. It is in this critical appreciation of the show that the genius of Svoboda can truly be seen: an object as simple as a conventional helium- or air-filled balloon was taken and used, not only as a potent visual metaphor for the play itself: its water, its hidden jewels, its search for simple truth and beauty; but also as a tangible visual appreciation of the director's style and of the acting-related aspirations of his youthful collaborators – in short, a potent visual coalescence of thought, theatrical framing and dramatic appreciation that led audiences to see both the play and the production for what they were. Although a lesser designer would perhaps never have seen their potential, looking back at Svoboda's last design for Shakespeare, we can now see 'these are pearls that were his eyes'.[4]

Notes

1   František Tröster (1904–68) was the most significant Czech designer of the mid-twentieth century. He worked with most major Central European directors of the inter-war avant-garde, and founded the Stage Design Department at DAMU (Prague) in 1946. He worked there for the rest of his life. Tröster achieved two hugely significant things in relation to world theatre design: (i) a shift from literalism to metaphorical expression, particularly involving architectural elements (Tröster was primarily an architect, not a painter); and (ii) the establishment of a practice of utilising new materials in a deliberately exploratory fashion wherever possible, in an attempt to find combinations of the unusual and the familiar. According to Oscar Niemeyer, Tröster's 'sculptural scenic architecture' was the beginning of modern stage design.

2   There were not many other Czech productions of Shakespeare's history plays during this period – with the exception of the 1987 production of *Henry IV* at the National (for which Jan Dušek did the scenography). With the benefit of hindsight, modern Czech scholars now acknowledge that the National was too afraid of the political implications of even *Richard III* – and Svoboda had by this stage of his career lost his desire to work on regional stages.

3   The historical phenomenon of 'Normalisation' in a Czechoslovakian context refers to the period 1969–1987. During these years (initially following the 1968 military

36 Christian M. Billing

intervention by Warsaw Pact armies and the replacement of the reformist Leader of the Communist Party of Czechoslovakia, Alexander Dubček, with the more hard-line and Soviet-servile Gustáv Husák) there was a consolidated attempt to restore centralist pro-Soviet version of Socialism and to re-establish Czechoslovakia as a compliant member of the Eastern bloc of socialist nations. 'Normalisation' involved five principal steps: (i) consolidation of political leadership in order to remove reformists and any pluralist philosophies; (ii) revocation or modification of any laws enacted by the reform movement; (iii) re-establishment of a centrally-controlled command economy to the detriment of attempts at liberating private enterprise; (iv) reinstatement of power to police authorities; and (v) development and consolidation of Czechoslovakian relations with other socialist nations, over and above any that had been developed with the West.

4   *Acknowledgements.* It would not have been possible to write this chapter without the selfless help of many individuals, who rightfully deserve an expression of my profound thanks here: Šárka Hejnová granted me access to her father's personal archive of productions in his former, now her own, home in Prague; Barbora Příhodová assisted me in my negotiations of that archive, as well as with the collections of the *Institut umění – Divadelní ústav*, Prague; Pavel Drábek translated numerous Czech-language reviews of productions that took place in Czechoslovakia, as well as obtaining DVD records of several key performances; Šárka Čermáková provided images and other documents from the archive of the *Divadlo J. K. Tyla, Plzeň*; Veronika Schandl both translated Hungarian reviews and obtained research materials on my behalf from the *Országos Színháztörténeti Múzeum és Intézet*, Budapest; Martin Hanoušek, Veronika Štefanová and other staff of the *Institut umění – Divadelní ústav*, Prague, helped with bibliographical matters and reviews relating to Czech evaluations of all Czech productions; Mariangela Tempera and Margaret Rose provided archival assistance and also forwarded materials from Italy. Like theatre making, then, the writing of theatre history is oftentimes a collaborative process, and particularly so when the *oeuvre* of a particular internationally renowned practitioner is far flung. The generosity of the individuals named above was exemplary. I thank them for their time, efforts, and their love of our discipline.

Bibliography

Bablet, Denis, *Josef Svoboda* (Lausanne: L'age D'homme, 2002).
Burian, Jarka, 'Josef Svoboda's Scenography for Shakespeare', in *Cross Currents: A Yearbook of Central European Culture*, Vol. 3 (Ann Arbor: University of Michigan Press, 1984), pp. 397–403.
Burian, Jarka, *The Scenography of Josef Svoboda* (Middletown, CT: Wesleyan University Press, 1974).
Burian, Jarka 'Hamlet in Post-war Czech Theatre', in Kennedy, Dennis, (ed.) *Foreign Shakespeare: Contemporary Performance* (Cambridge: Cambridge University Press, 1993).
Drábek, Pavel, *České pokusy o Shakespeara: Dějiny českých překladů Shakespeara doplněné antologií neznámých a vzácných textů z let 1782–1922* [Czech Attempts at Shakespeare: A History of Czech Translations of Shakespeare with an Anthology of Unknown and Rare Texts from the Years 1782–1922] (Brno: Větrné mlýny, 2012).
Flock, Sarah, *Rayonnement de la poétique d'Otomar Krejca en Belgique francophone*, Doctoral Dissertation Université Libre de Bruxelles, Faculté de Philosophie et Lettres (2010–11).
Hejna, Jakub (dir.) *Divadlo Svoboda [Theatre Svoboda]*, documentary film, produced by Jiří Konečný for Endorfilm, Prague 2011.
Svoboda, Josef, 'Nouveaux elements en scénographie', in *Scénographie: Le théâtre en Tchécoslovaquie* (Prague: Divadelní ústav, 1962), pp. 58–68.

Svoboda, Josef, 'The Role of Scenography in the Theatre', *The Times* (21/01/66) Interview.
Svoboda, Josef, *The Secret of Theatrical Space: The Memoirs of Josef Svoboda*, edited and translated by Jarka M. Burian (New York: Applause Theatre Books, 1992).
Svoboda, Josef, Personal Archive of Production Work (Prague).

Chapter 3

Scenography at the Royal Shakespeare Company 1963–1968

Towards an empty space

Liam Doona

> What is necessary however is an incomplete design; a design that has clarity without rigidity: one that could be called "open" as against "shut". This is the essence of theatrical making: a true theatre designer will think of his designs as being all the time in motion, in action, in relation to what the actor brings to a scene as it unfolds.[1]

Writing in 1968, Peter Brook outlines what has since become an established scenographic axiom; that in the theatre, the visual is vestigial; incomplete until the action of performance resolves the overall dramatic intention of the spatial and temporal moment. Embodied in the statement is an accumulation of learning and understanding about the role of scenography, much of which Brook owed to his participation in, and observation of developments at the Royal Shakespeare Company.

The RSC becomes between 1959 and 1968, under the lightning rod artistic direction of Peter Hall and his creative directorate of Peter Brook and Michel St Denis, the engine of a period of accelerated development and enquiry into "theatrical making". Having been prized in the stasis of the post-war years as an agency of social and cultural continuity, "Shakespeare" in the 1960s is reauthored and revisioned at the RSC as a globalised radical; un-attenuated by tradition and able to speak directly to and about the contemporary. It is a moment in which our understanding of Shakespeare's performance visuality, and scenography more broadly, is re-coined by Shakespeare's primary cultural agency.

Heavily influenced by his Cambridge tutor F.R. Leavis in his analytical scrutiny of text and meaning, and deliberately setting out to rediscover Shakespeare as a contemporary creative force, Peter Hall constructs the RSC as a critical and creative laboratory that purges a 200 year old pictorial tradition of stage design, and in doing so permanently unsettles the role, methods, and materiality of scenography. It is to be particularly from 1963 with the arrival of John Bury as Head of Design at the RSC and his scenography for *The Wars of The Roses* that a half-decade of practice and theory emerges which establishes these profound revisionings. With Peter Hall and John Barton's cycle of the Shakespeare histories staged though 1963 and 1964, Bury creates the antithesis of the dominant neo-romantic and visually episodic

Towards an empty space   39

tradition. His kinetic, rusting steel designs providing an early synthesis of a developing dialectic at the RSC – away from the rhetorical and the painterly and towards the sculpturally symbolic, the visceral and ultimately the metatheatrical.

Bury's disestablishment of pictorialism in effect signals a scenographic coup. The preceding School of Neo-romantic designers including such artists as Lilia De Nobli, Loudon Saint Hill, Desmond Heeley, James Bailey, and Leslie Hurry are disestablished and a new wave of young designers comes into place, including Sally Jacobs, Christopher Morley, Jocelyn Herbert, Ralph Koltai and Abdel Farrah. Informed by an innovative use of materials and a rediscovery of Elizabethan celerity, their flexible and open spaces though visually diverse, share a central characteristic, an anti-illusionistic purge of the directly representational, the decorative, and the superficial, a change which will ultimately lead to a dematerialisation of traditional scenography.

This reinvention is prefaced and informed by multiple, complex influences and contributions which ranged from the remarkable revelations of Peter Brook's six Stratford Shakespeares from 1945 to 1962,[2] to the publication of *Shakespeare Our Contemporary* by Jan Kott in 1961, The Berliner Ensemble's first visit to England in 1956 and the work of Joan Littlewood's Theatre Workshop. Mediated through Hall's creative directorate the period marks a dynamic convergence of new critical and scholarly thinking, absorbs wide-ranging European writing, staging and performance influences, and introduces a new aesthetic purpose to scenography, effectively emptying it of traditions and habits which had increasingly prescribed its visual potential.

Hall's departure from the RSC in 1968, to begin as artistic director of the National Theatre, concludes this period of radicalisation. Peter Brook's simultaneous publication of a new taxonomy of theatre, *The Empty Space*, effectively provides its coda manifesto and points towards the inevitable visual dénouement at the end of the decade, – *A Midsummer Night's Dream*. Designed by Sally Jacobs, it is a scenography fully unbuckled from the traditional obligation to provide referential or representational space.

Beginnings

> When I first went to Stratford in 1945 every conceivable value was buried in deadly sentimentality and complacent worthiness – a traditionalism approved largely by town, scholar and press.[3]

To understand the scale of scenographic achievement of Hall's RSC it is important to place its developments in a summary historical context and to briefly outline the landscape of Shakespearean production Hall and his collaborators were emerging from. During the first half of the twentieth century, scenography for Shakespeare had become increasingly contested. Whilst at the end of the nineteenth century William Poel had begun to argue against pictorial naturalism and for a return to an Elizabethan theatre form, following the turn of the century, others, Appia and

40   Liam Doona

Craig most notably, had argued that a visual language for Shakespeare cannot be found either in sceno-architectural precedent or in pictorial representationalism. Independently they develop visual theses for highly symbolic, abstracted spaces which will echo across twentieth-century scenographic development and coin early scenographic Modernism. During the 1920s and 1930s R.E. Jones in America, Leopold Jessner in Germany, Alexandra Exter in Russia and Paul Shelving in England, amongst many others, all contribute radical visual alternatives for Shakespeare which range from expressionism, symbolism, constructivism and high naturalism in modern dress. By the end of the 1940s European and American scenography for Shakespeare is a highly charged critical and creative field, though an effective anti-modernist school in Britain, led by designers such as Oliver Messel, Rex Whistler and their lieutenant at the then named Stratford Memorial Theatre, Leslie Hurry, will continue to promote a painterly and pictorial tradition.

By 1959 when Hall took up the role of Artistic Director at Stratford, the theatre could look back on 80 years of practice which had more than ably demonstrated this churning visuality. Despite Brook's gloomy post-war assessment, he speaks of a theatre which had periodically championed moments of extraordinary visual innovation – Komisarjevsky's designs for *The Merchant of Venice* in 1932, *Macbeth* in 1933, *King Lear* in 1936, *The Comedy of Errors* in 1938 all stand as moments of reinvention. The Motley collective's rationalisation of the stage and development of clear, elegant and stylish productions, Moseiwitch's muscular reinventions of a Jacobean multiplatform stage amongst others are all moments of success which attempt to break the hold of the Neo-Romantic. But the pre-war directorship at Stratford of William Bridges Adams to be "a custodian of eternal values" generally prevails in the 1940s and 1950s and cements the Neo-Romantics, pictorial style, seeking its inspiration more in nineteenth-century scenography than a development of the experimentalism of pre-war modernism.

Anthony Quayle, Hall's predecessor at Stratford, accurately conveys the manoeuvrability available to designers during the 1950s and the expectations of scenography:

> What degree of symmetry to aim at in the settings; how pictorial the setting may be; how much to make use of modern lighting equipment and how much to eschew it; whether to dress the characters in contemporary, Elizabethan costume or in the realistic dress of the period – these are some of the basic problems with which producer and designer wrestle with for months before ever a play goes into rehearsal. The work is made all the more fascinating by their knowledge that they may produce an answer which is both scholarly and theatrically effective, but that they can never produce a final and complete solution.[4]

For Quayle, Shakespeare is a set of more or less delineated alternatives. Designers such as Loudon Sainthill and James Bailey are in the ascendency. Theirs was work which colluded with the idea of Shakespeare as a Romantic writer and their emphasis was on an established visual rhetoric and materiality that could trace its aesthetic and technological ancestry directly back to Philippe de Loutherbourg's Romantic staging's of the eighteenth century. Their work was typically comprised of either firmly Elizabethan or Classical landscapes, highly pictorial and representational in their organisation, and occupied by actors in heightened re-constructions of period costume. These were production values which privileged an iconography of Classical painting and presented Shakespeare as a measure of traditional, conservative culture.

Peter Brook was the first post-war producer systematically to challenge this sensibility from within. Ironically, with the exception of a co-direction of the *Tempest* in 1963, he was not to direct a Shakespeare during the period in question. However, Brook's six Shakespeares at Stratford until 1962 each contribute to the radicalisation of scenography throughout the 1960s. Like Komisarjevsky before him, his productions at Stratford are always challenging, innovative and surprising. Each in some way provides a landmark in English scenography. His *Romeo and Juliet* of 1947 which reduced the visual landscape to ankle high city walls surrounding a blank stage backed by a brilliant blue cyclorama, and *Titus Andronicus* in 1955 which translated Lavinia's tongueless mouth and severed wrists to streaming red ribbons evidence an artist seeking a wholly authentic and innovative visuality. Set amongst the work of Leslie Hurry, Motley, Joseph Carl, James Bailey and other contemporaries at Stratford, these were moments of high visual daring and disruption.

Described by Barry Jackson as "the youngest earthquake I know",[5] Brook demonstrated the potential of Shakespearean scenography at Stratford to reach beyond established visuality and to begin to find new embodiments. Increasingly this is achieved by investing the productions in one major visual motif or symbol. Initially discovered in *Romeo and Juliet* in 1947 where, "The wings were filled with redundant items of expensive scenery",[6] Brook becomes ever more deliberate and testing in his clarification of scenographic purpose, as the visual ambition of his scenography shifts its reference points from the painterly to the sculptural and productions begin to value disruption over continuity, becoming increasingly conceptual in their visioning.

> One must remember that there are two forms of simplicity – the one that comes from a colourless and uninventive mind, and the real simplicity, which is the hardest thing to attain. Real simplicity comes when the imagination has purged itself of a thousand extravagances, stripping them down to an essence that has meaning and beauty.[7]

Brook offered Hall a clear insight into what such a purge might achieve in his 1962 production of *King Lear*. Immediately preceding John Bury's designs for *The Wars of the Roses* cycle it is a pivotal work and Brook's last direction of a Shakespeare until *Midsummer Night's Dream* in 1970.

Brook's creative restlessness had brought him to the Polish theorist Jan Kott by 1961. Familiar with the first French publication of *Shakespeare our Contemporary*,

42   Liam Doona

Brook recognised in it a manifesto which privileged a refreshed view of the plays and an approach which deliberately eschewed critical and visual precedence, seeking instead synchronicity with contemporary cultural and philosophical positions. Kott situates Shakespeare within the avant-garde of contemporary writing; specifically he cites Beckett's *Endgame* as a corollary of *Lear* and offers a succinct thematic; "The theme of *King Lear* is the decay and fall of the world."[8] This apparently simple distillation captures the moment that Shakespearean production is finally and permanently unbuckled from the nineteenth-century scenographic tradition at Stratford. It sets *Lear* outside the purely temporal and within the universal.

The impact of Kott on Brook was sufficient for him to halt his original visual concept:

> His first design had been a beautiful but harsh Renaissance world. The set was elaborate and the Stratford workshops had started to make it. Then Brook suddenly arrived in my office with a new model that was austere, spare, and hung with sheets of rusted iron... The play became all the more powerful because it was not illustrated literally.[9]

As director and designer Brook defined the key scenic components of *Lear* as two great rectangular canvas flats set symmetrically like open jaws. Within this anonymous, monumental space actors are costumed in heavy leather and canvas tabards. These have the effect of reducing the human silhouette to its simplest form, abstracted almost conical shapes. Brook's additions to the space are simple, rough, almost megalithic sculptural objects. Culturally anonymous, they speak only to extend the sense of a desolate, barren and inhospitable landscape beyond the flat, dead walls of the space. This is not only a pre-industrial, pre-modern world but it is a godless world, one where an apparently doomed humanity plays out futile, inevitably tragic power struggles.

For the storm scene Brook's master stroke is to introduce the sheets of steel used in theatre to create the sounds of thunder. Suspended above the stage they effectively split open an entire tradition of English scenography. These pieces are simultaneously the voicing of the storm, the unyielding material of the world of the play and a sculptural and sonic embodiment of Lear's collapse.

> Three steel sheets, discoloured with rust and time, were slowly flown in, like guillotine blades. Seeing the production in 1962 and watching these sheets inexorably descend they also brought to mind rough tongues of giant monsters. Then, they begin to vibrate, gently at first, making a distant growl, then more violently as the electric motors powering them accelerated, until they were shaking and buckling alarmingly above the solitary Gloucester: everyone else having rushed indoors for shelter.[10]

The identification of a key thematic and a correlating symbol or set of symbols describes the major methodological shift intrinsic to post-war scenographic

Modernism. The role of the design to resolve the sequential locations of the text within an overarching pictorial aesthetic template is replaced with the situating of a major, governing idea which outweighs in importance the topography of location in favour of a holistic, metaphorical or symbolic sculptural parallel. This underpinning concept, which may materialise in a variety of ways, establishes the grand vision of the production and means that all the events of the play are situated in direct relationship to this central visual idea. Whereas in Neo-Romantic design the scenographer is charged with the development of a sequence of vistas, here the designer is responsible for what is essentially a spatial sculpture, a sounding space which tunes the text to a newly revealed idea or meaning about its purpose or content.

In Brook's 1962 *Lear*, the accepted purpose of scenography to act as an index of an elsewhere is dispatched. Scenography here is its own referent with its own language of symbols. The logic and integrity of this world is entirely contained, rather as in the form of rituals, in its own materiality and spatial organisation. Brook's space for *Lear* is not a codified version or re-presentation of another actual historical or cultural location but instead, it intones its own world. With Brook's *Lear*, scenography at the RSC began to resonate with the materials and preoccupations not of classical painting, but of contemporary sister disciplines in the visual arts. The forms and textures finding a strong concurrence with the contemporaneous development in English sculpture were to be found, for example, in new English artists Lynn Chadwick, Reg Butler, Eduardo Paolozzi, William Turnbull and Bernard Meadows. Following the success of their joint show in the Venice Biennale of 1952 the critic Herbert Read wrote, "These new images belong to the iconography of despair, or of defiance...here are images of flights, frustrated sex, the geometry of fear."[11]

Whilst Brook's visuality laid out a new creative architecture, one which absorbed contemporary writing, philosophy and visual arts, it was one which Hall would only partly conform to in his first years of tenure. Hall was certainly a new broom but it would take some time for the stage to be completely swept clean.

Hall's priority from the outset of the RSC had been the establishment of an ensemble of performers. Inspired by the achievements of Berliner Ensemble, he recognised that in order to advance the performance of Shakespeare he needed to maintain an acting company which could be developed and trained to a shared contemporary performance understanding. This training element was to be substantially Michel St Denis' role. Beyond his ambitions for performers, Hall also clearly recognised the need for design excellence. However he did not initially advance one aesthetic over another and in the first phase of his tenure, design at the RSC was clearly in transition. Moseiwitch, Hurry and de Nobili featured amongst newer designers some of whom were to become central to the RSC; Bury, Jacobs, Koltai. Others would feature only briefly, including notably, Hall's initial choices as associate designers: Sean Kenny, Leslie Hurry and Desmond Heeley.

Amongst the multiple projects of expansion and development[12] he left some stones unturned. In his own productions Hall had yet been to find a scenographer

44   Liam Doona

who could keep pace with Brook. Indeed whilst a committed moderniser Hall was not, visually at least, a committed Modernist. Hall said of his regular collaborator, de Nobili,

> Her work was supremely romantic but never camp. She had a child's vision, an ability to look sadly at the world as if it were disintegrating into an over ripe autumn of browns, yellows and golds, with the occasional splash of blue or orange to show where the energy had been before the fall. Her sets were a cunning amalgam of painted cloths and gauzes. She knew all the tricks of the classic Italian scene painters; hers was a theatre of illusion, dark shadows and glowing highlights.[13]

If De Nobli's work was in direct succession with the Italian master painters she would certainly have recognised the last moment of full blown Neo-Romanticism Hall's RSC would preside over. Through Zeffirelli's production of *Othello* in 1961 with John Gielgud in the title role, Hall learned a valuable and never forgotten lesson about scenography.

Zeffirelli – an opera director – had designed a series of settings which owed more to the theatre of one hundred years before than to contemporary design.

> There were pillars, grills, battlements to be flown in and out; huge embossed doors to be erected vast flights of stairs to be put up and dismantled. Many of the sets were painted chocolate brown, so that when Gielgud, in his Othello makeup, stood against them, his face became immediately invisible. The dress rehearsal lasted five hours, at the end of which the unfortunate actors had not even got through the whole play. The first night lasted four and half hours … And was punctuated by the frantic sound of back stage hammerings … When the sets were in place, an exquisite stage picture, superbly lit and reminiscent of a Veronese painting was achieved – but only at the cost of the destruction of the play.[14]

Zeffirelli had been John Gielgud's choice of producer, and the price for Gielgud coming to Stratford. Convinced of the importance of bringing such leading actors to Stratford, Hall had agreed and laid the foundations for the largest disaster of his first period. As a result by the time of Brook's *Lear* in 1962, scenography at the RSC was effectively polarised. Brook stood to one side, the Neo-Romantics to the other. Hall's final work with Leslie Hurry, *Troilus and Cressida* in 1962, would see a kind of temporary compromise between the two schools. It was short lived and marked the end of Hall's creative partnership with Hurry.

> The production of *Troilus and Cressida*, in which the characters thrashed out their physical conflicts in a big sandpit designed by Leslie Hurry, started me on a journey through Shakespeare's political ironies which led to the War of the Roses and David Warner's Hamlet.[15]

This use of a 'real material' in a Hurry design sits outside the oeuvre of a designer whose instinct and aesthetic is genuinely Neo-Romantic. A painter by training and inclination Hurry had come to Stratford following success with ballet designs for Robert Helpmann and throughout the 1950s had offered some of the finest examples of Neo-Romantic design. Hurry had a masterful grasp of colour and line and his highly illusionistic settings shared de Nobili's understanding of chiaroscuro and illusion. But Troilus and Cressida is not recognisably a Hurry design. Whilst his costumes continue his love of classical allusion, the staging is quite different. Reduced to its key elements; a simple octagonal sand pit and a bloody cyclorama, it has none of Hurry's usual illusionistic gestures. But Troilus was a personal breakthrough for Hall.

> That production had a brilliantly innovative set (designed surprisingly by Leslie Hurry) of the utmost simplicity; it consisted of a shallow octagonal box filled with white sand, backed by a cyclorama the colour of dried blood. It suited the bleakness of the play's vision, and provided a superb background for the spectacular Homeric fight sequences, brilliantly lit and using mist (dry ice) for the first time at Stratford – a device then so unfamiliar that some of the critics thought it was steam.[16]

The development of the design had clearly been a challenging one for both Hall and Hurry. As Hall described in his autobiography:

> Leslie Hurry and I reached it by chance. We had a hexagonal shaped arena as the floor of our model setting, and I kept asking him to make it more like sand. I wanted it to be yellow– a colour his palette for the play did not readily encompass. Finally he rolled his grey eyes to heaven and said, "Why don't you just have real sand?" To, I think his surprise I jumped at the suggestion. And though we had to endure the jokes of the cast turning up for rehearsal clad in large sunglasses, and the scoffing of critics who thought real sand ridiculous, the texture and the movement of it made the production ring.[17]

Based on this discovery there remained for Hall a crucial element, where to find a designer who could collaborate on this new kind of Shakespearean production aesthetic.

John Bury

Within the mainstream of British stage design the reluctance to accept Modernism and to retain Neo-Romantic ideals had meant that post-war design innovation by European practitioners especially the Berliner Ensemble's Casper Neher and Karl von Appen had been explored and adopted only in isolated pockets. One of the most important of these was Theatre Workshop, a highly politicised cooperative theatre company formed on socialist principles and led by Joan Littlewood and Ewan MacColl.

46   Liam Doona

Theatre Workshop played a highly important role in the 1950s and 1960s in establishing an alternative theatre to the commercial, popular stage and developed, partly out of economic and technical necessity and partly out of political and aesthetic ideology, a visual language of production which coined a form of selective realism. Recycling found architectural materials and objects to create highly dynamic, fragmentary and expressive stage spaces.

By 1958 with their production of Shelagh Delaney's *A Taste of Honey*, the company has refined its aesthetic to a highly coherent approach to stage design which valued carefully selected architectural elements to construct both a coherent sense of a tangible world but also a highly theatrical symbol. *A Taste of Honey* emerges as part of a new canon of realist working-class drama of which John Osborne's *Look Back in Anger* is to the be the centrepiece. However, it does not conform to the traditional scenographic expectations of realism at the time, instead dealing with its multi-locational demands by simultaneously overlaying the visual remains of places to provide a sculptural, angular and dynamic multiple setting which deploys compositional mastery and a skillful use of lighting to, by turns, connect or dislocate the separate sculptural elements.

The designer of *A Taste of Honey* was partly trained chemist, John Bury, who had no art school training but progressed since the late 1940s through the open creative structure of Theatre Workshop to be lighting and set designer. Bury's work with Littlewood saw him occupy almost all possible positions in the company from performer to electrician, set builder and director. His grounding was therefore in the highly practical world of theatre making. It is a practice which values pragmatism as an aesthetic merit and which informs a visual style which is learned not at the easel or in the model box but on the rehearsal-room floor and in the workshop.

As early as 1954 when Bury designed *Richard II* for Theatre Workshop he established a clear, neo-Brechtian alternative to the aesthetic establishment. Coinciding with the Old Vic's production in the same year, the contrast with the highly pictorial central London production and Theatre Workshop's spare, monumental simplicity could not be starker. Bury's style, variously described by himself as "selective realism" or "unconventional realism" inherited some elements of Expressionism in that the choice and organisation of elements indicated distortion and their fragmented dispersal was intended to resonate with the central dramatic dilemma. His combined role of stage and lighting designer meant that he had none of the concerns of the neo-pictorialists for painted surfaces and illusion. Instead he was attracted to dynamic angular forms and strong textures, all of which created an exciting visual interplay when lit dramatically. Within these environments real objects and costumes could resonate beyond their naturalistic potential, acquiring a heightened poetic power without losing their reference to the real world.

Hall clearly recognised in Bury's designs[18] and his own experience of *Troillus* that locationally and temporally complex works could be given dramatic clarity and attack by revealing them through these neo-Brechtian performance spaces. By moving away from sequential vistas to symbolic platforms, the action could play without interruption, which allowed for the seamless visual experience to bring clarity and directness. Here, additionally, was a scenography which grounded the events rather than simply locating them, providing explanation and motivation. By making the scenography less archaeologically and topographically representational and more symbolically charged, the work became more accessible, more immediate and to use Hall's favourite term, more relevant.

The Wars of the Roses and after

But what did in fact the Grand Mechanism mean for Shakespeare? A succession of kings climbing and pushing one another off the grand staircase of history, or a wave of hot blood rising up to one's head and blinding the eyes? A natural order that has been violated, so that evil produces evil, every injury calls for revenge, every crime causes another? Or a cruel social order in which vassals and superiors are in conflict with each other, the kingdom is ruled like a farm and falls prey to the strongest? A naked struggle for power, or a violent beat of the human heart that reason cannot accelerate or stop, but a dead piece of sharp iron breaks once and for all? A dense and impenetrable night of history where dawn does not break, or a darkness that fills the human soul?[19]

When Hall began his planning for the great cycle of history plays, *Henry IV Parts 1 and 2, Henry V, Henry VI Parts 1, 2 and 3 and Richard III, The Wars of the Roses*, he did so with a real urgency to establish the pre-eminence of his company, cement its financial security and establish a new theatrical voicing of Shakespeare. In Bury he now had a designer with the visual skill and practical ability to describe the major visual journey the works would require within a coherent and practicable format, and one who could create a visuality appropriate to the critical and creative scrutiny he and his co-director John Barton would impose upon it.

As a designer who did not work through drawing and painting, Bury was an entirely new kind of practitioner at the RSC. Indeed, Bury had rejected Hall's initial offer of a meeting because he did not have a portfolio, but Bury was able to manifest an entirely new kind of highly physical scenography which along with work by Ralph Koltai and Sean Kenny was quickly gaining status. It is with Hall that Bury's materials centred approach synthesised into a wholly authentic scenographic method. In their two key productions of the period, *The Wars of the Roses* and *Hamlet*, the material of the environment becomes the means of manifesting the production's central concern. In *Wars of the Roses* it is metal, "dead, sharp iron". In *Hamlet* it is the cold, black reflections of marble. Bury and Hall's creative journey for *War of The Roses* began in a research visit to the armoury of Warwick Castle. Hall was attracted to the image and material of a sword. Its purpose and materiality clearly spoke of generations of power struggle. It was both a material and an object which embodied purpose and history. Its flat shape provided the killing edge but, as Bury recognised in his designs, its materiality meant it could perform as a table, a floor, a wall, whilst still retaining its core symbolic meaning.

48 Liam Doona

The sword embodied what Kott had conceptualised as the "Grand Mechanism", the killing machine of history, a self-perpetuating and always present battle for power. In this object Hall and Bury found the exquisite coincidence of text and visuality which Kott's discussion of the Shakespeare histories required and Hall envisaged. However, it was not simply a logo. This was an element which could inform all aspects of performance and which would directly influence the speaking, the music and the performance style. It brought a specific language of sound, movement, weight, texture and colour. Working through the central visual motif, Bury's scenography now needed to facilitate multiple internal and external locations in England and France and to communicate the grinding power struggles of the texts.

Two giant metal clad doors which were able to open or close the space provided a means of managing the overall scale of the playing space and moving for example between exteriors and interiors, their movement effectively wiping away one scene and discovering the next. Treated as rusted steel on one side and copper on the other, they could create the shift between England and France. The addition of bare trees provided a sense of landscape beyond. Bury's brilliance here is not only in developing the central theme symbolically, but in extending that symbolism into the nature of the scenographic shifts between location. Rather than an episodic approach where scene changes are managed in darkness or behind a curtain, Bury choreographs the scenery so that each movement is a visual reminder of the grinding action of events in this "great steel cage of war".[20] Setting the entire scenography on a one in eight rake, a steep slope leading down to the audience, had the effect of making the world seem ready to fall into the auditorium at any moment, heightening the sense of danger and immediacy.

Unusually for the RSC, Bury also lit the production. Working entirely with open white light, Bury used intensity and direction in place of colour. The effect was to heighten the textured complexity of the surfaces and to emphasise the monolithic, sculptural qualities of the space. This was a new kind of post Brechtian realism, a visual epic created by the convergence of all production elements through a single guiding thematic. Bury had shifted scenography to a new materiality following which it became almost impossible to use the painterly or illusionistic techniques of the neo-romantics without the effect seeming ironic or simply implausible. Ralph Koltai was to further abstract and extend this new materiality in a remarkable world of objects for the 1965 production of *The Jew of Malta*. His highly sculptural scenography used combinations of found and made objects, beautifully composed, to create a sense of historically laden landscapes.

Whilst both designers deeply invested in the latent power of materials to function symbolically, the effect of their scenographies is quite different. Bury's spaces are genuinely scenographic in that they are completed by the presence of performers. They are forms designed to specifically support moments of drama. Koltai's works are more independently sculptural and abstract, existing in empathetic parallel to the text. Taken together, Koltai and Bury by 1965 represent contrasting approaches in this new school of materiality with Farrah's use of plastics in the 1963 *Tempest* and

Jocelyn Herbert's use of wire mesh for *Richard III* in 1961 being further examples. The tempo of design innovation at the RSC was gaining pace as new designers with their highly challenging approaches to space and materials gained confidence and tested the boundaries of scenographic materiality ever further.

By 1966, as Head of Design, Bury had been able to lead design practice at the RSC over an extended period and to create a clear visual style which supported Hall's refreshed approach to Shakespearean performance. But it is an approach which was to be quickly unsettled by a combination of aesthetic and pragmatic concerns. Bury recognised that in order to develop and build a distinctive visual approach whilst working with a diverse group of designers some restraining aesthetic template would need to be put in place. Additionally he recognised that the RSC budgets were extremely finite and a means of extending the potential of this budget was essential. Bury explained, "we wanted to feel in different directions – but we didn't want to have stage hands changing scenery every night and building different shape stages etc. So, we started to create the 'box situation' the grey box with standard floor and standard rake, in which everybody had to work."[21]

By creating a supposedly neutral stage space which provided a sense of scenic focus and containment, Bury had intended to maximise the visual potential of any element placed within it. In his later plans for the Aldwych Theatre, the RSC's London home from the early 1980s, he developed this idea further.

> The other thing we were very keen on is that we wanted to continue with our theory that a production needs its own amount of scenery, and nobody else's amount. By which I mean that the problem of a conventional stage is that if you want to do a production – say a Beckett – or something which needs a chair and dustbin and nothing else – then you have to create an enormous amount of scenery to hide the lighting battens and stage manager and the rest of it. It costs just as much to put on this low budget production as it does a high budget production, because of the huge volume of stage that has to be filled.[22]

The preceding period had clearly evidenced that materiality conveys specific scenographic significance, but the playing out of that significance across an entire scenographic landscape such as for the *Wars of the Roses* was not always desirable or practicable.

The Hall/Bury *Hamlet* of 1965 captures this moment of transition as the dark containing chamber begins to appear within which an inset marble floor communicates the central materialist concept. However, it is in the costume detail of Hamlet's rough red woollen scarf that its audience recognises a young student, very much their contemporary. An advantage of the "box situation" is being discovered in the capacity to bestow amplified significance and focus through the deliberate overall reduction of visual elements.

At the same time as Hall and Bury were preparing the *Hamlet* of 1965, Peter Brook's parallel investigations into the Artaud inspired Theatre of Cruelty are

50   Liam Doona

climaxing in his production of *The Persecution and Assassination of Jean-Paul Marat as Performed by the Inmates of the Asylum of Charenton Under the Direction of the Marquis de Sade* by Peter Weiss.[23] Working with the designer Sally Jacobs who had been attracted by the idea of Brook's highly experimental London workshops, the *Marat/Sade* design signals the end of the highly materialist works of the early to mid-1960s as working with Bury's "box situation", scenography begins to purposefully dematerialise towards empty chambers which architecturally bound the performance space, but are topographically ambiguous.

Marat/Sade's play within a play concept allowed Brook and Jacobs to examine concepts of a metatheatrical scenography using a basic chamber, container, or open box which resonates the dramatic locus of the text primarily through the costumes and properties, but simultaneously reminds us of its own theatricality. Jacobs expresses the walls of the box as rough brick, potentially supporting the implied topography of the fictional asylum but equally capable of being read as the bare walls of the real theatre. This deliberate playing out of the liminality of performance, balancing on the threshold of the real and the fictional, is a signature of Brook/Jacob's work. With *Marat/Sade*, scenography becomes about the theatre as the dramatic and scenographic site, as "theatre making" itself begins to express its own ritual and symbolic matrices. Jacob's design certainly acknowledges the architecture of the fictional asylum, but it does so in a way which deliberately blends or confuses it with the architecture of the theatre itself. There is no longer a sense of the fictional scenographic world continuing beyond its walls. Here rather the world of the play exists only within this chamber and the world beyond is explicitly that of the contemporary audience. It is a scenography which is returning again to question its role as index. Where scenographic surfaces and boundaries have previously served as a mediator between the visioned, fictional world we can see and its implied world continuing beyond, in *Marat/Sade* this implied world is actual and inhabited by the audience. It is Brook's first "open box".

In *Marat/Sade* the materiality of scenography is becoming the architecture of the space itself. The juxtaposition offered at the RSC by 1965/66 of the monumental symbols of Koltai and Bury and the bounded spatial absence of Jacobs and Brook is stark, but both approaches emerge from an identical concern to understand theatrical space.

Christopher Morley's arrival at the RSC in 1966 is at the vanguard of the next phase of design revolution, much of which will substantially occur under Trevor Nunn's direction following Hall's departure. Morley's instinct, like Jacobs, is for an economy of visuality which privileges the performer in space over and above the materiality of the built scenography and it is largely through Morley that the chamber designs of the late 1960s are developed. Whilst certainly not explicitly a school of minimalism Morley and Jacobs are to create spaces which are highly objective and topographically unencumbered as part of continuing to examine the requirements around scenographic representationalism. However, their shift towards a form of scenographic minimalism demonstrates that simplicity of form does not equate with simplicity of experience. Indeed the deliberate openness has the additional benefit of providing the creative ensemble with the maximum period of experimentation and discovery, as the scenographic chamber does not prescribe action but allows for change, discovery and development.

Ironically Morley's first design, due to budget constraints is essentially a borrowing of Bury's *Hamlet*. Morley and Nunn's vison of their first RSC production, *The Revengers Tragedy* returns decadence to the RSC stage but in a wholly new form. Locating the text within Bury's black world, Morley isolates the performers in an even greater darkness than Bury had achieved.

> Christopher Morley, the designer, has conceived the whole evening as a carnival of stark blacks, whites, and glittering silver. The masked court whirls in a torchlit pavane out of a sable limbo into diseased phosphorescence. The scenes of charnel-poetry take on a funereal pomp: at the other end of the scale, the duchess's idiot sons appear as chalk-faced clowns from a silent film, bickering and cuffing like Laurel and Hardy in ruffs.[24]

Costumes take a recognisable seventeenth century-silhouette but disguise their cheapness (they are made from lining material) beneath the encrusted, swirling patterns of silver formed from painted latex drips and swirls. The effect in Tourneur's study of sexuality and revenge is one of evil luxuriating in itself, characters isolated in pools of glistening white light. The impact of performers materialising in apparently empty space is mesmeric and confirms the new visual direction of spaces which are increasingly ambiguous in their cultural and architectural motifs but gain specificity through their costumes and properties.

An empty space

By his own admission Hall would see the last period of his tenure as losing the energy and direction in place before 1966. Hall's tenure had seen a highly energised, ultimately exhausting, engagement with new and challenging forms of theatre making which, within a brief and intense period, radically transformed British theatre's visuality and enabled the development of an authentic English school of scenography, diverse in its outputs but collectively prizing visual economy over pictorial exuberance.

This English School had in *The Empty Space* its own distinctive rubric which would be a long-standing critical companion piece to theatre making and describe a transformed understanding of the role of the scenographer, particularly in relationship to the classical text. By 1968 the idea of the designer as décorateur, or mise-en-scène as a pictorial assemblage of an historical topography have become obsolete. Shakespeare as the site for innovation and experimentation is established as is the need for all design to emerge not from precedent or an accepted template, but from close critical scrutiny of the text and parallel creative enquiry and innovation.

Hall's objective rediscovery of text, the realpolitik impetus of Kott and the increasing exchange of cognisance between scenography and the visual arts more

52   Liam Doona

broadly, jolts design for Shakespeare out of its familiar territories and establishes it as one the primary challenges of contemporary stage design. It is a point at which British theatre moves beyond a polarised dialectic to a more complex – perhaps ultimately more confusing – but infinitely richer landscape of visual practice.

Historically, no other body of dramatic writing can be said to have played such a profound and formative role in the evolution of scenography as Shakespeare's, and it is in large part because of the RSC's sustained investigations and developments we continue to see these texts as endlessly mutable. Ultimately Hall, Bury and Brook's shared legacy was in a revolution which did not argue for a single point of view or a single visuality, but which argued for an empty space in which to examine the myriad alternatives which the times, the resources and the concerns may prompt. The role of the designer in this process of rejection and renewal, stripping away precedent and unsettling previous interpretations is now central to the practice of staging Shakespeare and to re-coining the texts in the currency of contemporary audiences.

> In life there is a myth; we ourselves can never go back on anything. New leaves never turn, clocks never go back, we can never have a second chance. In the theatre the slate is wiped clean all the time.[25]

Notes

1   Peter Brook (1990) *The Empty Space*, London, Penguin. p. 114.
2   *Love's Labour's Lost* (1946); *Romeo and Juliet* (1947); *Measure for Measure* (1950); *Titus Andronicus* (1955); *The Tempest* (1957); *King Lear* (1962).
3   Peter Brook (1990) *The Empty Space*, London. Penguin, p. 51.
4   Ivor Brown and Anthony Quayle (1951) *Shakespeare Memorial Theatre 1948 –1950. A Photographic Record*, London Reinhardt and Evans, p. 17.
5   Michael Kustow (2005) *Peter Brook: A Biography*, London. Bloomsbury, p. 43.
6   Peter Brook (1999) *Threads of Time*, Methuen.
7   Michael Kustow (2005) *Peter Brook: A Biography*, London, Bloomsbury, p. 55.
8   Jan Kott (1974) *Shakespeare Our Contemporary*, Norton and Co., New York, p. 152.
9   Peter Hall (2000) *Making an Exhibition of Myself*, Oberon, p. 206.
10 Michael Kustow (2005) *Peter Brook A Biography*, London, Bloomsbury, p. 125.
11 Herbert Read, *New Aspect of British Sculpture 1952*, quoted in *Geometry of Fear* catalogue. Exhibition curated by Ann Jones, with Jill Constantine and Natalie Rudd.
12 Hall set in place the staging of 43 new productions between 1960 and 1963 and re-designed the Stratford stage to provide a deeper forestage.
13 Peter Hall (2000) *Making and Exhibition of Myself*, Oberon, p. 118.
14 Sally Beauman (1982) *The Royal Shakespeare Company*, Oxford, Oxford University Press, p. 247.
15 Peter Hall (2000) *Making and Exhibition of Myself*, Oberon, p. 116.
16 Sally Beauman (1982) *The Royal Shakespeare Company*, Oxford, Oxford University Press, p. 246.
17 Peter Hall (2000) *Making and Exhibition of Myself*, Oberon, p. 167.
18 Bury also designed *Macbeth* directed by Donald McWhinnie in 1961 at the RSC.
19 Jan Kott (1974) *Shakespeare our Contemporary*, New York, p. 30.
20 Dennis Kennedy (1996) *Looking at Shakespeare*, Cambridge, Cambridge University Press, p. 179.

Towards an empty space 53

21 David Addenbrooke, *The Royal Shakespeare Company*, p 216.
22 David Addenbrooke, The Royal Shakespeare Company, p 217.
23 The RSC's commitment to writing other than Shakespeare had been an essential part of Hall's strategy to attract and retain a company of word class performers and to contextualise Shakespeare both amongst his historical contemporaries for example Marlowe and new writing. Hall's commitment to Pinter for example begins at the RSC which under the direction of Peter Daubney hosts an international season of visiting theatre work and produces works by Durrenmat, Vian and Hochhuth.
24 Ronald Bryden (1966) *The Observer*, 9 October.
25 Peter Brook (1990) *The Empty Space*, London: Penguin, p. 157.

Chapter 4

Karl-Ernst Herrmann
Unfolding Shakespeare's space

Klaus van den Berg

Unfolding and visual field

In his exploration of visual history in twentieth-century Shakespeare productions, Dennis Kennedy observed that Shakespeare's plays are generally "'open' texts" which offer few physical characteristics of locations.[1] In contrast, the "visual field of a production" (13), consisting not only of the scenographic elements on stage but also of awareness of the venue's architecture, its integration into an urban context, and the overall perception of space at a moment in time, can be rather complex. The divergence between the dearth of physical actuality and the rich force field consisting of a repository of historical spaces for any Shakespeare performance requires a careful unfolding of space in production that has become one of the measurements of a designer's substantive contribution to performance history. With regard to Shakespeare's "open text," it means to unfold a world that is mostly out of sight in the plays' composition as a result of the bare stage Shakespeare employed for his productions. As Shakespeare's plays have moved farther away from their historical period, greater skill of scenographic transformation is required to establish a visual field that allows the text to move through a sequence of images and to unfold the repository of spaces inside the visual field.

In the well-endowed and de-centralized German theatre landscape, which supplies large ensembles, financial support, and an educated audience, Shakespeare's plays have had a long and diverse history of scenographic solutions. Like no other author, Shakespeare's plays have been a site for competing visions and artistic ideals. Starting with the first detailed creations under Johann Wolfgang von Goethe at the Weimar Court Theatre in the eighteenth and early nineteenth centuries, Shakespeare's plays have been a force field for ideological contests between, for example, Max Reinhardt's lavish and romantic view of Shakespeare, Leopold Jessner's expressionist versions or the Nazi's co-opting the "open text" for shaping their own visual reality at the Schaupielhaus Berlin throughout the 1930s. Furthermore, the availability of many excellent and suggestive German translations has increased the likelihood for visionary Shakespeare productions in the German theatre.

From a historiographical perspective, the post-World War II era in Germany became a contested political and artistic force field that not only increased the potential for visual complexity but also the challenge for rendering the space of Shakespeare's open text legible. Germany's military, political, and cultural defeat in 1945 did not put an end to the various strands of Shakespeare interpretations but rechanneled the existing artistic potential as many directors, actors, and designers continued their work in the 1950s and 1960s within a new political framework. Germany, now divided until reunification in 1990, experienced a fundamental loss of home and culture, a recalibration of ideology through the superimposition of American democracy and capitalism (West) and the Soviet-style communism (East). While both the newly founded Federal Republic of Germany and German Democratic Republic struggled with their own histories and managed the new ideologies by developing a repertory of plays speaking to this situation,[2] Shakespeare's plays remained a convenient artistic site to re-invent visual realities and to restructure social and political experience.[3] Post-war audiences, deprived of a positive cultural and political vision in the midst of devastation left by World War II and the ensuing cold war, continued to be receptive for Shakespeare's histories and many of his tragedies that dealt with political issues such as individual leadership and succession of political power as well as comedies that engaged new worlds such as Arden and Illyria in two perennial Shakespeare favorites *As You Like It* and *Twelfth Night*, respectively.

Working in the context of this historically charged period, Karl-Ernst Herrmann has shaped the development of German design at its various stages over the past half-century. From the late 1960s, when Herrmann began working at the Bremen Theatre, which had then become the hub of conceptual experimentation in directing and design, to more recent designs in Salzburg, Prague, Brussels, Paris, Amsterdam, and Madrid, Herrmann, much like designers such as Josef Svoboda, Robert Wilson and Robert LePage—has accepted the convergence of design and directing emphasizing scenography as the center of performance. In his work with influential directors such as Claus Peymann, George Tabori, and, above all, Peter Stein, Herrmann began to comprehend Shakespeare, much like other authors since the Renaissance, as a bourgeois writer who was operating in the social and economic constraints of emerging capitalism. Herrmann learned how to represent plays as a repository of spaces—both of the author's own historical era and as spaces embedded as precursors of modernity—that needed to be ultimately rendered visible in the production design. In a way, Herrmann began to enforce the idea of the play as what Walter Benjamin has labeled as an image space: a constellation of a theatrical scene, or a stage for the writer's own age, and a latent space of modernity. The intense work with Stein, especially on the two large Shakespeare projects *Shakespeare's Memory* and *As You Like It*, facilitated Herrmann's aspiration of creating a meaningful environment for the actors to exist and to support the director in unfolding a sequence of spaces in the course of the performance.

In this chapter, I trace the development of Herrmann's visual logic in a two-step process: first, at the center of my discussion are two of Herrmann's historic Shakespeare productions, *Shakespeare's Memory* and *As You Like It*. In my analysis, I show that Herrmann not only developed core principles for approaching

56 Klaus van den Berg

Shakespeare design but also, in turn, that these design principles became seminal for other authors. Second, to make transparent the successful development of this approach I frame this discussion with two productions, one that preceded and one that succeeded those Shakespeare productions. I argue that Herrmann's design for Peter Stein's famous *Peer Gynt* production in 1971 exposed one essential principle for the visual logic of his Shakespeare productions and for the equally famous *Othello* production at the Vienna Burgtheater directed by George Tabori in 1990, which represents in many ways a refinement of his solution for *As You Like It*.[4] Ultimately, I claim that *Shakespeare's Memory* and *As You Like It* contributed to his overall design method of creating an image space: explored as historical force field, they represent Herrmann's refinement of design as an art form of unfolding space for contemporary interpretations.

Herrmann and German Shakespeare design

In his long career now spanning more than forty years, Herrmann has progressed from assisting the well-known German designer Wilfried Minks to becoming his own director and scenographer in the best-known theatres across Europe.[5] Following his assistantship with Minks, Herrmann spent the formative years of his professional career at the Schaubühne Berlin working, above all, with Peter Stein and Klaus Michael Grüber on by now legendary productions such as Ibsen's *Peer Gynt* (1971), Kleist's *Prince of Homburg* (1972), Gorky's *Summer Folk* (1974), Shakespeare's *As You Like It* (1977), Botho Strauss' *Big and Little* as well as *Three Acts of Recognition* (both in 1978), and Aeschylus' *Oresteia* (1980). In the 1980s, Herrmann worked frequently at the Schauspielhaus Bochum and Burgtheater Vienna under the artistic leadership of the once founding member of the Schaubühne Berlin, Claus Peymann, where he contributed designs to Shakespeare productions such as *The Winter's Tale* (Bochum 1983), *Richard III* and *The Tempest* both directed by Peymann in Vienna, and *Othello*, directed by George Tabori. Since the 1990s, Herrmann preferred the union of designer and director creating a body of significant productions including operas such as the Mozart's *La Clemenza di Tito* and *Cosi fan tutte*[6] that led him to design for all major European stages such as the Brussels Opera and the Salzburg Festival.

Despite the quantitatively limited output in Shakespeare productions, Herrmann's visual approach to Shakespeare has been distinct and influential. Within the context of post-World War II Germany, Herrmann's collaboration with Peter Stein on *Shakespeare's Memory* (1976) and *As You Like It* (1977), stands out not only as one of the most productive relationships between designer and director but also one of the most fascinating historical configurations: their work contrasts with a number of alternatives in the German theatre at the beginning of the 1970s and has become a deliberate counter model to Shakespeare approaches prevalent in post-war Germany. In East Germany Bertolt Brecht and his designers Karl von Appen, Teo Otto and Caspar Neher had left a very productive scenographic model that focused on integrating textual and visual dramaturgy for

Unfolding Shakespeare's space   57

subsequent generations of German designers.[7] However, Brecht's attempt to build his own theatre, the Berliner Ensemble, and the pressure from the Communist regime to focus on plays representing socialist realism, left only limited time producing Shakespeare within the context of Marxist aesthetics. Brecht's controversial adaptation of *Coriolanus*, completed in 1953, was only produced after his death in 1964 by his successors at the Berliner Ensemble. One of Brecht's intellectual heirs, Heiner Müller, followed Brecht's path of stage adaptations and crafted a number of plays based on Shakespeare originals. Those play adaptations amount to designed landscapes rather than plays in the traditional sense in which Müller montaged Shakespeare and contemporary scenes toward images.[8] Adaptations such as *Macbeth, Hamletmachine, Anatomy of Titus Fall of Rome: A Shakespeare Commentary* are extraordinary in foregrounding spatial issues at the same time Stein and Herrmann began to work on their own productions of Shakespeare at the Schaubühne in the 1970s.

In the Western part of the divided Germany, one of Stein's most significant directing influences had been the actor Fritz Kortner who transferred his experience from the German expressionist theatre in the 1920s and his cultural experience of an outsider as a Jew. Kortner who, as an actor, had been one of the most famous Shylock interpreters, had created a significant body of Shakespeare productions ranging from *Julies Caesar* (1955), *As You Like It* (1956) *Henry IV* (1956), *Hamlet* (1957), *Timon of Athens* (1961), *Othello* (1962 and 1965), and *The Tempest* (1968), many of them produced at the Kammerspiele Munich.[9] Kortner brought his unique way of grinding out thoughtful script interpretations to those productions, albeit within the bourgeois tradition of a subsidized theatre system and no claims to conceptual reworking. Stein would refine Kortner's method of developing a dramaturgical approach in the context of the 1960s counterculture under the influence of Marxist philosophy and Brechtian interpretations. In contrast, the German-born British director Peter Zadek intervened drastically into Shakespeare's text with precisely the intention to shake up the in-depth but orderly productions delivered by many of Germany's post-war directors and designers. Zadek had worked first with Herrmann's mentor Wilfried Minks on a production of *Henry V* (1964) and *Measure for Measure* (Bremen 1967) that inaugurated a Shakespeare style begun in Bremen and subsequently continued in Hamburg and Bochum that was colorful, playful, sometimes vulgar, flashy and gaudy.[10] With regard to scenography, the results were, as Marvin Carlson has pointed out, sometimes stunning as Zadek chose "unconventional spaces (*Lear* in a cinema, *Hamlet* in an abandoned factory)."[11] In contrast, George Tabori offered dramaturgically grounded interpretations that also stimulated a carefully crafted scenography, although his productions of *The Merchant of Venice* (originally planned to be performed at the concentration camp Dachau) and *Othello* (at the Vienna Burgtheater) often intervened into the text as well. Brecht's and Müller's adaptation process, Kortner's probing but more conventional productions, and Zadek's pop art solutions to *The Merchant of Venice, King Lear, Othello, Hamlet*, and *The Winter's Tale* in Hamburg and Bochum left an opening for Herrmann's individual

58 Klaus van den Berg

scenographic approach to Shakespeare which sought to identify a visual logic drawn on a historical and critical text analysis.[12]

Image space: site of unfolding complexity

Herrmann's work with Shakespeare must be seen in this highly charged political environment of the late 1960s and early 1970s dominated by the revolt of young artists against the political and cultural establishment. As has been widely documented, the Berlin Schaubühne, the location for Herrmann's initial design approach, operated as a collective and followed a very political path similar to the Berliner Ensemble and the work of its designers Karl von Appen and Caspar Neher. The revolt in the German art scene in the 1960s was fueled through a profound interest in critical theory, particularly Theodor Adorno's aesthetic theory and Walter Benjamin's media theory. One of many critical ideas Adorno and Benjamin contributed was a rethinking of image space and the underlying forces of spatial representation. Particularly, Benjamin's idea that art works must be perceived image space, a force field of cultural, economic, and technological forces became a powerful idea in the context in which Herrmann's work began to take shape.[13]

Benjamin had deployed image space mass as a key concept of his critical theory, in which he articulated a new kind of theatrical stage prefigured in the urban environment and in the spatial experience of modernity (streets and architecture). His idea was to eliminate the theatre of illusion and replace it with a stage that performed as a visual field in which location and image lay open similar to a display case in which actors shared deliberate gestures. Above all, Benjamin's notion of theatricality—either in historical scenes or in the actual theatre—is helpful to excavate Herrmann's contribution to Shakespeare design: the notion that each scene is essentially a constellation of locations (original theatre space, locations suggested in the play, and contemporary performance space) folded into an image. In Benjamin's sense, design operates like an exhibition site in which physical space, role-playing, scenography, and spectatorship form a constellation ripe for transformation and re-visioning.

At the core of Herrmann's scenography is this idea of the theatrical scene as a complex image space. The 1979 exhibition catalog *Inszenierte Räume* (*Staged Spaces*) that documents Herrmann's early career features numerous variations on a theme of his work:[14] the shaping of a theatrical scene with windows and doors that provide access to other spaces. Moreover, his sketches constantly reveal an ostensibly unified space with complex details: floors, walls, ceilings with varying textures and patterns, a simple chair, and the actor at the center of the space, all elements structuring a room that has become the signature of Herrmann's style. The catalog features an entire page labeled "Zimmerskizzen," literally room sketches, in which one can follow Herrmann's desire to unfold variations of window and door configurations and how he places the human figure within those configurations (Herrmann n.p.). Opposite Herrmann's sketches is a brief text entitled "Refuge for the Homeless" taken from Theodor Adorno's *Minima Moralia*.[15] The text defines the modern private sphere as one of loss of safety (*Geborgenheit*), and contentment; instead of living spaces they are configured as "Schauplatz," a theatrical scene staging insights into human existence. These scenes are what critic Walter Benjamin labeled *thought images*: not realistic representations but visual configurations rife with historical experience and constructed to unfold contemporary action.

The endpoint of image space, the visual logic that Herrmann developed through his Shakespeare productions, can be readily seen in two of Herrmann's most iconic productions. Thomas Bernhard's *Heldenplatz* (1988) and Anton Chekhov's *The Cherry Orchard* (1989) feature those carefully constructed configurations of windows and doors to help directors stage two plays that have become bookends of modernity: the loss of home in pre-revolutionary Russia and the problematic home in a post-war society with lingering fascist traits in late twentieth-century Austria. In Herrmann's visual world, theatrical space is a primal scene that contains a repository of spaces both inscribed by their authors and imagined by directors and designers with potential to unfold movement. In the case of Bernhard's *Heldenplatz*, Herrmann conceived a home with oversized windows, towering above their inhabitants of a seemingly regular Viennese apartment and placed into the wall so that the characters barely managed to look outside. In addition, Herrmann surrounded the windows with a number of gigantic closet doors. At the point when all closet doors were swung open, it displayed the point of the Nazi past that is Bernhard's topic: the windows to the past are enormous in size but the characters are not well positioned to see through it.

Herrmann's Shakespeare productions in the 1970s and 1980s were instrumental in developing this method. He executed this sense of theatrical scene in one of his vaunted designs for Shakespeare's *Richard III* directed by Claus Peymann at the Burgtheater Vienna in 1987. The two central features of Herrmann's design were first, a stage floor with an oversize gully hole into which Richard could dispose his victims and through which they reappeared at the end, and second, a system of rods functioning as barriers that divided and changed the empty space of the acting areas throughout the performance.[16] In a post-show discussion with the audience, the actress Annemarie Düringer lauded Herrmann's design stating "Karl-Ernst Herrmann finally provides us simply with space and air to act. To Act! This is today's Shakespeare stage. It enables our acting to create a scene."[17] In a recent speech in honor of Herrmann's career, Herrmann Beil, one of Germany's leading dramaturgs, who has also been one of Herrmann's collaborators for more than thirty years at numerous prominent German theatres, extended Düringer's praise from a critical perspective. Beil identified the concept of unfolding (*entfalten*) action as a key signature of Herrmann's work that enables directors to orchestrate a play inside a theatrical space. As Wilhelm Hortmann suggests in his assessment of Herrmann's design for *Richard III*, the spectator realizes that Herrmann's bleak and uninviting environment inscribed a type of action that had been conceptualized in conjunction with director and dramaturg.[18]

Image and the display of cultural critique

Despite the limited number of actual Shakespeare productions, critics such as Peter Iden have claimed that Shakespeare was a fulcrum for the Schaubühne in building a performance approach. For artistic director Stein, Shakespeare was the "incarnation" of a modern writer whose work and biography already contained elements of early and late bourgeois existence, and who was intrigued by Shakespeare's own economic position, political vision and dramatic quality to wrestle with the material.[19] In Stein's view, each play, canon or new work must be placed in a constellation with Shakespeare, and this interrelationship should be a source for action in any performance. All members of the Schaubühne were drawn into the discovery of the author as a historical subject, the ruptures of an age, the conflicts between a preceding and the coming age (in this case the Middle Ages and Renaissance), and to experiment with ideas of how cultural ideas might be presented visually. This method of quasi scientific engagement as a grounding for each production stood in stark contrast to most German production approaches in the 1970s and challenged the designers to conceive visuality as a repository of historical spaces drawn from a complex context.

Before designing any Shakespeare play for the Schaubühne, Herrmann created the design for its production of *Peer Gynt* in 1971 that contained seminal strategies for *As You Like It*. Historically, Ibsen represented the high modernist version of bourgeois society, and *Peer Gynt* served as a vehicle for a far-reaching critique of how the bourgeois concept of individualism had failed from the nineteenth century into the later part of the twentieth century. The company engaged in large-scale research, similar to their later Shakespeare productions of *Shakespeare's Memory* (1976) and *As You Like It* (1977), to inscribe a cultural reading of the play: Stein drew a parallel between Peer's journey and nineteenth-century adventure novels, especially those of Karl May, that were inscribed into the memory of German culture. In conjunction with their reading of Marxist philosophy, the production team read Peer as a representative victim of the economic conditions of the nineteenth century: it drew a link between workers' repetitive labor in confined factory spaces and their neurotic desire for individuality and singularity that Peer enacts. Thus, the company performed Peer as a petty bourgeois turned colonial adventurer, an idea that led them to split the role of Peer among eight actors who acted out the various faces of this character while denying the audience the experience of a complete and universal self.[20]

The production offered Herrmann a chance to envision a cultural critique of the panoramas and bourgeois interiors, which formed the material of nineteenth-century aestheticism. Anticipating a strategy he would use later for Shakespeare, Herrmann reworked the entire Schaubühne theatre literally into an exhibition space to expose the visual consciousness of the nineteenth century. Herrmann designed *Peer Gynt* as a gigantic landscape that proved not only convenient for the episodic structure of the play. In a literal attempt to turn the Schaubühne theatre into an exhibition space, the theatre's actual proscenium was dismantled and the

Unfolding Shakespeare's space 61

Figure 4.1 Peer Gynt, production photograph showing the exhibition space and nineteenth-century visual consciousness (Berlin, 1971)

Source: Image from the Deutsches Theatermuseum München, copyright Deutsches Theatermuseum München, Archiv Abisag Tüllmann, reproduced with permission

theatre transformed into an oversized arena. Into this space, Herrmann built a sand-colored platform, which was flanked on its long sides by high bleachers for the audience that would return for *As You Like It*. The locations of the play were mounted on the platform, like a landscape, from a ditch signifying the sea on one end to a large rock on the other side signifying the mountains. In this experiment with a museum-like staging, individual set pieces were transformed to serve multiple purposes; for example, the rock opened up to reveal a bourgeois salon during the scene in the troll kingdom demonstrating Herrmann's penchant for openings as means to conceal and reveal actions thus controlling the configuration of the image. Herrmann's set here linked the ideas of the 1960s environmental theatre with the panorama effects typical for the nineteenth-century visual consciousness: he crammed the platform full with scenic locations and objects employing a museum-like display to expose it as a monument to failed individualism.

Herrmann's visual approach of excavating the nineteenth-century consciousness and its presentation as an exhibition space allowed Stein to develop a gestus in the Brechtian sense. For example, at the end of the performance Stein linked the icon of the nineteenth century, the camera, along with an icon of twentieth century, mass marketing, to comment on the failure of individualism as a source of social progress. For the final tableau the reunion between Solveig and Peer was rendered as a trivial work of kitsch. When Peer lay on Solveig's lap in front of her mountain hut, workers began to dismantle the set pieces of this scene and carried Peer and Solveig in their frozen position center stage. While a photographer shot a picture of the redemption tableau for eternity, conveyor belts transported Peer Gynt souvenirs to the audience to take home.

Herrmann and Stein created a Shakespeare performance at the Schaubühne for the first time in 1976. The historical moment had arrived to offer an alternative to the pop art productions by Peter Zadek that had gained traction in the mid-1970s and to develop a distinct visual method. Stein disliked Zadek's interventionist ways of approaching Shakespeare, and he decided to produce a large-scale preliminary show, a hybrid of documentary and theatre, *Shakespeare's Memory,* that would in its gigantic scope and dramaturgical seriousness a clear alternative to Zadek. Instead of what Stein called blunt interventions ("Zugriffe")[21] he brought the same research and dramaturgical approach that he had used for *Peer Gynt* to bare for the spatial concept of *Shakespeare's Memory*: instead of what Stein conceived as spatial gimmicks, he required the creation of a critical performance space.

Similarly to its treatment of the nineteenth century for *Peer Gynt*, the Schaubühne embarked on excavating the consciousness of the Elizabethan age. Herrmann's design for *Shakespeare's Memory* might be called a massive preliminary study to *As You Like It*. Historically, the visual approach to *Shakespeare's Memory* was a transition between Herrmann's critical display case for *Peer Gynt* to his much more refined scenography for *As You Like It*. Many critics have lamented the artistic failure of *Shakespeare's Memory* in turning massive research into the same effective show and design concept that *As You Like It* proved to become.[22] While Herrmann had managed to draw the research for *Peer Gynt* into a congenial image space that allowed an unfolding of the action, the ensemble's research of the Renaissance period neither produced a coherent dramaturgical approach nor a finished script. The two-day event transpired into an un-curated museum rather than an integrated visual concept.

Much like the subsequent performance of *As You Like It*, *Shakespeare's Memory* was staged in a Berlin film studio. Due to its vast scope, Herrmann employed the principles of a topographical landscape. He built a rectangular platform into the film studio surrounding it by paintings that evoked scenes from Renaissance lives.[23] While Herrmann proved in later productions such as Mozart's *La Clemenza di Tito* that much more efficient design elements could produce similar effects of movement and recalling historical staging elements within the confines of the proscenium stage, in the case of *Shakespeare's Memory* he approached visual representation through "associative logic":[24] instead of a dramaturgical conception that allowed spaces and actions to unfold, Herrmann laid bare the ruptures of an age visually. In a way, Herrmann created what one might call a traditional view of a museum inside a film studio by either juxtaposing Elizabethan spaces or offering them sequentially using the method of processional staging. For example, Herrmann assembled a number of miniature spaces that accommodated the

Unfolding Shakespeare's space   63

Figure 4.2 Shakespeare's Memory, production photograph showing Herrmann's landscape of Elizabethan spaces (Berlin, 1976)

Source: Image from the private collection of Ruth Walz, copyright Ruth Walz, reproduced with permission

Schaubühne's hybrid mix of performance and documentary.[25] Among them were an Elizabethan banquet hall created by rolling out tables; a citation of Leonardo da Vinci's theatre represented by circular arrangement of benches in an adjacent space; a real museum with displays that illustrated Elizabethan ideas; a maze of passages; a structure of cables and figures to visualize the newly discovered perspective (constructed in such a way that it amounted to a prison of perspectives); and a life-size reproduction of the stern of an Elizabethan ship.[26] This sequence of Renaissance spaces cumulated in what the company called a "Shakespeare Island," a heap at the center of the hall on which the company simultaneously performed scenes from multiple plays.

Figure 4.3 *Shakespeare's Memory*, production photograph showing Herrmann's rendering of the effects of perspective in a 3-D space (Berlin, 1976)

Source: Image from the private collection of Ruth Walz, copyright Ruth Walz, reproduced with permission

Figure 4.4 *Shakespeare's Memory*, production photograph showing the stern of an Elizabethan ship (Berlin, 1976)

Source: Image from the private collection of Ruth Walz, copyright Ruth Walz, reproduced with permission

Shakespeare's Memory drew the ire of even well-wishing critics since the extensive layout of spaces and texts lacked coherence. Peter Iden particularly criticized what he called the Shakespeare "potpourri," a sample of widely dispersed texts that lacked any dramaturgical plot line.[27] The performance, above all, concealed what critics have generally identified as the Schaubühne's strength: to provide insights and an artistically convincing critical view of Shakespeare. By the same token, the show's arbitrariness also subverted what has become one of Herrmann's strength: developing an image that relies on an efficient unfolding of a complex space.

Shakespeare's court: image space of modernity

One may read Herrmann's design for *As You Like It* as a paradigm for excavating an image of Shakespeare's modernity. *As You Like It* may not seem the most obvious choice of interpreting Shakespeare as an early modern writer in the economic and sociological sense, but the play invokes the aporias and the power politics of Elizabethan court society.[28] As Jan Kott argued in his essay "Bitter Arkadien", which the Schaubühne included in a book-length documentation of their performance, this comedy reproduces the same social and political history than the tragedies: it features the escape of the rightful ruler from court into the forest of Arden after an unsuccessful political battle.[29] The play dramatizes political retreat and focuses subsequently on the social regrouping in an alternative location. Much like the Renaissance and Baroque courts all over Europe, the Elizabethan court had become an early modern space that increasingly lacked the justification of a metaphysical power as *raison d'être*. Thus, rulers increasingly turned their courts into sites of spectacle to assert power, which, in turn, hastened the need for developing alternative models of escape.[30] In the play Shakespeare creates Arden as a contrasting model to the court and presents a central character, Rosalind, who as a woman disguised as a man playing a woman seducing a man orchestrates the spectacle in the forest. However, Kott argues that Arden is not a romantic utopia but a site in which capitalist laws rule, which was precisely the Schaubühne's critical position in examining the conditions of society from a modern perspective.[31] Arden is a much more severe place than portrayed in many sentimentalized Shakespeare productions. For Herrmann it was paramount to create a transparency of this visual reality and place the spectator in an active viewing position to observe it.

Despite its unwieldiness, *Shakespeare's Memory* provided the textual nucleus and inspiration for *As You Like It*. In *Shakespeare's Memory*, selected scenes such as II.1 (the first Arden scene) and later scenes had appeared in conjunction with scenes from *The Tempest* to draw the audience already into Shakespeare's world. In *Shakespeare's Memory*, the forest of Arden primarily figured as a "magical land" in which the "city person must be prepared to see wondrous and unexpected things."[32] It took another year of research to develop a coherent critical performance approach and for Herrmann to create a modern image of Arden.

Joslin McKinney and Philip Butterworth have reminded us that the dramatic text generally operates "as a conditioner of image."[33] This is even more the case for

66 Klaus van den Berg

translations and adaptations as they contain multiple layers of interpretation and adaptation crucial for visual meaning. The Schaubühne used the first German Shakespeare translation, a prose version by Johann Joachim Eschenburg, a close Lessing adviser, which had emerged from the spirit of the German enlightenment. It integrated into Eschenburg's version translations of songs stemming from the more famous Schlegel/Tieck translation thus mixing enlightenment and romantic literary registers. Eschenburg's translation offers a very vivid and direct representation of the visual world, and the Schaubühne adapted Shakespeare's action at crucial turning points setting in relief the production's political message with consequences for the image space Herrmann was to produce: one can escape into the forest but there is no return to the court.

As the Schaubühne used the more flexible venue of the film studio in Berlin Spandau for this production, Herrmann was at liberty to inscribe the emblems of Elizabethan times in a modern appearance. His solution was a complex image in which the practices of the Elizabethan stage were dissolved into a bi-furcated space: Herrmann displayed the court and Arden simultaneously inside the film studio, a configuration of competing spaces which were not only linked in the mind of actors and audiences but which both had to traverse in the course of the evening.

Herrmann's exhibition catalog *Inszenierte Räume* includes a sketch of Herrmann's vision for *As You Like It* that displays the image of the two contrasting spaces.[34] The court space, designed for the action corresponding roughly to the play's Act 1 through II.3 was a sparse and open hall; the other, for the scenes in the forest, was an environmentally complex version of Arden. Herrmann installed a small door connecting the two spaces through which the audience passed to enter Arden similar to the parties of Duke Senior and his band of exiles, Orlando and Adam, and Rosalind with Celia and Touchstone. Herrmann's drawing represents a preliminary stage of the design process that still lacked the placement of the audience inside the Arden environment, but it speaks to the display character of both spaces, to Herrmann's method of exposing the locations to the modern gaze of the audience, and to his attempt of integrating both spaces into an image inside the film studio. A podium located at the center of the court space and a podium at the opposite end in the forest mark the contrasting political and philosophical beginning and endpoints of the journey for actors and audience (Herrmann n.p.). Herrmann's finished ground plan included a similar albeit more differentiated solution of both spaces: the square-shaped court space had mutated into a longer rectangle that featured a number of different acting areas matching the multiple acting areas in the forest. It also featured a central podium in the court space for the fight between Orlando and Charles, while Arden now included a lake as the structuring part of the axis that conceptually linked the two spaces. The passage from court to forest, originally conceived as small, became much larger due to audience seating arrangement, which consumed much more space than in the original drawing, and due to one of Stein's ideas of how to stage the ending of the play.

The court space in Herrmann's design was a sleek image of modernity that offers simplicity combined with dramaturgical complexity. The cold and austere

Figure 4.5 As You Like It, production photograph showing Herrmann's rendering of the Elizabethan court as an image of modernity (Berlin, 1977)

Source: Image from the private collection of Ruth Walz, copyright Ruth Walz, reproduced with permission

space was designed as a long and narrow room, closed up by walls and high ceilings. The space sported Herrmann's typical textures such as ceiling moldings, wall openings and a floor where the audience stood.[35] Into the wall surfaces Herrmann carved openings that marked the historical and functional complexity of his space. Except for the wall stage left, each wall featured an opening: Herrmann placed a door on the ground level with an archway above inside one of the narrow walls; the wall adjacent to Arden received the door for the actors and audience to escape into the forest. In the wall that formed the main façade, Herrmann placed an arched entryway high above the audience that could be reached via a steep staircase. The acting areas were restricted to very small runways along the walls, which allowed the actors to move to any of the space's three sides.

The court space for *As You Like It* may be considered a paradigmatic solution for Herrmann's future career.[36] It has become an expression for what Walter Benjamin referred to as image space: a constellation that contains both past and contemporary expression of space. The court space combines the cultural and political situation (significant to Stein's political view of Shakespeare as an early bourgeois writer of modernity) and a repository of historical spaces. The carefully installed details of white space drew on numerous stylistic traditions through which Herrmann offered Stein a point of entry for rendering the play in modern terms. Despite the sleek, sparse and efficient quality that marks a modern space, Herrmann's layout clearly drew on an image of the Elizabethan theatre itself with a mostly empty stage and ample space for audience members surrounding around the stage. In addition, the high arches recall the loggias and processional arches of the Renaissance; the abstractness, the blending of white space with black costumes recall the dynamics of the expressionist stages; and the placement of this setting into the film studio recalls the display character in the Western consumer society effectively.

The complexity of Herrmann's image became transparent in the director's unfolding of the plot and how the visual arrangement shaped its interpretation. Herrmann's image of the court allowed the director to exhibit the court system in its formality and political isolationism. Since the acting areas were narrow and attached to the walls, any entrance by Duke Frederick or Rosalind and her cousin Celia were cut short turning them into cautious appearances in the public sphere. In the opening tableau that defined the nature of the performance, Duke Frederick's court appeared especially cold and uncanny: since the actors could only perform on the narrow walkway, they moved carefully along the wall, and each walk became a very calculated move symptomatically of a court under the power of a usurper. On the narrow wall stage left Duke Frederick's movements to ascend to his small seating area created less the impression of majesty and power than of restraint. Furthermore, the wide dimensions of the hall also allowed for distribution of courtiers throughout the space, which added a feel of continuous surveillance at court.[37] Since the costumes were mostly dark, the characters appeared as if blotted onto the wide, impersonal, and bleached space. Another related effect of the design, which amplified the display character of the space, was that the actors' moved along the walls similar to animals pacing in cages. In some ways, the doors, which looked small in relation to the high walls recalled Sergei Eisenstein's use of doors in the movie *Ivan the Terrible* in which the small exits shape the characters' actions.

Herrmann's space also supported and emphasized the display of calculated social and political gestures. For example, Herrmann placed a chair that doubles as Duke Frederick's throne at the narrow wall, framed by two staircases leading up to the area. Their placements away from the central focus of the space foregrounded both the throns as sites of surveillance and isolation. Similarly, the design empowered Stein to magnify gestures and social behavior of Elizabethan society already suggested in the text. When, for example, Rosalind (Jutta Lampe) handed Orlando

Figure 4.6 As You Like It, production photograph showing Orlando (Michael König) and Charles (Günter Nordhoff) and the audience surrounding the platform for the wrestling match (Berlin, 1977)

Source: Image from the private collection of Ruth Walz, copyright Ruth Walz, reproduced with permission

(Michael König) her chain as a token of admiration and support, Stein exploited the levels of the space to magnify the gesture. Rosalind (Jutta Lampe), standing on the raised platform with Celia nearby leaning on her body, slowly bowed down to Orlando letting the chain float into his hand.[38]

Arden: environment as force field

The visual logic of a museum is to display multiple rooms (or objects) in relation to each other. Applying this logic, Herrmann built the forest of Arden as an image corresponding to the modernity of the court space into the film studio.[39] Unlike the emblematic function of the forest on the Elizabethan stage or its imaginary presentation in a theatre of representation within a proscenium stage, Herrmann, following the model developed in *Peer Gynt* and *Shakespeare's Memory*, treated the forest as a complex environment with multi-faceted locations. For the transfer to Arden, Herrmann made actors and audience change locations and perspective. After streaming through the door connecting court space and Arden, the audience faced a gigantic tree and a lake on the opposite side of the film studio. Unlike the court space, in which the audience stood, much like Elizabethan groundlings at the bottom of the stage, spectators were now seated on raised bleachers that were

Figure 4.7 As You Like It, production photograph showing Herrmann's rendering of the forest of Arden as modern panorama (Berlin, 1977)

Source: Image from the private collection of Ruth Walz, copyright Ruth Walz, reproduced with permission

arranged roughly as a thrust stage to look down onto the action. Furthermore, Herrmann had created walkways behind the bleachers, and he distributed individual sites on elevated platforms amidst the audience. Reversing the design idea for the central island he had created for *Shakespeare's Memory*, he left empty the space between bleachers, platforms, and lake covering it only with leaves. The visual emblem that connected the various staging areas was the name "Rosalind" painted in large letters on the floor.[40]

The visual logic for Herrmann's all-embracing environment of Arden may be construed from two moments in the performance. In the first Arden scene (II.1), the production intervened with the script linking vision and reality directly when Duke Senior and his exiles were introduced. At the moment when Amiens intoned the song "Blow, blow, thou winter wind," the Schaubühne version added a new line "Im Wald ist die Wahrheit" (In the forest is the truth,) to the refrain "Heiho, sing heiho" (AYLI II.7, Video 1:00:36). For Stein who was nothing if not comprehensive, this intervention signaled an all-embracing inspection of the forest. Stein was in need of a comprehensive yet practical solution. Consequently, Herrmann displayed multiple parts of a forest in the film studio to accommodate Stein's detailed social and political analysis of a spatial environment that required the simultaneous presence of all locations. Furthermore, Herrmann's modern sense of

Unfolding Shakespeare's space 71

space visualized Arden, instead of accepting the linearity of Shakespeare's script that leads audiences into different parts of the forest, by transforming linear scene progression into a spatial image of a forest with all its fragmented parts. This fragmented vision of Arden sharpened the moment of discovery at the play's climactic moment: in the Schaubühne version, Rosalind and Celia appeared in Renaissance costumes riding on a float in the tradition of medieval and Renaissance processional wagons. When she revealed herself to her father, Duke Senior, Orlando, and Phebe as a complex object of desire, Duke Senior exclaims: "If there be truth in sight, you are my daughter" (ASYL V.4). For the audience "Truth in sight" became an intricate constellation of realities, an image of Rosalind's virtuoso theatricality and multi-faceted identity and the multi-faceted forest she had traversed for the past three hours. For the Schaubühne there was no easy solution to this image: the experience of Herrmann's Arden was too dense, rich, and real to make a return to court possible.

Generally, Herrmann's image of Arden was crafted as a visual field that included highly focused locations mounted on platforms amidst the audience, more extensive areas of the forest at either end of the space, and, depending on the audience's seating, locations behind their seats. Much like his design for the court, Herrmann created the forest as an image space that displayed multiple locations in the forest and enabled seamlessly—and sometimes simultaneously—unfolding of the action. Instead of exits and entrances that would define locations in traditional *As You Like It* performances, Herrmann foregrounded the cinematic interlacing of actions. The simultaneous display of locations allowed Stein a very detailed reading of the social reality for each group inhabiting their particular corner of the forest, and the audience could observe each of them at their pace. Herrmann employed here a strategy he had already applied in his design for Gorky's *Summer Folk* (1974) breaking a seemingly closed environment open so that it dissolved into the staging of smaller stories: aside from the lake which is not assigned to any character and became an image of transformative action, Herrmann differentiated a thicket for Duke Senior and his exiles, Rosalind's homestead, a special location for Audrey's hut where Touchstone was biding his time with working-class activities and Shakespeare's sexual humor,[41] and separate walkways that Jacques preferred wandering.[42]

Matching the complexity of the court space, Herrmann created a diverse environment comprised of thickets, prickly bushes, woodpiles, dense wooded areas, lakes, and meadows. The textures of the different parts of the forest corresponded to the subtle textures for the court space. While the long sides of the film studio were reserved for the mixed placement of audience bleachers, elevated platforms, and difficult to surmount wood piles, Herrmann created two distinct areas opposite each other: on the side adjacent to the court space, he placed a very dense and difficult to penetrate wall of trees; on the opposite side, Herrmann built a large tree with adjacent lake and meadow that offered a much more open atmosphere. The open meadow drew together the entire space: leaves partially covered the stage floor and, above all, the name Rosalind painted in large letters as a visual emblem for the integral figure of the multi-faceted action.

Instead of creating a romantic retreat for court dwellers, Stein and Herrmann took Shakespeare literally when the Duke describes the hardship that he and his fellow exiles must endure. It is this harsh world that the Duke accepts as "good counselor" and that the Schaubühne production foregrounded (ASYL II.1). Herrmann's design favors a difficult to penetrate thicket over an aesthetically beautiful patch of woods. For example, the exhausted Adam who accompanied Orlando into the forest lay amidst thicket of twigs, bushes, so that it became a difficult effort for Orlando to remove him from that spot (video 1:15:14). Similarly, Herrmann located the scenes with Duke Senior in front of a dense section of the wood that visually underscored how difficult the escape from the court had been and how difficult any return would be. It was equally dark, and character movement through

Figure 4.8 As You Like It, production photograph showing Jutta Lampe (Rosalind) near the lake (Berlin, 1977)

Source: Image from the private collection of Ruth Walz, copyright Ruth Walz, reproduced with permission

Unfolding Shakespeare's space 73

the forest was literally tough.[43] In this arduous environment, the meadow and lake at the far end of the hall offered a contrasting space to the court and visual relief from the dense forest Herrmann erected in other parts of the hall.

Herrmann's organization of Arden helped to interpret several themes of the play's dramaturgy through complex imagery. Herrmann used here a hybrid approach of mixing theatrical design (some painted scenery of woods) with real natural images (lake filled with real water) posing the choices of theatricality and realness to both Rosalind and the audiences. Since all locations were present simultaneously, the poems Orlando hung on trees exercised a stronger and prolonged visual presence onstage as the audience had the choice of observing them while another scene was in progress. The areas behind the audience's bleachers found Jacques walking in solitude and marveling at the presence of a fool in the forest (Video 0:54:20). Having the name Rosalind painted in large letters on the stage floor allowed the actress Jutta Lampe to spread out sexually on the large letters indulging in Orlando's desire for her (video 1:07:20). Stein exploited a similar play with narcissist desire, when Phebe marveled at her physical reflection in the water (Video 1:23:55). As the performance progressed, the lake became the preferred place for Rosalind's encounters with Phebe and Orlando. The simultaneous presence of real water and painted scenery offered many opportunities to display the theatricality of the action. In a very dense image of illusory love, Stein had Phebe's admiration of her own reflection followed by her prospective lover Silvius carrying her away and laying her in front of a nature painting (Video 1:31: 33). Furthermore, the realness of the water was underscored late in the play when Lampe as Rosalind shed her disguise publicly that she maintained in the forest throughout the play and took a bath mostly naked (video 1:41:52)—an image where Stein combined the staging of reality (bathing/cleaning in the forest) with shedding layers of identity.

One of Herrmann's favorite strategies to shape action through images occurred at the end of the performance. First, just before Rosalind revealed herself as woman and daughter of Duke Senior, Stein staged the escape of Duke Frederick and his warriors from the court (only reported in the play) as a difficult struggle to penetrate the thicket of the forest; at the end of the extended sequence, the Duke and his fighters shed their armory sinking exhausted to the stage floor (0:12:15) where we would find them at the end of the performance for the Duke to deliver the epilogue. At that point, the forest resembled a devastated and devastating environment. Second, immediately following this scene, one side of the woods opened like a curtain creating an informal gate for a processional wagon carrying Rosalind and Celia, now in female Renaissance costumes, accompanied by Hymen, re-entering the forest in a highly formal manner. In many subsequent productions of his career, Herrmann drew on staging practices from earlier ages creating startling anachronistic effects. After Rosalind revealed herself as daughter of the rightful Duke, the entire court community (sans Jacques) prepared to return to the court. Herrmann's design allowed for an ironic interpretation of that attempt to return. When the processional wagon carried everyone back toward the court space, it became disentangled in the forest with much comic effect, stopping the return and happy ending in its tracks. All characters immediately disembarked and limped back into the forest (Video 0:02:35). Herrmann crafted a visual solution for the Schaubühne's modern dramaturgical concept that a happy return to the original space and former social and political space is impossible. Stein's conclusion was that the society would not return to the court; instead, all must deal with a contemporary image of Arden. Herrmann had built a door of escape from the court—both for the audience and the actors—but that same door was not a route for a return passage.

Herrmann, who has excelled at finding modern solutions for historical staging practices, delivered with his Berlin Arden a very modern re-visioning of the panorama—in many ways, a refinement of his scenography for *Peer Gynt* in 1971. Panoramas became popular in the nineteenth century offering breathtaking views of landscapes that created illusions of reality. As Walter Benjamin diagnosed in his *Arcades Project*, panoramas attempted to bring nature into a kind of theatre, were illusions bordered on dreams and phantasmagorias, and became precursors of the silent-film era.[44] The cyclorama, a special form of the panorama, was introduced into the theatre in the late nineteenth century to heighten the sense of illusion. Unlike those applications in the theatre, Herrmann pursued the opposite intention, that is,

Figure 4.9 As You Like It, production photograph showing the arrival of a processional wagon in Arden (Berlin, 1977)

Source: Image from the private collection of Ruth Walz, copyright Ruth Walz, reproduced with permission

to break the illusion and create an image space to support the director in achieving a critical reading of the play. For *As You Like It* the panorama was a component of the image space but mediated by Herrmann's visual strategies. Similar to his design for *Peer Gynt*, Herrmann set in relief the illusory nature of panoramas by creating the appearance of a panoramic vision inside a film studio. Since the panoramas had contributed, historically, to the emergence of cinema, Herrmann decided to interlace both forms of spectacle for the audience that afforded it a critical view of theatricality of either one. Displaying a panoramic vision of Arden inside a film studio, walls and beams partially exposed, created a dialectic vision of panoramas and a conscious viewing of the fragmented nature of the cinematic treatment of panorama. However, by distributing the audience among the various parts of the panorama, Herrmann emphasized the audience's viewing of a fragmented and disconnected reality and compelled it to perceive a bi-furcated image. Generally, Herrmann presented the modern version of Arden like the workings of a modern city—the context of Berlin and its audience—in which a panorama cannot be grasped fully anymore—neither spatially in a fully developed and manipulated way nor in the linear sequence that Shakespeare's text outlined.

Herrmann's *Othello*: modifying the image

Herrmann's image for the court setting for *As You Like It* has spawned a number of re-embodiments for his later designs of Shakespeare, contemporary plays and operas. One of his most successful applications of a critical image turned performance space was for George Tabori's production of *Othello* at the Burgtheater Vienna.[45] Despite *Othello's* more unified plot structure, the play still poses the challenge of discovering a scenography that unfolds its plot structure through the locations of an image space. Similar to his image of the court, Herrmann created a configuration of walls with openings that could be turned into a complex scenography altering the configuration. Herrmann created the image of a boxing ring with one corner extending into the audience. Instead of the closed space for *As You Like It*, he designed a square space by erecting two flexible walls in a 90-degree angle as background and employing only two railings to complete the square. The image was divided into three planes that could be alternatively lit: a stage floor whose apex was pointed directly at the audience; walls that were divided into two parts: one plane about eight feet high, the other much taller above. The walls were constructed as flexible folding partitions so that one or two-door configurations (or a mirror) could be installed in the stage left wall for alternative scenes.[46] Characteristically, Herrmann added only a few significant furniture pieces that became the structuring feature of the performance: a table to survey military strategy at the beginning, later a grand piano for parts of the performance in Cyprus, and for the tragic finale, a platform bed with high curtains surrounding it.

Herrmann reprised the simplicity of the court space for *As You Like It* and the complexity of its operation through visual configurations. Again, Herrmann applied something of a visual rebus to inscribe the dynamic elements of the

Figure 4.10 Othello, production photograph showing Othello (Gert Voss) and Iago (Ignaz Kirchner) inside the boxing ring with piano at centre (Vienna, 1990)

Source: Image from the Archiv Burgtheater Vienna, Copyright Oliver Herrmann, Burgtheater Archiv, reproduced with permission

Elizabethan stage (back wall and two doors) and turn them into a modern image that enabled Tabori to draw a very modern performance from the actors. For example, a conversation between Othello and Iago took place in the front corner of the metaphoric boxing ring suggesting the physical if not psychological battle between protagonist and antagonist. For Desdemona's death, the walls turned dark engulfing Othello's body, while the floor remained bright with white curtains surrounding the bed and Desdemona, all naked on the bed. Herrmann placed a mirror in front of the doorframe downstage providing the image with even more complexity. The mirror marked not only the enclosedness of the space but also reflected part of the action back to the audience, so the audience could reflect, in the spirit of the Brechtian idea of theatre, the complex racial and psychological process enacted in this by now hall of mirrors.

Image space and restructuring vision

Following his work with prominent directors such as Stein, Peymann and Tabori on Shakespeare productions, Herrmann gradually adapted the union of director and designer based on the design strategies he had developed. Aside from his work on Chekhov and Thomas Bernhardt, Herrmann won acclaim for his production of

Mozart's *La Clemenza di Tito* at the Opera National de Paris. In the work on Mozart, Herrmann expanded even more the spatial potential of his design concept he had successfully created for *As You Like It* and *Othello*. On the surface Herrmann again offered the image of a sparse room with a few chairs surrounded by white walls and a white ceiling (adorned by a circular opening in ceiling and walls). However, under the surface of this design lurked an even more refined and sophisticated mechanism than lay dormant in *As You Like It* and *Othello*. The white walls were subdivided into lower and higher segments that offered endless possibilities for projections and light configurations; again, Herrmann worked with multiple doors, which, in turn, were inserted into even larger openings. To complete the detailed structure, Herrmann had divided the floor into larger tiles. Overall, the design concept might be considered analogous to a modern airplane wing: it may appear as a complete unit but in reality it is comprised of multiple parts and emerges in various looks supporting different flight phases.

This design concept accommodated the staging practices of opera in the seventeenth and eighteenth centuries that relied on the theatrical effects from changing scenery. Surprisingly, the modern looking design supported the entire machinery of Mozart's *opera seria* and unfolded the action from underneath the surface with the precision of modern technology. Herrmann employed his design to create vistas and perspectives—he even managed to simulate a *scena per angelo* in the style of the Galli-Bibienas. The doors became even more versatile and refined tools: they opened for a character to enter; they served as a passage of larger vehicles or for technological display; they might become light filled or dark for physically and emotionally closed dark spaces. Herrmann's show, for which he acted as designer and director in conjunction with his wife Ursel Herrmann, had become able not only to provide an echo of a historical stage such as the Elizabethan stage in *As You Like It*, but now a more technologized version of this space was capable of revealing the entire repository of eighteenth-century spaces.

While some critics were uneasy with the overall success of the Schaubühne Shakespeare enterprise at the time of production in the 1970s,[47] there is very little doubt that Karl-Ernst Herrmann reached a plateau in his career with his method of designing *As You Like It* and consolidated this position with other Shakespeare productions in the 1980s. On a long list of stellar German designers of Shakespeare, Herrmann has achieved success on a high level and developed a distinctive approach that I have outlined in this essay by examining a few paradigmatic productions. What is at stake in the area of Shakespeare design is to identify a genuine solution in the rich tradition of German design in the twentieth century that answers theoretical and historical challenges for a new age. In this endeavor Herrmann has benefited from collaborating with many top directors such as Peter Stein, Claus Peymann and George Tabori; together they have sought to excavate the modernity in Shakespeare and identifying a visual signature that displayed the historical and modern Shakespeare without resorting to questionable visual strategies. Conversely, while it may have been less noted, it is highly probable that Herrmann's working method strongly shaped the work of such a diverse group of directors.

78 Klaus van den Berg

I have claimed that the unique approach of Herrmann's work can be identified within the context of critical theory. Herrmann's scenography has its origin in this tradition of positing performance space as a scene (*Schauplatz*) shaped within a force field of technology, economy and historiography. In response Herrmann devised his idea of a new kind of theatrical stage: not a place for mimesis, but a politically and aesthetically contested site for struggle and transformation, and thus a medium that can restructure historical experience. Herrmann's designs are frequently solutions to this cultural sense of space that arose from the loss of home so prevalent in the modern experience, from the crisis of bourgeois aesthetics, and the need to uncover a design approach that would neither get caught in the traps of the phantasmagorias of commercial theatres, illusionism, abstract design, or an adaptation of favorable cultural trends.

From the start Herrmann defined the theatrical scene as a practical and theoretical model to shape an image space that could integrate historical experience inside a modern shell. I have argued that performance space, in the productions covered in this chapter, is not a space of representation but exactly this kind of Benjaminian scene, an image space that can reveal a repository of historical experiences. Herrmann has built a model of theatricality based on the unassuming room of his early career that offers variations of vision and movement through its gaps without committing to any fixed cultural and aesthetic parameters. In this sense Herrmann's designs have made an invaluable contribution to Shakespeare by incorporating effortlessly Shakespearean performance practices within the fold of a modern shell. Thus, Herrmann has pointed to another Shakespeare performance aesthetics: it is the unfolding of those spaces during performance, a dramaturgy of space that substitutes imitation, abstraction, or authenticity as design method. Michael Patterson quietly hinted at the success of this unfolding strategy in 1981, without making special references to critical theory, calling the audience experience of *As You Like It* a "restructuring" of vision.[48] The above discussion has identified and recognized this process; it also has made transparent why Herrmann ultimately proceeded to become a scenographer.

Notes

1   D. Kennedy, *A Visual History of Twentieth-Century Performance*, 2nd ed., Cambridge: Cambridge University Press, 2001, p.12.
2   In the west Sartre and Beckett seemed perfectly suited to address the desolate intellectual and political situation while the eastern block emphasized plays (or interpretation of plays) in the style of socialist realism.
3   Heiner Muller, one of the most important Shakespeare adaptors, inscribed strong design elements in his adaptations of *Macbeth* (1971), *Hamlet* (1977), and *Titus Andronicus* (1984).
4   The production of *As You Like It* is well-documented in reviews, and a film based on the performance.
5   The assistantship with Minks has a noted Shakespeare connection since Minks designed some of the most famous pop art productions directed by Peter Zadek—especially *Measure for Measure* in Bremen in the 1960s and 1970s.

Unfolding Shakespeare's space 79

6 Often in partnership with his wife Ursel Herrmann.
7 See K. van den Berg, "Contemporary German Scenography: Surging Images and Spaces for Action," *Contemporary Theatre Review*, 18.1, 2008, 7–8.
8 J. Kolb, *The Theater of Heiner Müller*, Cambridge: Cambridge University Press, 1998, pp. 87–103.
9 Stein assisted Kortner at this theatre.
10 M. Carlson, "Peter Zadek: The Outsider Who Has Come Inside," *Theatre Research International*, 32.3, 2007, 236–238.
11 Carlson (2007), 237.
12 The analysis supported at the Schaubühne Berlin closely aligns with an approach pursued by the Frankfurt School. In this chapter I focus on the topic of the image, which Walter Benjamin, and to some extent Theodor Adorno, applied to art works.
13 In this context Walter Benjamin's critical work is of particular note since he closely collaborated with Brecht on the latter's innovative theatre model of a dialectic theatre. W. Benjamin, "What is Epic Theatre?", trans. H. Zohn, eds. H. Eiland, M. Jennings. *Walter Benjamin. Selected Writings*. Vol. 4. Cambridge, MA: Belknap Press, 2003, pp. 302–309.
14 K.E. Herrmann, E. Wonder, *Inszenierte Räume*, Hamburg: Kunstverein, 1979.
15 T. Adorno, *Minima Moralia*, trans, E.F.N. Jephcott, London: Verso, 1974, pp. 38–39; Herrmann n.p.
16 The image is reproduced in M. Carlson, *Theatre is more Beautiful than War*, Iowa City: Iowa University Press, 2009: p. 61 and W. Hortmann, *Shakespeare on the German Stage. The Twentieth Century*, Cambridge: Cambridge University Press, 1998: p. 337.
17 H. Beil, "Kommen Se rinn, da können Se raus kieken. Laudatio auf Karl-Ernst Herrmann" www.hein-heckroth-ges.de/hermann-beil-kommen-se-rinn-da-koen-nen-se-raus-kieken.html (last accessed May 27, 2013)
18 Hortmann p. 337.
19 P. Iden, *Die Schaubühne am Halleschen Ufer 1970–1979*, Frankfurt: Fischer, 1982: p. 211.
20 Schaubühne am Halleschen Ufer, ed. *Peer Gynt. Ein Schauspiel aus dem neuzehnten Jahrhundert*, Berlin: Albert Nentrich, 1971.
21 Iden, p. 211.
22 Ibid., p. 213.
23 P. Lackner, "Stein's Path to Shakespeare," *The Drama Review* 21.2, 1977, 82.
24 Ibid., p. 87.
25 Iden, p. 220.
26 Ibid., p. 213.
27 Ibid., p. 220.
28 Lackner, 81. Play selection at the Schaubühne was not just subordinated to dramaturgical considerations but originated from the ensemble desire to cast as many of its members in good size roles and avoid the traditional system of lead actors.
29 J. Kott, *Shakespeare Heute*, trans. P. Lachmann, Munich, DTV, 1980, p. 274.
30 W. Benjamin, *Ursprung des bürgerlichen Trauerspiels*, Frankfurt: Suhrkamp, 1955.
31 Kott, p. 278.
32 Lackner, p. 87.
33 J. McKinney, P. Butterworth, *The Cambridge Introduction to Scenography*, Cambridge: Cambridge University Press, 2009, p. 83.
34 The catalog lacks page numbers.
35 The film version was shot without the audience present, and the floor was covered with leaves.
36 It anticipated design solutions for Botho Strauss' *Kalldewey Farce*, Mozart's *La Clemenza di Tito* and *Cosi fan tutte*, Shakespeare's *Othello* and *Richard III*.
37 This effect is no doubt much stronger in the film version, since it was produced without the presence of the audience and thus offered isolated views of the court space.

38 Peter Stein's film version intensified this gesture by shooting the moment from the side capturing Duke Frederick sitting alone in the far distance.

39 Herrmann pioneered the strategy of flexible space for the Schaubühne, which became a regular opportunity when the ensemble moved into Erich Mendelsohn's building in 1980. The renovated cinema offers flexible audience-stage configurations.

40 For detailed reviews of *As You Like It* see Kennedy, pp. 261–265.

41 For example, when Audrey makes butter, Touchstone operates the device in a very sexual manner.

42 Michael Patterson provides an exhaustive list of all the activities in the forest. M. Patterson, *Peter Stein*, Cambridge: Cambridge University Press, 1981, pp. 139–140.

43 Rolf Michaelis has argued that Herrmann's design method and visual themes are closely tied to his collaboration with a few high caliber directors such as Peter Stein, Claus Peymann and George Tabori at the Schaubühne Berlin and the Burgtheater Vienna. R. Michaelis, "Eine Liebe nach dem Tod," Zeit Online Jan 19, 1990 www.zeit.de/1990/04/eine- liebe-nach-dem-tod (last accessed May 30, 2013).

44 W. Benjamin, *The Arcades Project*, eds. H. Eiland, K. McLaughlin, Cambridge, MA: Belknap Press, 1999, p. 532.

45 As critic Rolf Michaelis has argued Herrmann's Shakespeare productions must be seen as linked in their visual themes and approach in which he worked with very few directors of caliber such as Peter Stein, Claus Peymann and George Tabori at renowned theatres such as the Schaubühne Berlin, and the Burgtheater Vienna. R. Michaelis, "Eine Liebe nach dem Tod," *Zeit Online* Jan 19, 1990 www.zeit.de/1990/04/eine-liebe-nach-dem-tod (last accessed May 30, 2013).

46 In the two-door configuration one centrally located in the left wall, the other one downstage left.

47 Patterson, p. 138 and p. 149.

48 Patterson, p. 149.

Chapter 5

Ming Cho Lee

Arnold Aronson

Ming Cho Lee is generally considered one of the most significant figures in American design in the second half of the twentieth century. In the 1960s and 1970s he transformed the American approach to scenic design, moving it from a largely pictorial style dominated by the poetic realism of his mentor Jo Mielziner, to a sculptural, emblematic, and architectural approach. The decorative was emphatically rejected in favor of more spatial and architectonic decor; the horizontal gave way to a verticality virtually unknown in the American theatre. Along the way Lee explored new or non-traditional scenic materials to give the stage a more industrial or contemporary feel. There were multiple sources for his innovations, notably the Constructivist-inspired work of his other mentor, Boris Aronson, as well as his training in Chinese landscape painting which he studied as a teenager growing up in Shanghai. But ultimately the inspiration was Bertolt Brecht. Lee's passionate belief in the political and social efficacy of art led to a functional, utilitarian design that emphasized the stage-as-stage. His impact was felt not only in theatre but in opera and dance—he designed for the New York City Opera, the Metropolitan Opera, Martha Graham and the Joffrey Ballet among many others—but his most immediate impact was on American Shakespearean production as resident designer for the New York Shakespeare Festival for eleven years, beginning with the opening of the Delacorte Theatre in Central Park in 1962. Starting in the late 1960s he also began designing for major regional theatres across the country, which often meant more Shakespeare. Lee's career trajectory was closer to that of European scenographers—he did relatively little Broadway (despite a Tony award for *K2* in 1983 he found little success there) but instead thrived in institutional theatres with their greater emphasis on classics. All told, from an undergraduate production of *Much Ado About Nothing* at Occidental College in 1953 through *Antony and Cleopatra* at the Guthrie Theatre in Minneapolis in 2002 he designed some sixty productions of Shakespeare's plays, not counting several operas and ballets based on works from the canon.

Shakespeare has been performed in English-speaking North America since at least 1730 and was a staple of the popular stage throughout the nineteenth century. Scenographically, it was no different from the melodramas and well-made plays of the era, employing pictorial realism and naturalism and created largely from stock scenery. The repertoire, right up through World War II, however, was fairly limited, more often than not providing vehicles for star actors; consequently, a design that foregrounded the performer was more valued than a conceptual approach. Several of the Broadway productions of Shakespeare throughout the twentieth century were British imports, frequently from the Old Vic, and thus brought the early and mid-twentieth-century scenic conventions of the English stage. The scenographically realistic approach to Shakespeare implies a literal reading of the text—a belief that the dramatic locales are actual places (or at least have the potential to be actualized) that must be recreated on the stage in order to complete the act of reception. It is illusionistic, placing the characters within a physical setting that references the real world.

Scenographically there were two important American contributions from the first half of the twentieth century—the designs of Robert Edmond Jones, especially in his productions with director Arthur Hopkins and actor John Barrymore, and the productions of *wunderkind* Orson Welles. With productions of *Richard III* (1920), *Macbeth* (1921), and *Hamlet* (1922), Jones introduced expressionist techniques, including Jessner-like steps, monumental structures seemingly inspired by Edward Gordon Craig, and space sculpted by light, clearly influenced by Adolphe Appia. The goal was to move away from specifically realized locales and to bring out the underlying and emotional qualities of the texts. Illusionistic, pictorial decor was replaced by a depiction of an interior, symbolic landscape, but the stage was, nonetheless, scenographically transformed. Welles, on the other hand, devised the first concept productions in the U.S. including the "voodoo" *Macbeth* (1936) set in Haiti and the fascist-themed *Julius Caesar* (1937). Scholar Dennis Kennedy believes that *Macbeth* was "the first major production of Shakespeare in English to select a locale for the action that was overtly foreign to the spirit of the play."[1] Such a strategy overlays a very specific sign system on top of the existing one, perhaps on the assumption that the original setting may no longer be relevant or resonate in the contemporary world. While the specificity of the new visual motif may illuminate the text for a modern audience, it all too often runs the risk of imposing interpretive limitations.

In the post-war era, scenographic and staging innovations first emerged in the new Shakespeare festivals—the Stratford Shakespearean Festival in Canada (1953), the American Shakespeare Festival in Stratford, Connecticut (1955), and the New York Shakespeare Festival which began as the Shakespeare Workshop in 1954 and found a permanent home at the Delacorte Theatre in New York's Central Park in 1962. Stratford, Ontario, was the most significant in terms of staging because it was there that artistic director Tyrone Guthrie and his designer, Tanya Moiseiwitch, essentially introduced the "open stage" or thrust stage to North America. Had Ming Cho Lee seen this type of stage and Moiseiwitch's architectural unit sets prior to his employment at the New York Shakespeare Festival his work might have taken a somewhat different turn. But his major exposure to Shakespeare in the 1950s was at the festival in Connecticut with its barn-like auditorium and end stage. In 1956, the festival's second season, John Houseman became artistic director and hired the Armenian designer Rouben Ter-Arutunian (who was born in Tbilisi, Georgia, trained in Berlin, and came to the United States in 1951). Ter-Arutunian devised a setting that served, with some variations or additions, for six productions over two seasons. It consisted of a backdrop of horizontal slats that functioned like Venetian blinds. The result was a kind of unit set, analogous to the basic architectural setting of the Elizabethan stage in its consistency from show to show (though not in its structure), but it consisted of designed scenery consisting of flexible constructed scenic units. Lee readily admits that he borrowed the idea of slats from Ter-Arutunian for some productions of opera he had designed at the Peabody Conservatory of Music in Baltimore and his early Off-Broadway ventures.

New York Shakespeare Festival

The New York Shakespeare Festival had been performing on a temporary stage in Central Park for several years before finally erecting a permanent outdoor structure across the Turtle Pond from the Belvedere Castle, a pseudo-Romanesque structure perched on a high rock. Eldon Elder, who had been the resident designer for the Shakespeare Festival, designed the Delacorte Theatre, but was fired when producer Joseph Papp discovered that he was also working for the American Shakespeare Festival in Connecticut. The young and relatively inexperienced Ming Cho Lee—at that point his resume, aside from assistant work, consisted primarily of dance and regional opera, the latter mostly at the Peabody Conservatory of Music in Baltimore—was brought in and was asked to make some changes to the still-under-construction theatre, mostly relating to the placement of lighting and scenic towers. In subsequent seasons he would oversee some other changes that improved the relationship between stage and auditorium. The stage of the 2,300-seat Delacorte as designed by Elder resembled that of the Tyrone Guthrie-designed Stratford Shakespeare Festival in Ontario, Canada, with a polygonal thrust and broad steps leading down to the auditorium on five sides. While it had the openness of the Ontario theatre, it lacked the concomitant intimacy. It was not simply that it was an outdoor theatre, but the forty-eight foot wide stage and the depth of the auditorium—far greater than at the Guthrie-designed space—distanced the audience from the stage and made intimate scenes difficult. There was also the question of competing with nature and the city—how to incorporate the surrounding environment which was part of the theatre's appeal, without overwhelming the production. There was little precedent for such an undertaking. There was also the question of the stage itself. While today the thrust stage is ubiquitous, and aprons and thrusts are often added to traditional proscenium stages, in 1962 it was still a rarity.[2] Perhaps Lee's greatest challenge in that first season was learning how to design for such a large and open thrust stage. Gerald Freedman, a resident director at the New York Shakespeare Festival who directed *The Tempest*, Lee's second production of the 1962 season, stated, "When we started, there was an encrustation of Theatre Guild productions of Shakespeare. They were all proscenium dominated. What I know I brought to the collaboration was not the idea of the thrust, but how you use a thrust. Some of that came from my work on Broadway musicals. I brought a musical theatre sensibility, which meshed with my understanding of classical theatre. It was presentational."[3] (Lee traveled to Stratford in the spring of 1963 to see how that theatre worked, but he designed his first season at the Delacorte without benefit of this research.)

The Delacorte opened in June 1962 with *The Merchant of Venice* co-directed by Joseph Papp and Gladys Vaughan. In many ways it was the physical demands of this unusual stage that shaped the decor as much as any Brechtian-inspired ideas about design or current thoughts about Shakespearean scenography. Lee intuitively grasped that in order to focus the gaze of the audience on the stage while still incorporating the surrounding park and skyline, there was a strong need for a framing device, and the scenery would need a far greater height than most stages. The environment has to "control the action," as Lee put it, "When people sitting in the front row look up at an actor, if they see the park, Fifth Avenue and the sky, they lose all interest. But if they look at the actors' faces and there is some surface or line or whatever that belongs to the environment of the show—through which you see the sky—then you feel that the performers are acting within something. The scenery creates an inner volume and nature is the other volume."[4]

Lee's solution was to frame the stage with two latticework towers upstage right and left, with Venetian lancet arches, shutters (using Ter-Arutunian's slats), and symmetrical flights of open steps with graceful arcs leading to upper platforms. The towers were, at times, connected by a bridge that could slide on and offstage thereby creating multiple locations by altering the spatial arrangement of the stage while also offering a raised stage area. Two tapestry panels unfurled upwards from the stage floor between slender upstage poles, providing appropriately evocative backdrops for Portia's house and the courtroom scene. This relatively simple scenic vocabulary, with its delicate scaffolding structure, was able to suggest a Venetian locale while at the same time allowing the lake, the Belvedere Castle, and the nighttime park to be continuously present. The delicacy of the latticework made the towers appear almost like tracery against the cityscape. There was real architectural detail, yet the overall effect was almost abstract.

It was evocative of place while never allowing the audience to forget that it was looking at a stage set located within an urban park. Lee's Brechtianism had steered him from the predominantly decorative vocabulary of the day toward the functional and overtly theatrical (one could discern echoes of Brecht's designer Teo Otto whom Lee acknowledges as an influence on the development of his aesthetic), but some of it was dictated by the practical demands (and budget) of the venue.

Lee's second production that summer was *The Tempest*, directed by Freedman. The basic scenic structure of towers and bridge remained, largely for financial reasons, but tensions arose between Lee and Freedman regarding aesthetics and the overall look of the set—tensions that would recur, to varying degrees over the next few years. Freedman tended to be more focused on staging than theme and his

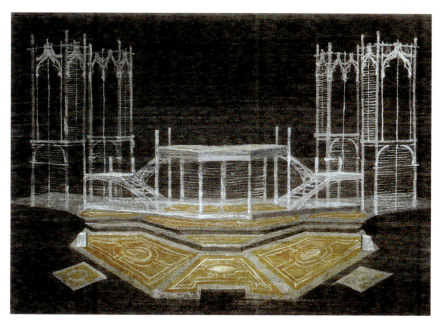

Figure 5.1 Merchant of Venice, sketch, New York Shakespeare Festival, 1962
Source: Photo courtesy of Ming Cho Lee

inclination was more decorative—he wanted a "pretty set" in Lee's words, including a realistic ship and island—whereas Lee wanted a set that more directly addressed the political or social themes of the play. Freedman did get a more or less realistic ship-like structure that utilized the movable bridge from *Merchant* for the opening scene. But the overall design was a cobweb-like construction superimposed on the underlying scenic structure, from which trees seemed to emerge supporting the upper stage on the bridge. The effect was almost surreal. The stage floor was painted with what appeared to be bubbles or perhaps a stylized impression of sea foam. The combination of styles did not really work. The skeletal towers with their fragmented slats or shutters and the web-like and globular elements seemed to come from different productions. Interestingly, Lee's unhappiness with Freedman's approach seemed to be echoed in the *New York Times* review, which noted that Freedman rejected any deep investigation of themes in favor of "lightness and grace" (July 17, 1962). Nonetheless, Lee and Freedman went on to a productive artistic partnership, working on twenty-three productions together, as well as a lifelong personal friendship.

This production also marked the start of one of the great creative collaborations of the twentieth century. Freedman brought in costume designer Theoni Aldredge; Lee's lighting assistant, Martin Aronstein, would eventually become the festival lighting designer (through the first two seasons, Lee designed his own lights). The

86   Arnold Aronson

three designers worked together on thirty-five productions at the Shakespeare Festival and elsewhere, about two-thirds of these with Freedman.

Although the English Renaissance stages of Shakespeare's time may have been "open-air," they were enclosed, allowing Shakespeare to create scenes of great intimacy, something that posed a dilemma for Lee at the Delacorte. Judith Crist, in her review of *Merchant* in the *New York Herald Tribune*, noted the spatial problems created by the vast open stage; "The stage ... is somehow bare; the Rialto is deserted, with only a couple of players pausing to converse from time to time. Only in a masque scene ... is any use made of the afar reaches of the stage" (June 27, 1962). Lee was aware of the difficulties: "When I was trying to create an interior, or a sense of interior, let's say the scene between Shylock and Jessica where they are inside, no matter how we moved the damn thing in [the movable bridge], it still looked like they were outside the house."[5] It was for precisely this reason that Lee sought to redesign the stage for future seasons. For the 1963 season he eliminated the movable bridge and created a unit set that would function as the basic structure for all three productions. The fundamental unit was a raised platform upstage, situated about eight feet above the stage and composed of three angular sections to mirror the front of the stage. It was reached by steps on either side, each with a landing about halfway up. Tall posts rose up behind the stage. Lee thought of this as an Elizabethan stage, though it was actually closer in spirit to a Greek than an Elizabethan theatre, which was actually appropriate for the open Delacorte stage. At this time the Shakespearean stage was mostly understood by the John Cranford Adams model which posited an "above" and an "inner below" or discovery space. While that model has long since been rejected by scholars—it was not supported by the evidence, and more important, would not have worked with the sightlines of the essentially circular Globe and its onstage pillars—it actually worked remarkably well on the broad thrust of the Delacorte. The upper level not only provided a stage that met the eye-level of much of the audience, it allowed for fluid movement between scenes. And the space below the upper platform—the inner below, as it were—was in full view of the entire audience on the broad open stage of the Delacorte.

The new set provided for fluid staging on two distinct levels, although it eliminated the possibility of scenic wagons rolling on and offstage, meaning that any set changes were done manually. It also provided a strong sense of enclosure for interior scenes on the stage level, seeming to solve one of the problems of the previous year, but there were still issues with the first production of the 1963 season, *Antony and Cleopatra*. Despite the tall posts rising up behind the stage, the upper level tended to flatten the action below, reinforcing a horizontal visual field and subverting some of the grandeur created by the vertical elements. This was not helped by director Joseph Papp who had not quite figured out how to best exploit the fluidity that the new configuration provided. In act four, for instance, the wounded Antony is brought to Cleopatra's monument and raised up to her chamber—but it was done rather awkwardly, lifting him from the stage to the upper level, which was confusing to the audience since he could easily have been carried up the stairs.

For the next production, *As You Like It*, Lee and director Freedman had a better grasp of how to utilize the new configuration. This time, given the apparent frivolity of the play, Lee was willing to be romantic and decorative, and took the paintings of Rococo artists Watteau and Fragonard as inspiration. He surrounded the set with three-dimensional trees, abstract clouds and tree fragments in front of the upper level; there was a working fountain. The ornamentation helped unify the upper and lower levels, and the trees and clouds allowed the eye to flow from downstage upward toward the sky. For all its frothiness, the setting possessed much of what had already become signature elements of Lee's style: scaffolding, vertical poles, skeletal sets, horizontal shutters and slats. The poetic sensibility of Mielziner and the structural and emblematic vocabulary of Boris Aronson can all be seen within this work. But now it came together in an identifiable style and became a template of sorts for subsequent Delacorte productions.

The final show of the 1964 season, *Electra*, though obviously not Shakespeare, needs to be mentioned because it was a breakthrough for Lee and a landmark in American scenography. Lee eliminated the raised upper stage but kept the basic ground plan, with a raked central thrust and ramps on either side leading to an imposing central doorway. The true innovation was in the upstage scenic units. What appear to be three massive fragments of stone wall—made from carved Styrofoam—were hung from pipe scaffolding that followed the upstage angles of the stage. Significantly, the three units floated, not touching each other, the floor or the top of the pipe structure. At the time, at least in the American theatre, it was revolutionary. While the rock walls might be described as "realistic" in terms of look and texture, it was really a nonliteral, nonrepresentational set. These were emblematic, iconic units that announced the stage-as-stage. Although Lee's subsequent sets rarely moved entirely into the realm of the abstract and iconic, except in his dance designs for Martha Graham and Joffrey Ballet, he was now freed from a commitment to the representational.

Of the subsequent Shakespeare productions, the 1966 *Richard III* most closely resembled *Electra* with emblematic walls of consisting of sculpted heraldic slabs mounted on vertical poles. Two raised platforms of unequal height are set against the back walls at left and right, reached by simple wooden staircases. As with *Electra* the scenic pieces did not touch the floor and there were gaps between them. Instead of stone, these were intended to look like corroded copper, the chaotic detritus of war. Interestingly, the effect was somewhat collage-like, a harbinger of a soon-to-emerge technique of Lee's designs.

As with most of Shakespeare's plays, there are multiple locales, moving among a street, the palace, in front of the Tower, and so forth. But the specificity of the locales is secondary to the atmospheric world of the play—a site of mythological grandeur, battle, and the transfer of power. Lee's set, an iconic environment, created a space in which Richard would rise and fall and the new order emerge.

Interestingly, although the pipe grid of *Electra* was first and foremost a functional structure—it had been there all along in many of the Delacorte sets, though often encased within wooden sleeves—it was also an aesthetic scenic component, and

Figure 5.2 Richard III, model, New York Shakespeare Festival, 1966
Source: Photo courtesy of Ming Cho Lee

subsequent sets increasingly foregrounded this device so that by the mid-1960s, metal pipe grids and scaffolding had become the most iconic aspect of Lee's work. But unlike the ethereal skeletal structures of his mentor Jo Mielziner (see, most notably, *Death of a Salesman*), Lee's architecture was closer in spirit to the Russian Constructivists and embodied a gritty, industrial look. While the geography of the stage was not quite that of the Globe or other theatres of the time, Lee, more than anyone in the American theatre, created a modern equivalent to the architectural and emblematic stage of the English Renaissance.

The middle show of the 1966 Shakespeare Festival season, *Measure for Measure*, foregrounded verticality and industrial scaffolding as almost nothing before had at the Delacorte. Moreover, the set was something radically different, for both the Shakespeare Festival and Lee: a very frontal white brick façade with a kind of fire escape structure and steep industrial stairs leading up from either side.

Director Michael Kahn, who came from the Off-Off Broadway world having had recently directed the "Motel" segment of *America Hurrah* at La MaMa, wanted neither abstraction nor a historically accurate Vienna. He wanted the set to look like New York City's meat market district, now a chic area but at the time an area of low-rise brick tenements and warehouses. This was not, however, intended to be an illusionistic set—essentially it was a fragment, a quotation of the neighborhood. The pipework's verticality counteracted the potential squatness of the

Figure 5.3 Measure for Measure, ½" model, New York Shakespeare Festival, 1966
Source: Photo courtesy of Ming Cho Lee

building, and the metal structure provided the upper stage area that Lee had incorporated into most of the previous Delacorte sets—but now it was an integral part of the architecture. The fire escape even created an "inner below" that would become the setting for the jail scenes by placing a construction of metal bars below the balcony. The effect was hard, cold, and disturbing in its brutality. In some way this harkened back to Welles-like strategy of resituating a play in a more contemporary environment, except that here, Kahn was not implying a direct metaphoric correlation between the setting and the play. However, setting it in a modern urban environment helped foreground the inherent tensions in the play between comedy and near tragedy, between the fairytale like construct of the story and the harsh selfishness and cruelty of certain characters. The starkness and industrial quality of the set also shattered any aura of stereotypical "Shakespeare-ness." This was a kind of Brechtian alienation intended to force the audience to confront the ideas of the play shorn of its usual cultural trappings.

Vertical pipes and scaffolding continued, notably in productions of *Romeo and Juliet* (1968), *Timon of Athens* (1971), and *Hamlet* (1972)—which employed a double revolving stage to emphasize the ever-changing perspectives and angles of Elsinore—but a more conceptual and modernist approach was taken in the 1971 production of *Cymbeline* with the young director A.J. Antoon. Antoon was happy with Lee's scaffolding but wanted the set to look like an office building, so Lee added

Figure 5.4 Hamlet, ½" model, New York Shakespeare Festival, 1972
Source: Photo courtesy of Ming Cho Lee

black Plexiglas panels and made the stage floor shiny black. The reflective panels inspired the actor Sam Waterston, who played Cloten, to develop an ongoing comic routine about catching his own reflection. In a sense this completed a kind of evolution. Just as the pictorial settings allowed *characters* to interact with a dramatic environment, Lee's sets now encouraged *actors* to interact with a theatrical environment.

In 1967 the Shakespeare Festival converted the former Astor Library near the East Village into the Public Theater, a multi-theatre space for the production of new plays. Lee was responsible for designing two of the new spaces, the Anspacher and Newman theatres. The Anspacher, in a way, was Lee's response to the Delacorte—a relatively small thrust stage enveloped by an intimate 275-seat auditorium. Lee designed several of the productions in the space over the next few years, including the musical that opened the new theatre, *Hair* (he would not, however, design the show when it moved to Broadway). Most of the shows he designed there used pipe scaffolding, but the significant innovation, beginning with *Hair*, was collage. The scaffolding became a framework for posters, images, and emblematic and iconic scenic elements and this approach reached an apotheosis of sorts back at the Delacorte with *Two Gentlemen of Verona* (1971) and *Much Ado about Nothing* (1972), both of which moved to Broadway after their seasons in the park.

The former was reconceived as an inventive, celebratory rock musical by downtown director Mel Shapiro, with music by *Hair* composer Galt MacDermot and the book adapted by playwright John Guare whose Off-Broadway hit, *The House of Blue Leaves*, had opened earlier that year. Shapiro initially was not happy about the scaffolding, insisting that musicals were horizontal, not vertical, but he came to embrace the idea. Lee painted the pipes orange and red and added architectural elements such as window cornices and fire escape-like balconies that evoked both New York and Italy. To allow for the change from Verona to Milan, there were Venetian blinds with images of Verona painted on one side, and Milan on the other. Lee employed advertising graphics for the latter, referencing the commercial billboards that punctuate modern-day Milan. The overall effect was not unlike the collage for *Hair*, though less dense; there was a much greater sense of space breathing through the whole structure.

Much Ado About Nothing was fundamentally another scaffold-and-collage set—some of the structure and complex staircase pattern, in fact, came from *Hamlet*—but it was really a celebratory decorative design. Director A.J. Antoon

Figure 5.5 Two Gentlemen of Verona, model, New York Shakespeare Festival, 1971
Source: Phtoo courtesy of Ming Cho Lee

Figure 5.6 Much Ado About Nothing, model, New York Shakespeare Festival, 1972
Source: Photo courtesy of Ming Cho Lee

situated the action in 1912, in what Lee called America's "age of confidence," and the atmosphere was that of a summer evening in a small town. "No great social comment, nothing Brechtian," says Lee. "Just do it and the play itself will say all the things that are pretty horrendous."

Scott Joplin's ragtime music provided the soundtrack; Dogberry and company were played as Keystone Kops; canoes floated into view on a turntable, as did a Model T Ford. Lee's first impulse was to have the scenery floating off the floor as he had done several times since *Electra*, but Antoon wanted billboards, so Lee designed a background collage of advertising images and photogravure blowups of Teddy Roosevelt and others, firmly planted on the ground. *New York Times* critic Clive Barnes, described the Broadway set (which was virtually identical to that in the park) as "a lovely wooden construction of complex terraces, platforms, catwalks and alcoves that remarkably gives the mood and style of early 20th-century American architecture. ... The total effect is startling and yet beguilingly attractive." (November 13, 1972). Lee acknowledges that "I was breaking all the rules I had set up for the park. It was deliberately decorative and it was realistic, but because of the collage the look was not *real* realism. It was filled with wonderful touches, as if you were right in the midst of 1912, living with these people."

Much Ado was Lee's final production for Shakespeare in the Park. After eleven seasons and twenty-seven plays from the canon, American Shakespeare no longer looked the same. In 1962 the majority of Shakespeare productions either were realistic, pseudo-expressionist, or monumental. Lee introduced a presentational, multi-level, sculptural, emblematic, and iconic scenography frequently relying on metal and wood as basic materials. But at the same time, he had gotten into a rut. Writing in the *New York Times* of July 9, 1972, Julius Novick pointed out

> how very conventional most of Joseph Papp's Shakespeare productions have been. ... much of the time it has been a matter of finding an appropriate period for the costumes, getting Ming Cho Lee to design another of his scaffoldy settings, and very straightforwardly getting the thing on.

At the end of the 1972 season, even Lee's mentor, Jo Mielziner, wrote him a note saying he was repeating himself.

Regional theatre

In 1967 Lee designed his first production at the Arena Stage in Washington, D.C., *The Crucible*, which began a long association with that theatre as well as the start of a career that took him to most of the major regional theatres in the country. His first Shakespeare done outside the New York Shakespeare Festival was *King Lear* in 1968 for the Repertory Theatre of Lincoln Center—technically not a regional theatre, but conceptually similar. Nonetheless, with Freedman directing and Aldredge designing costumes, it was essentially the festival creative team. Freedman's concept was that as Lear lost the trappings of power and humanity, the set would be stripped away as well, leaving an almost bare stage by the end. He also wanted a somewhat rough and primitive feel, which Lee achieved through the use of a wooden platform, wooden superstructure, and erosion cloth as the background, as well as a large heraldic-like emblem at the rear. If one had to choose an iconic Ming Cho Lee set of the period it would be hard to do better than this *Lear*.

It turned out, however, to be one of Lee's more poorly received designs because he did not fully understand the challenges of the notoriously problematic Vivian Beaumont Theatre until it was too late. The Mielziner-designed space tried, with little success, to combine a thrust and proscenium. Lee attempted to use the great depth of the stage, and it looked fine under house lights. But as soon as the set was seen under stage lights it became lost in the cavernous space.

In 1971 Lee designed *Henry IV Part 1*, directed by Gordon Davidson, at the Mark Taper Forum in Los Angeles. The Taper, opened in 1967, is a circular building in the midst of the rectangular campus of the Los Angeles Music Center. The buildings were designed by architect Welton Becket, but again the theatre itself was designed by Jo Mielziner; though by not attempting to combine two forms of stage it was architecturally more successful. The stage is a thrust surrounded by a semi-circular amphitheatre—no deep proscenium stage behind—and much more intimate and not as fan-shaped as the Delacorte. Lee had designed a very frontal

Figure 5.7 King Lear, model, Repertory Theatre of Lincoln Center, 1968. Over the course of the play the scenery was stripped away. By the storm scene, all that remained were the four wooden posts and a white cyclorama

Source: Photo courtesy of Ming Cho Lee

Volpone there earlier in the year, closer in style to *Much Ado* than to the earlier emblematic Shakespeare productions. For *Henry IV*, however, Lee covered the thrust with wooden planks (another Lee stylistic trope that became ubiquitous in the American theatre), angled and placed to make the stage floor irregular and asymmetrical. The towering set was fronted by massive wooden beams and a façade that combined emblematic elements and stonework—"an outer surround that represented the world of the political struggle," according to Lee—reminiscent of *Richard III* at the Delacorte. Perhaps because it was indoors in an enclosed space, it had a grandeur that was sometimes lost in the Delacorte productions. Perhaps most intriguing, the centerline was set at a diagonal that created a subconscious disorientation for the audience. Looking at a photo of the set it is virtually impossible to identify the centerline. Lee believed that one of the things that distinguished *Henry IV Part 1* from the other Shakespearean histories was the focus on private life in juxtaposition to public display. The asymmetry of the set allowed for alcoves and niches—private spaces within the architecture of power.

Figure 5.8 Henry IV, Part 1, Mark Taper Forum, 1971
Source: Photo courtesy of Center Theatre Group

In 1978 Lee was teamed with Romanian director Liviu Ciulei for a production of *Hamlet* at Arena Stage and it changed the way Lee worked with directors. It also led to one of his first Shakespeare designs that did not depend on the formula from the Delacorte.[6] Ciulei's conceptual approach and visual sensibility (he sometimes designed his own sets) was highly stimulating for Lee who thrived on the intellectual give and take of the discussions they had. It also allowed him to break out of his established patterns and try something radically new. Lee had been intrigued by a production Santo Loquasto had designed for Arena in which he had taken out a section of the stage floor to reveal the basement below. For *Hamlet*, Lee proposed taking out the whole floor, then raising the playing space higher, allowing the audience to see beneath the stage. He designed a stage floor of dark polished wood, inspired by a church he had seen in England, with the brick vaulting and foundations visible beneath it, "so that underneath is rotten but on top it is very, very clean and polished," explained Lee. The raised stage was framed by low benches but was otherwise barren, save for the occasional piece of furniture such as a tangerine-colored desk for Polonius, a gold chaise for Gertrude, and a dinner table where Ophelia went mad, so that actors were isolated in a kind of theatrical void.

Entrances and exits were made through the labyrinth of this ominous, vaulted underworld –the ghost, Hamlet on his way to confront the praying King; Polonius was murdered there and Laertes burst from below to avenge Ophelia. Almost accidentally, Lee had discovered a kind of inverse verticality. Instead of vertical polls ascending above the stage, there was seemingly unfathomable depth beneath the stage; the audience was witnessing only what transpired at the pinnacle of this subterranean structure, which threatened the stability of the visible world. Ciulei had originally suggested mirrors as a dominant visual motif, and while Lee rejected the idea (he felt it would wind up as second-rate Josef Svoboda), the pit was lined with Plexiglas that created a reflective surface, providing the audience with views of the underside of the stage and parts of the walls not otherwise visible to them, as well as extended and sometimes distorted glimpses of characters coming and going. This was a *Hamlet* revealed through architecture.

The 1972 *Hamlet* at the Delacorte had created a maze of crisscrossing ramps ascending through a vertical maze. Characters moved on a tenuous, unstable network above the ground. The world of the Arena *Hamlet* was the reverse. The visible world rested on a dark, unknowable underworld from which all the characters emerged and to which they all descended. The architecture of the set thus became inextricably bound up with the text and the dark world of Elsinore.

This was a stimulating and productive collaboration for Lee, replicated in the production of Molière's *Don Juan* the following year. But after that, unfortunately, he never worked with Ciulei again.

In the latter part of his career Lee established close relationships with two theatre companies: the Actors Theatre of Louisville where he worked with artistic director Jon Jory on five Shakespeare productions (*The Tempest, Antony and Cleopatra, Romeo and Juliet, The Comedy of Errors*, and *Othello*); and the Shakespeare Theatre in Washington, D.C. where three of the seven shows he did between 1995 and 2005 were by Shakespeare (*Macbeth* directed by Joe Dowling, and *King John* and *Merchant of Venice* with artistic director Michael Kahn).

None of the productions at Louisville could be considered groundbreaking or innovative, but neither were they derivative. They emerged from long discussions between Jory and Lee about the themes, meanings, and implications of the plays, in which Lee functioned as much as a dramaturg as designer. The basic set for *The Tempest* was a mound that Jory described as "post-apocalyptic sand dunes"; Prospero's cell was a ruined Palladian structure. For *Antony and Cleopatra* Jory had the idea of depicting the nearly twenty locales of the play through color rather than architecture so Lee created a set of sliding panels painted in primary colors. *Romeo and Juliet* (1994), however, had an interesting postmodern touch. Having already done the play at the Delacorte in 1968 and Circle in the Square in 1977, as well a ballet version for Pacific Northwest Ballet in 1987, Lee did not want to do another Renaissance set for the 1994 Louisville production. Jory wanted to draw a connection between authoritarianism in the family and totalitarian societies and this led at first to the notion of setting the play in pre-fascist Italy, just before the rise of Mussolini. But the monumentality and minimal decoration of fascist architecture did not mesh well with the sense of artistic decadence that Jory was also looking for. One day at Yale, Lee walked past the drawing table of one of his students and on it was a book called *Inside Rome* lying open to an image of an eighteenth-century Roman courtyard painted with decorative frescoes, three window balconies, and Ionic columns. Lee felt it was perfect and used it as the basis for his set. The absolutely frontal, two-story façade, with pediments and painted columns, provided a certain monumentality while being offset by the elegant yet playful rococo frescoes. But Lee added one other touch that transformed the set from the merely decorative to the truly theatrical: bright white utilitarian, industrial stairwells on either side with walls seemingly made of concrete. The juxtaposition of the two radically opposite sensibilities emphasized the artificiality of the world of the Montagues and Capulets, a world of illusion surrounded by a cold, hard brutality.

Lee did two productions of *Othello* during this period, one in 1994 at Stratford, Ontario directed by Brian Bedford, and the second at Louisville in 1998. For Stratford Lee set the production in 1939, not long before the U.S. entry into World War II. Venice became Washington, D.C., and Cyprus was a colonial outpost suggestive of the Philippines. This was as close as Lee ever came to translating a Shakespearean set into a recognizable contemporary setting. However, he kept it strongly emblematic through the motif of a black and white setting, inspired in part by a production of Verdi's *Otello* designed by Timothy O'Brien that not only reflected the theme of the play but also created a stark contrast between the two

Figure 5.9 Romeo and Juliet, ½" model, Actors Theatre of Louisville, 1994
Source: Photo courtesy of Ming Cho Lee

worlds. For act one in Venice, the set was shiny black, evoking both elegance and a place of intrigue. For the remainder of the play in Cyprus, it was suggestive of colonial architecture—stark white with minimal decor, except for downstage, which retained the shiny black surface and threw the rest of the set into relief.

The Louisville *Othello* four years later was, Lee declared—speaking more as a spectator than designer—"The best *Othello* I had ever experienced." The contrast between the two locales in this production was created through a juxtaposition of beauty and ugliness. For the first act, there was a backdrop based on a fifteenth-century painting by Carlo Crivelli (which Lee would use again in 2005 for *Lorenzaccio* at the Shakespeare Theatre). The painting is grotesque, but with a richness of tone that created a Venetian atmosphere. The photorealism that Lee had been experimenting with in the 1980s was now turned into something harsh for the Cyprus portion of the play. Lee was inspired by the architecture of many American consulates:

> You think, 'Here is America,' but instead you walk into a Holiday Inn. I envisioned Othello and Desdemona living in totally soulless Holiday Inn. So in one sense it is absolutely abstract. On the other hand it is absolutely real.

But Lee took it even farther, eliminating anything attractive or comforting; it was based less on minimalist hotel design and more on concrete and glass industrial structures. When Jory first saw it he was struck by its ugliness, declaring it "hard to look at," though he also pointed out that it was ugly "in a beautiful way, as anything by Ming would be."[7]

Lee's first production with the Shakespeare Theatre—*Macbeth* in 1995—was a somewhat frustrating experience as Lee felt that Joe Dowling provided little guidance, but the set was one of the more striking of the latter part of Lee's career, reminiscent of Eastern European neo-expressionism. Lee created a spare, off-white box whose stage right wall curved into the wooden plank floor. Visible through the portals of the blood-stained back wall was a field of wheat, while a barren, blood-red tree, resembling a diseased heart and arteries, dominated the set and provided a structure for the witches to climb on. Stacy Keach, who was playing Macbeth, insisted on an "above," an upper gallery for certain scenes, so Lee provided metal scaffolding upstage—a sort of final echo of his early scenic vocabulary. None of this evolved from any coherent conceptual idea, but despite the haphazard genesis, the set worked remarkably well, and the bloody tree was a perfect metaphor for the play.

King John is one of Shakespeare's less-frequently produced plays, perhaps because it sits uneasily between history and farce, lacking the grandeur and intrigue of the other history plays. Initially Kahn and Lee saw it primarily as a political play and Lee designed a parapet with a red balcony and a gate below, which allowed a rostrum for speeches. There were towers on either side, which moved in and out to delineate the different scenes. Once again, the basic ground plan was a formal box perforated by rectangular openings. During rehearsals, however, it became clear

Figure 5.10 *Macbeth*, model, directed by Joe Dowling, Shakespeare Theatre Company, 1995
Source: Photo courtesy of Shakespeare Theatre Company

Figure 5.11 *King John*, directed by Michael Kahn, Shakespeare Theatre, 1999
Source: Photo Carol Rosegg

that the strength of the play lay in the moments of personal interaction among the characters. It was not the cold, impersonal political play both he and Kahn had imagined. Rather, the very human characters moved within an impersonal world. As this became apparent, scenic elements were added to mitigate the original formality of the design.

The Merchant of Venice followed later that spring with what Lee refers to, with some justification, as a "safe set," essentially a Shakespeare in the Park Renaissance set adapted for a proscenium stage. "If you do it in the period," Lee asserts, "you cannot do a bad set. And I did not do a bad set. But it was not a great set."

Conclusion

Lee's great innovations in theatre design in general and for Shakespeare in particular came mostly in the 1960s and 1970s. As with any young artist there was an energy and sense of daring, a desire to break with the past, and the ability to see things in new ways. Of particular note was the cross-fertilization among genres. During these years Lee was doing opera, dance, and theatre in almost equal measure, something few, if any, of his contemporaries could claim, and each fed off the other. Also, more than most of his colleagues he was working for institutions. While none of these institutions, save for the Metropolitan Opera, were very well funded, he still had the resources that came with such organizations, part of which was the possibility of developing ongoing relationships with certain directors and other designers. And within theatre, alongside Shakespeare and other classics, he was doing new plays and musicals. No other designer of his generation could claim such a wealth of experience and opportunity. But Lee's most innovative creations came most often when working with adventurous or iconoclastic directors such as A.J. Antoon and especially Liviu Ciulei. Except for the late collaborations with Michael Kahn, those opportunities were unfortunately few and far between in the latter half of his career.

As Lee worked increasingly in the regional theatres and opera companies outside of New York his work became less visible and had a decreasing impact on the development of American scenography. Meanwhile, other scenographic approaches, notably postmodernism, seemed to overtake him. But his work actually continued to be constantly new and surprising. It is just that the most daring productions—with Cloud Gate Dance Theatre of Taiwan, productions of *Death of a Salesman* at both Stratford and Oregon Shakespeare Festival, *A Touch of the Poet* at Oregon, *Carmina Burana* for Pacific Northwest Ballet, *The Woman Warrior* at Berkeley Repertory Theatre and two other theatres, *The Hollow Lands* at South Coast Rep, and many more—were no longer those of Shakespeare. But all the years of confronting the spatial, temporal, and visual demands of Shakespeare inevitably continued to shape his aesthetic. Lee retired from designing in 2005, though he continues to teach at the Yale School of Drama.

Notes

1. Dennis Kennedy. *Looking at Shakespeare: A Visual History of Twentieth-Century Performance*. (Cambridge: Cambridge U.P., 1993), 145.
2. The Circle in the Square, an Off-Broadway theatre in a converted night club, had a deep thrust—almost an alley stage—that dated to 1951. While this had some influence on the soon-to-emerge Off-Off Broadway movement, it had little immediate effect on more mainstream theatres. The Guthrie-designed theatre in Minneapolis, modeled closely on the one at Stratford, Ontario, opened in 1963, a year after the Delacorte. In the postwar era, however, some theatres experimented with theatre-in-the-round.
3. Personal interview, November 11, 2010
4. Arnold Aronson, *American Set Design* (New York: Theatre Communications Group, 1985), 92.
5. All quotes from Lee are from personal interviews conducted between 2010 and 2013 unless otherwise noted.
6. Lee's *Julius Caesar* in the round at Arena in 1975 and *Romeo and Juliet* on the long narrow thrust at Circle in the Square in New York in 1977 were shaped by the physical demands of those theatres, but in spirit they were not far removed from his earlier Shakespearean designs.
7. Personal interview, October 18, 2012.

Chapter 6

Alison Chitty – the public sketch

Hilary Baxter

Alison Chitty is one of the key British Theatre Designers working across the last decades of the twentieth century and the first two decades of the twenty-first. Her influence is widespread yet subtle in terms of the impact of her design work for theatre productions and her influence upon subsequent generations of theatre designers. She was awarded an OBE in 2004 (Officer of the Most Excellent Order of the British Empire) and in 2009 elected as a Royal Designer for Industry.[1] She has been recognized for her exemplary design work with two Olivier awards in 2001 and 2007[2] and a Young Vic award in 2008.[3] She has worked as a theatre designer for all of her professional life, mainly in the subsidized theatre such as the Royal National Theatre (RNT) rather than commercially for the West End. Chitty's designs are most recognizable through her distinctive drawings and sketches than for a specific style of work, as her designs for productions range broadly from gritty new pieces for stage or screen (*Secrets and Lies*, Leigh 1996) to classic Shakespeare productions and most recently new operas for the Royal Opera House (Sir Harrison Birtwistle, Sir Michael Tippett).

Chitty's collaborations with eminent British directors on productions of Shakespeare in the late twentieth century will be used here to define her contribution to contemporary Theatre Design and I am concentrating on her design work for two particular watershed productions of Shakespeare since Chitty has mainly concentrated on designing operas for the past decade. I have deliberately chosen to focus on the two productions outside of the Royal Shakespeare Company (RSC) as the examples I am analysing that represent her contribution to designing Shakespeare. These two productions, one for Riverside Studios and the other for the National Theatre (now the RNT), are more in keeping with the overall profile of her work within a varied artistic programme also concerned with new writing rather than one with the remit of re-interpreting a series of classics.

I have identified three key elements with Chitty's designs for Shakespeare: First, that the use of storyboards and drawings is a crucial part of her design work to develop her ideas organically. How her close collaboration with directors creates integration of the set and costume design with all the other elements of the performance and finally to articulate how Chitty works with the audience as part of her design process.

Alison Chitty – the public sketch 103

In a storyboard for her iconic theatre production of *Julius Caesar* (directed by Peter Gill) at the Riverside Studios, London in 1980, Alison Chitty depicted a white space, sparsely inhabited, with a piece of stage floor that is being hoisted by fly lines, then a table and later a tent. Characters enter, talk to others, often grouping and re-grouping until in the final scene a body lies on the ground, while the group stand apart uncertain, guilty. Chitty explains how the storyboard is an important part of the design process:

> In a storyboard I draw the key moments of each scene, which shows me the shape and structure of the play and where the actors need to be, so that I can design a space to hold them.' She goes on to add 'It's what I call designing from the inside out – not from the outside in.'[4]

This storyboard is created at a point when neither designer nor director will have a clear idea of what the finished production will look like. It is easy to overlook this when viewed much later, as a sense of inevitability is engendered, rather than reminding us that Chitty and Gill were engaged in the early stages of creating a production, a collaborative journey.

This storyboard of eighteen ink drawings, all on the same page and using quickly drawn boxes, shows each scene of the play, the use of space and the movement of characters through the whole production as series of lines. The individual drawings seem quite small, and the overall impression is that of fluid movement both in line and potential stage pictures. The lines are quick and definite, with some parts of the drawings left blank to throw emphasis into different areas of the indicated stage space, but for the fact that they accurately capture elements of staging such as the details of the back wall, lines of the floorboards and the movement of the actors. Individual characters are not distinguishable except in relation to other groups or characters, but energetically inhabit the space whether in soliloquy, conversing in pairs or forming a team, a mob, or opposing sides.

In general, storyboard sketches are not usually intended to be seen, however, Chitty published this complete set of drawings as a finished piece of work having also published two more detailed storyboard sketches from this production. This storyboard confirms Chitty's reputation as a visual collaborator, and is a public statement of her belief that to communicate visually as a designer at all stages of the process is important not only to the designer's understanding of the piece but as a key tool for the director as well. These storyboards reveal what was being discussed between designer and director at a very early stage of the production process, not only in the design details such as the floorboards but also the use of the space with stage pictures involving individuals and groups of performers. In this way, which is almost cartoonish, the whole play can be viewed and understood visually and very simply. The explicit use of big group scenes and frequent use of the ensemble as spectators of other smaller scenes indicates an initial interpretation of the text to constantly build tension in this way, which inevitably leads to violence.

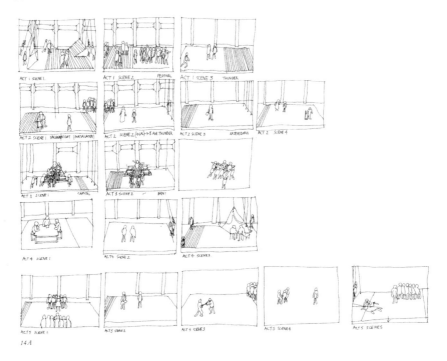

Figure 6.1 Storyboard drawings for Julius Caesar by Alison Chitty, 1980
Source: Courtesy of British Theatre Design

Early design decisions indicated in this first storyboard carry right through to the final production, notably the floorboards and the parallel pillars in the back wall (the pillars might have been part of the actual brick wall structure of the Riverside Studio space). Other elements are added in later sketches to emphasize the political context, always working towards expressing the shocking violence of the murder in the text.

The view of the stage in the first drawings are as if from a traditional theatre perspective seated in the back of the stalls or dress circle, where the floor is an important visual for the audience. But in the Riverside Studio, seating was raked from the same level as the stage floor, meaning that the back wall was far more important when viewed in production. This shift is reflected in other storyboard drawings for *Julius Caesar,* which were published earlier in date but later in the design process of the same production. One drawing is partially coloured and employs the outline sketch of two men and floorboards, but this time the back wall has been postered over with grey and sand coloured sheets of paper. There is also a legend in Latin (mainly obscured) over which has been carefully but boldly daubed in red paint 'Caius Julius Caesar'. The use of the red paint on an otherwise pale neutral background, with little other detail, immediately makes the visual impact: rough, immediate and politically charged. This sketch was originally accompanied by a photograph of the production showing something of the same background but with an actor being carried at shoulder height on a litter, the Latin legend showing on the wall behind. The tones of the photograph are mixed; half the stage is in heavy dark shadow, the rest is in warm light but with texture picked up on the back wall and the posters. It seems that the red lettering is imminent but has not yet arrived. The tense political atmosphere has been achieved. Chitty commented that:

> I began to see how with very little you could express a lot and also how that meant it was possible to change from one scene to another in a very fluid way, and of course in Shakespeare that's so crucial.[5]

The original storyboard drawings and the subsequent coloured version followed by the photograph give a clear indication of Chitty's design process in three different stages working with the text to support Peter Gill's direction. Initially, the ideas are forming, suggestions rather than details, giving room for other collaborators to also inhabit the world, actors developing characters, the lighting designer to create mood and focus, and the director to bring all of the separate elements into a single unified piece.

In a second coloured *Julius Caesar* drawing, the costumes are beginning to be more defined. There are two characters standing together who appear to be both male, wearing trousers. One has banded details across the legs, the other similar lines across the lower arms and an 'epaulette' shoulder detail all visually relating to period costumes. At this stage of the design process, all elements are beginning to be tested in terms of their potential. From the photograph of the production, it can be seen that these tentative details of dress were pared down to a simple and stylized sports clothes scheme, a fact commented upon by John Peters in his review for *The Sunday Times* newspaper:

> The men all wore identical grey sweaters, tunics and trousers with leg warmers and soft grey leather shoes – except Caesar who had a robe, presumably to indicate seniority. The scene was laid for a political conflict performed as a violent ballet.[6]

Chitty explains her approach to costume, "I think if you use the word 'clothes' it helps you have a different relationship with what you're doing and it's as simple as that."[7]

These clothes for *Julius Caesar* were very different from those that Chitty had designed for a previous Shakespeare with Peter Gill. For *Measure for Measure*, the previous season, she had found secondhand velvet curtains, which she asked to be specially dyed into beautiful rich colours. These were then cut into stylized period costume shapes, using boned stays for the women's bodices with full-length skirts

106 Hilary Baxter

Figure 6.2 Julius Caesar, designed by Alison Chitty, Riverside Studios, 1980
Source: Photo Donald Cooper

and long robes with heavy sleeves and cuffs for the men. The drape of the softened velvet gave the clothes elegant sweeping bold shapes, where new fabric would have been bulky with a stiffer movement. The set for *Measure for Measure* also used recycled materials; house doors intended for disposal were stained and varnished, then mounted against the brick wall of the back of the stage space. The variety of panelling and differences in size and detail of the doors gave textural interest, as they formed a line across the back of the stage. The floor was brick, which linked with the back wall. In this way, Chitty created a setting that could become a visual metaphor for the whole piece. Not specific to any one scene or particular event, but a visual comment on the world of the whole piece, allowing for the possibilities of lighting and staging to interpret the piece and inhabit the space as needed. This slightly abstracted visual comment using real details (doors) in a non-realistic manner (lined up) firstly gives us, as the audience, permission to decide for themselves what the doors might mean or where they might lead to if opened. The doors can obviously be used as real doors that people might use, or seem to use or washed over with coloured light to abstract even further for other scenes. This abstract even poetic use of visuals was utilized by Chitty as her response to the challenges of dealing with a difficult Shakespeare. Contemporary reviews of this production comment on the pared down nature of the design, the tiles on the floor and the use of the bare brick wall on which the doors were mounted. This paring down to key details, use of the elements of the theatre space itself and the slight abstraction without overpowering the performance is, I suggest, one of Chitty's main contributions to designing for Shakespeare.

Peter Gill has been recorded talking about how he first asked to work with Chitty. When he was the artistic director at Riverside Studios, Gill was very confident about getting very young designers to take on big commissions, and so when he was planning to put on *Measure for Measure*, he asked Chitty to take the commission, as he had seen some of her drawings in a Theatre Design exhibition. He explains, "She has a marvellous eye…'based on realising the text but in a poetic way'… an enormous sense of colour, very, very good clothes indeed."[8] Chitty says that she realised during their first collaboration that:

> I was looking for what Peter didn't know he wanted but would know when he saw it, and that's actually what I did all the time. I mean that's how you design anyway – you don't know what you're going to get. You've no idea what it is but you try and find it and when you see it you go; "Oh well, it must be that."[9]

Gill has commented that they have a shared aesthetic, because of her early work in the theatre-in-the-round at Stoke and his first productions without any budgets. His reflection is that that together they might have a tendency to oversimplify, but his final comment confirms that it is the quality of the collaborative creative relationship that has become important in their working together:

> Alison is very sympathetic to work with, she's a great team member she then did all the productions after that … she had a light touch and she was very good with people… she drew very well.[10]

Gill's comment indicates here his respect for Chitty as an artist and collaborator. The lightness of touch he refers to is manifest in their work together on the Riverside Shakespeare productions where the aesthetic is carefully stripped away. Nothing purely decorative or overly fancy has been indulged giving a completeness of shared vision to the production where all elements of performance work together. This pared back approach is neither bland nor timid as it can often be rich and stylish. They created complete visual worlds which framed the Shakespearean text for a contemporary audience, not through complex conceptual decisions but through creative working of ideas within the rehearsal process. This completeness of a production is the aim of many UK designers and directors.

Chitty herself studied Theatre Design as a full time undergraduate degree at the Central School of Art and Design in London. Designer Ralph Koltai was Head of the department (1965–72), working closely with Robin Don and Nadine Bayliss, who were all working professionally with Koltai, as well as teaching with him. The ethos of the course was concentrated on developing professional practice, primarily learning from the professional work of the tutors, informally assisting them, attending dress rehearsals and so on, an integration of study, practice and friendships.

108 Hilary Baxter

Reflecting on her time there she has commented that "I feel that I have invented my process, I am not aware that I had a process from Central", and goes on to say, "My own philosophy is to be a designer not a decorator and that's a fine line but that's where I come from."[11] After graduating in 1970, she competed for a bursary from the Arts Council[12] and subsequently was offered a sponsored placement in the Victoria Theatre in Stoke-on-Trent[13] where she stayed for four years as designer and a further four as Head of Design.

In her time at Stoke she designed over forty productions, many of which were new plays from the writers in residence.[14] As Chitty says of her early work for this theatre-in-the-round:

> The most important thing about this theatre was that everybody looked down onto the floor. And so the floor was an incredibly important visual element, and the floors became my passion out of this I'm sure. It started as I said with tons and tons and tons of floor cloths that were swung in and out.[15]

The fluidity of this system of scene change, all in front of the audience, is very much part of Chitty's approach to design and is a feature of much of her work, particularly in her design for Shakespeare. Working for a theatre-in-the-round meant that the audience also became part of her design and this demonstrates that Chitty as a designer had to consider how the piece would play in front of this uncertain visual element:

> In the winter the lights could be much brighter than they could in the summer because in the summer everybody came in their white T-shirts and their pink things and their pale blue this and whatever they were all wearing. But in the winter they were all in their navy blues and their browns ... so the whole space felt darker and in the summer the whole space felt lighter.[16]

This intensive period of design work for the same theatre gave Chitty the opportunity to develop her work process, and from which she has based her design approach for her later major work, "I believe that to make space for the audience to take part, they have a better time. If when you express any place, every single element is expressed, it's a kind of dead experience for an audience."[17] This 'spareness' is particularly important when designing for Shakespeare, as the text allows for many different interpretations of character work and requires fluidity both during and between scenes. An assistant of Chitty's refers to it as 'economy of gesture' saying that she shows restraint in her set design, preferring the simple statement with extravagant details concentrated in the props and costumes, when appropriate.[18]

In 1980, Gill left the Riverside Studios[19] having been invited to be an Associate Director at the National Theatre.[20] He asked to take a creative team with him, one of whom was Alison Chitty. The size and scale of the operation was much larger than either Chitty or Gill had worked on previously with three working theatre spaces. Despite anxieties over her ability to cope and work within such a complex organization, with all the workshops and backstage teams to support this scale of production, her work with Gill was well received, including the unusually visually sumptuous *Venice Preserv'd* for the Lyttleton proscenium arch theatre.

In her professional sphere, Chitty has formed long-lasting collaborative partnerships with several directors, Peter Gill, Mike Leigh (best known for his gritty film direction) and Sir Peter Hall. Director of the National Theatre from 1973–1988, Hall was the director responsible for moving the NT (now RNT) to its current site on the South Bank, and had previously worked closely with John Bury, one of the major British Theatre Designers since the 1950s. By 1987, Chitty had become the NT Resident Designer and was working closely with Peter Hall, designing another Shakespearian Caesar, *Antony and Cleopatra*, which starred Antony Hopkins as Antony and Judi Dench[21] as Cleopatra.

As an insight to his method of working Hall says that: "change is part of the creative collaboration of the theatre" and he insists on the right of a creative person to respond in the final stages of production to make improvements to the overall quality of the final piece, to produce the best result possible:

> A director's job is to get the best out of the designer… A designer has to be open to this process; he should not produce what he thinks the director *should* have before they have seen together what they can find. In my experience, the greater the designer, the more open he is to experiment and risk.[22]

In other words, a director must allow the designer experimentation time, to explore visually, the world of the play and to work though ideas in collaboration, to come to a solution together, which neither had previously conceived. Hall expects his designers to experiment and take risks.

For *Antony and Cleopatra*, Chitty was designing now for the Olivier stage (the largest of the three NT stages) which is a big open space, modelled on the ancient Greek theatre at Epidaurus, where the banked seats of the auditorium look down onto the stage floor giving prominence to the design of the floor and the relationship of the performer to the audience. Peter Hall refers to this as "one of my happiest times in the theatre" and begins to describe a way of working organically which he believes to be important and contrasts this with designers that impose an idea on a production:

> We had rehearsed for a month, with the designer, Alison Chitty, sketching obsessively, before any models were made or any costume decision taken. Such circumstances are rare, however. With this production, at the National Theatre in London, there was the luxury of twelve weeks' rehearsal. Normally, because of deadlines, budgeting, contractors' time, and other pressures, the design has to be ready even before rehearsals begin, with a danger that it is not organic but imposed.[23]

110 Hilary Baxter

The indulgence of a twelve-week rehearsal period for one production was and still is an extremely lavish provision and indicated the importance of this production in the schedule. This was commented on by Chitty herself, who gives the designer's perspective:

> It was very complicated agreeing a design – we couldn't really agree anything and really Peter didn't want a design at that point because we were going to rehearse for twelve weeks I think – it's a famous production where we had twelve weeks rehearsal – and he didn't really want a set I don't think at that point and I was struggling to try and find a set… and it was very complicated and we didn't really have anything until the day before we started rehearsal which was fine, it was absolutely fine.[24]

Although Chitty is very measured in her reflection, the inability to agree on any starting point for creating sets, costumes and props is very difficult in such a large organization, where the pressures of scheduling multiple productions means that there are many departments that will be pushing a designer for their decisions. Chitty also comments "He's famous for when he doesn't like something, he empties it all out and then we start again."[25]

For *Antony and Cleopatra*, Hall and Chitty had discussed several possible ways of staging the piece with a complete sense of the world and sky, using circles and domes and relating them to the Olivier space. They had both read and were inspired by Harley Granville-Barker's essay which describes it as a play of action, which they wanted to embrace in their use of stage space and had decided to keep the Roman colours in cool tones (steel blue, etc.) whereas the Egyptians were to be hot, sexy and sensual (russets, reds). Chitty was also visually inspired by paintings from the Renaissance, and used colour and textiles from this period to create an appropriately evocative mise-en-scène. In one of the interviews made by Tirzah Lowen (who was documenting Hall's process on this production) during the rehearsal process, Chitty says that she was trying "to get the effect of a corner of a Renaissance painting, with a glimpse of ruins, light and shadow in folds of material…"[26] Lowen also describes the model as presented to the cast:

> Against a deep maroon cyclorama, on a rounded floor area, stands an inner semi-circle. This is made up of three sections – two curved side walls and a central set of doors, pillared and pedimented – each of which can retreat or advance along floor-tracks, separately or together, to form varying configurations.[27]

In the RNT archive, the technical drawing of the working ground plan shows exactly the different placing of the pieces for each scene. There is great flexibility in this use of space. The action can move easily as the central pieces essentially track backwards and forwards. In this open staging for such a large space, there is a need for other careful design work to direct the eye of the audience, as Hall said, "We will have a problem clarifying when we are in Egypt, when in Rome, but costumes, props and lighting will help."[28] Chitty's process of sitting in rehearsal and sketching, suggesting solutions and then reflecting on the design decisions as a continuous part of the production's development is, I suggest, an important element of her collaborative approach. Being a key observer as the actors work through the scenes, being able to see the groupings and interpretations gives an insight into the shapes that their costumes will make in movement and aids the design process.

Few of the drawings and none of the sketches made for this *Antony and Cleopatra* have been put in the public domain; Chitty's main visual concept for the costumes was to create a "sixteenth-century view of the classical world,"[29] avoiding the traditional version of classical garments of knee length togas for the Romans or the Cleopatra-cliché Egyptian snake headdresses. This was intended to show the audience that the play should not be seen in purely historically correct details. Shakespeare did not travel to Rome. He is writing about passion and power. This, I suggest, can be seen in the sumptuous detailing on Cleopatra's costume and the gloriously deep rich red colour used for the set design.

In Chitty's early costume design for Antony, he wears a long loose kaftan-type coat with huge hanging sleeves over an open shirt, long boots and a soft hat or head covering. In Cleopatra's first costume drawing, she is also wearing a loose gown over a high-waisted front opening dress. Her sleeves are long and hanging loosely, but this time with a tight under-sleeve detail. To the side of the drawing, there is also a line sketch of the back view:

> I also write notes on them and I try and draw the backs of things, if backs of things are important or unusual or specific, and often I draw details of makeup or helmets, little details of things I put on the same page. I like the drawings to be a bit cluttered, I mean, clear but I always put a note on of which scene the clothes are worn in and when the change is or whether they've got a quick change. I put notes like that on, as much information as I can.[30]

It is well documented that Judi Dench had reservations about her casting as Cleopatra, which she described to Peter Hall in very self-deprecating terms, suggesting that she is too old and too short to play such an iconic beautiful figure. In such an instance, Chitty, as costume designer, has first to enable Dench to feel herself to be the powerful, mythological ruler, and then convince the audience to believe that is so. This was achieved by such careful costume work that Lowen observes "In designing the costumes, Alison Chitty has extended the personality of each actor to mesh with the character they play."[31] In other words, the time spent observing and sketching in the rehearsal room enables the eye of the designer to become well attuned to the movement and shape of each individual body, not just the developing characteristics of the performance, but the inherent physicality of the performer, which will never be totally left behind.

Given the decorated style of the garments, very few could be taken from the stock, so the sixty or so costumes were made by the wardrobe department at the

112 Hilary Baxter

Figure 6.3 *Antony and Cleopatra*, costume Design for Cleopatra played by Dame Judi Dench, Royal National Theatre, 1987

Source: Photo Hilary Baxter

NT. The costume notes evidence the amount of sketching that Chitty produces and also the materials from which the costumes were made, exotic and textured fabrics mixed with stripes both bold and subtle for variety.

The pages for Cleopatra show that her costume reflects her emotional journey through the performance. In the first scenes she is wearing cream, light gold touches mixed with brown, the second costume is warmer, more bronze, light rust colour, and more gold. The third is blue but with a strong green edge, the gold is darker, purple, with a brash gold cloak. Finally there are dark purples, red, gold with a coral pink, more bronze glitter, all very sensually dramatic. It is this bold and confident use of colour that makes Chitty's costume design work individual. Her designer's vision can develop organically with that of the director, satisfy all the needs of the actors, and still be bold and gorgeous as a visual statement. The audience and press response was enthusiastic,[32] there were many mentions of Chitty's sets and costumes, the gorgeous use of colours, the sensuality of the visuals. Peter Hall was also awarded the Best Director for *Antony and Cleopatra* at the Evening Standard Drama Awards in November 1987. It was a seminal production.

Chitty has also been influential through her involvement with the 'Motley' Theatre Design course (currently resting). The course was originally launched in

Alison Chitty – the public sketch   113

1966 by Stephen Arlen[33] and Margaret 'Percy' Harris,[34] based on the approach to design from the Old Vic School.[35] When the course moved to Covent Garden it became the 'Motley' course. Harris was the course director up until her death in 2000, at which point Chitty took over. Chitty explains her take on the Motley course philosophy as:

> Inspired by the work of the Royal Court (theatre) where the priorities and passions are on the text and the performer and we go into the design of every production through the text and the performer. That doesn't mean to say that we don't design, or we don't have loads of scenery but what is the absolutely crucial central element to any piece of theatre is what somebody's got to say and who's going to say it and that's where we start.[36]

As an educator, Chitty was honoured with a Sir Misha Black medal in 2007, as recognition of her work at the Motley school in Drury Lane, London, cited as "maintaining the excitement and freedom of imagination" together with an ethos of diversity.[37] Sadly the course last recruited in 2010 because despite the successful achievements of its alumni, existing outside of the university-fication of postgraduate study became too difficult in terms of recruiting students. The importance of a mainly practice based study (rather than an academic approach such as a Masters), which was successful in bringing students from a diverse range of undergraduate studies gave a rich mix of interests and informed the design work produced. The access that Motley students had to contemporary London productions through their high-calibre tutors and opportunities to join production meetings, costume fittings and other professional situations gave the Motley designers a confidence in their design careers combined with an more idiosyncratic and individual design style, rather than say a design college style. This is particularly important when designing for Shakespeare, where the familiarity of the text calls for a more unusual, visual style to re-invigorate the text for a modern audience, which is not at all the same for a new play introducing a new narrative.

That teaching is an important part of Chitty's working life is clear as she talks about her attitude to taking her assistants to meetings:

> I think they should go to anything they possibly can and that's how they learn and that's how they like being with you, and maybe they stay a bit longer with you and they all, they always leave in the end, but all of mine have always just become my great pals.[38]

This integration of personal life and teaching is, I suggest a direct link to her own education under Koltai. Chitty has a good reputation for nurturing her assistants and other members of her team and there are clear distinctions in her working method in terms of what she will use an assistant to do, and what she completes herself:

I couldn't have anybody else paint the model. That is what – it's idiosyncratic and it's me. Same with costume drawings, I mean I couldn't get anybody – some people get other people to do their costume drawings. I mean I can't even contemplate what that must be. Anyway, I enjoy it, you know, it's a pleasure.[39]

In conclusion, it is clear that Chitty, whilst perhaps not primarily considered a pioneer in terms of her innovation to the debates of Theatre Design, has subtly contributed an enormous amount to the contemporary practices through her productions and teaching. Her vivid use of colour and bold costume designs show that Theatre Design can be both simply effective and visually exciting. She is fully prepared to match the creative process of demanding directors with continuous production and reflection to achieve the best possible solution. She takes enormous care to ensure that the actors will be supported by her work. There is no doubt that Chitty's career has flourished in the subsidized theatre in Britain, during a period where government funding was made available across the sector, but her willingness to share and support the careers of others through her teaching also has ensured that her processes and influences have extended beyond her immediate circle of collaborators. I would also suggest that it is her honesty as a collaborator and a visual artist, reflected in her conversation with Michael Tippet regarding a design solution for his *Garden of Remembrance* when Chitty said to him, "I can't seem to design this. I don't know what it is and I don't know... I don't know what it should be." And he said: "Oh... It's a place where roses are."[40] She goes onto say, "And it sort of totally released me...? as he said it I thought: 'Oh...' and I could imagine these roses just blowing in the wind, just floating across the space."[41] This last comment reveals exactly how as a designer, she responds to the spoken poetic image, enabling a text or piece of music to be staged in front of an audience, as well as understanding completely her role in their experience of the performance.

To conclude by considering Chitty's legacy, I suggest that she has contributed hugely to the development of Theatre Design practice, particularly by her willingness to strip away superficial details, using the bare elements needed for the production, even the unadorned theatre walls as theatrical elements in their own right, inhabiting her stage space with carefully detailed characters. In this way her visual languages for Shakespeare create a compete world for the text, supporting performers to achieve the great and powerful characterizations. This inspires the audience to believe that their experience is multi-sensory, tactile and visually satisfying, with the action flowing smoothly from one setting to another, contributing pace and tension to the production. Alison Chitty is the designer-artist working from the inside of the text to give it a fresh life for contemporary audiences.

Notes

1   The distinction Royal Designer for Industry (RDI) was established by the RSA in 1936 to enhance the status of designers in industry and encourage a high standard of indus-

Alison Chitty – the public sketch   115

trial design. Only 200 designers are able to hold the distinction RDI at any one time, there are now 130 RDIs and 56 Honorary RDIs. Chitty's citation: "A leading stage designer for 25 years, Alison Chitty has designed for the leading theatre and opera companies both in the UK and worldwide. Her aesthetic has been consistent in its pursuit of expressing the playwright's words or the composer's music with simplicity of form and colour. She understands the power of space and her work avoids the superfluous gesture and concentrates on strong narrative, wit, and striking aesthetics. Her costume designs also reflect the same passion, character, and attention to detail. Her film work includes Mike Leigh's *Life is Sweet*, *Naked*, and *Secrets and Lies*. Chitty is also Director of the Motley Theatre Design School in Covent Garden, nurturing the talent of future production designers.

2   Both for costume design on productions at the RNT: 2001 for *Remembrance of Things Past* and in 2007 for *The Voysey Inheritance*.

3   For under acknowledged inspirational workers in the theatre.

4   Alison Chitty quoted in John Goodwin *British Theatre Design: The Modern Age* (1989) p. 32.

5   I am indebted to Liz Wright for allowing me to use the unpublished transcriptions of her National Life Story Oral History interviews with Alison Chitty available from the British Library by appointment.

6   John Peter, *The Sunday Times*, 25 May 1980.

7   Liz Wright transcript of National Life Story Oral History interviews with Alison Chitty op.cit.

8   British Library National Life Story Oral History interviews "The legacy of the English Stage Company' Peter Gill interviewed by Harriet Devine.

9   Liz Wright transcript of National Life Story Oral History interviews with Alison Chitty op.cit.

10   British Library National Life Story Oral History interviews: Peter Gill op.cit.

11   Liz Wright transcript of National Life Story Oral History interviews with Alison Chitty op.cit.

12   of Great Britain.

13   Artistic Director Peter Cheeseman.

14   Including Alan Plater, Sean Compton.

15   Liz Wright transcript of National Life Story Oral History interviews with Alison Chitty op.cit.

16   Ibid.

17   Ibid.

18   David Neat, Chitty's design assistant for Antony & Cleopatra in conversation with the author 16 January 2013.

19   West London Theatre Critic, John Thaxter wrote: "It is no exaggeration to say that Gill's four years as director have taken Riverside to a leading position in British theatre; … with his own productions (notably The Cherry Orchard and this year's Julius Caesar)."

20   Now Royal National Theatre usually abbreviated to RNT.

21   Now honoured as a Dame.

22   Peter Hall Foreword in John Goodwin *British Theatre Design: The Modern Age* (1989) pp. 12–16.

23   Ibid.

24   Ibid.

25   Ibid.

26   Alison Chitty quoted in Tirzah Lowen, *Peter Hall Directs 'Antony and Cleopatra'*, p. 10.

27   Tirzah Lowen, *Peter Hall Directs 'Antony and Cleopatra'*, p. 9.

28   Peter Hall quoted in Tirzah Lowen, *Peter Hall Directs 'Antony and Cleopatra'*, p. 9.

29   Alison Chitty quoted in Tirzah Lowen *Peter Hall Directs 'Antony and Cleopatra'*, p. xiv.

30 Liz Wright transcript of National Life Story Oral History interviews with Alison Chitty op. cit.
31 Tirzah Lowen *Peter Hall directs 'Antony and Cleopatra'*, p. 122.
32 see Tirzah Lowen *Peter Hall directs 'Antony and Cleopatra'*, p. 154.
33 Managing Director of Sadler's Wells Opera.
34 Designer and part of the 'Motley' design triumvirate.
35 The school has been known under a series of different names, as it tended to take the name of the location, in a series of temporary studios.
36 Liz Wright transcript of National Life Story Oral History interviews with Alison Chitty op. cit.
37 Copyright © 2012 the Sir Misha Black Awards.
38 Liz Wright transcript of National Life Story Oral History interviews with Alison Chitty op. cit.
39 Ibid.
40 Ibid.
41 Ibid.

Bibliography

British Library. *"National Life Stories: An Oral History of British Theatre Design"*, London: The British Sound Archive. Available at www.bl.uk/website_search/search?q=cache:Pf6 Dw0yVsbcJ:www.collectbritain.co.uk/reshelp/findhelprestype/sound/ohist/ohcoll/ ohperf/performingarts.html+video&site=public&client=public&proxystylesheet= public&output=xml_no_dtd&ie=UTF-8&access=p&oe=UTF-8

British Library *" National Life Stories: The Legacy of the English Stage Company"*, London: The British Sound Archive. Available at www.bl.uk/website_search/search?q=cache:Pf6 Dw0yVsbcJ:www.collectbritain.co.uk/reshelp/findhelprestype/sound/ohist/ohcoll/ ohperf/performingarts.html+video&site=public&client=public&proxystylesheet= public&output=xml_no_dtd&ie=UTF-8&access=p&oe=UTF-8

British Theatre Design, 1979–1983 (1983)(Catalogue of an Exhibition presented by the Society of British Theatre Designers) Oxford: Holywell Press.

British Theatre Design, 1983–1987 (1987) (Catalogue of an Exhibition of a Collection, presented by the Society of British Theatre Designers) Faringdon: Twynam Publishing.

Goodwin, John, ed. (1989) *British Theatre Design: The Modern Age*. London: Weidenfeld & Nicholson. Foreword by Peter Hall, pp. 12–14.

Granville Barker, Harley (1993) *Anthony and Cleopatra, Granville Barker's Prefaces to Shakespeare,* London: Nick Hern Books Ltd and the RNT by arrangement with Batsford.

Howard, Pamela. (2002) *What is Scenography?* London: Routledge.

Lowen, Tirzah. (1990) *Peter Hall directs Anthony and Cleopatra*. London: Methuen Drama.

McKinnon, Peter and Eric Fielding, eds. (2012) *World Scenography* 1975–1990, Taiwan: OISTAT.

Mullin, Michael. (1996) *Design by Motley*. London: Associated University Presses.

Rosenfeld, Sybil. (1973) *A Short History of Scene Design in Great Britain*. Oxford: Blackwell.

Websites

www.ahds.rhul.ac.uk/ahdscollections/docroot/shakespeare/performancedetails.do?perform anceId=11379

www.debretts.com/

www.mishablackawards.org.uk/medal/chitty
www.motleytheatredesign.co.uk/history/index.html
www.nationaltheatre.org.uk/video/olivier-theatre-overview
http://ralphkoltai.com/biography/
www.spokeo.com/Peter+Gill+1
www.thersa.org/__data/assets/pdf_file/0012/250041/RSA-RDI-press-notice-2009.pdf
www.thestage.co.uk/news/2008/07/designer-chitty-presented-with-2008-young-vic-award/

Chapter 7

Robert Wilson

Maria Shevtsova

Principles

It is impossible to separate Wilson the stage designer from Wilson the director, since he has united these two roles consistently throughout his career. He can be described as an *auteur* director, in the wake of the two major figures of twentieth-century theatre, Vsevolod Meyerhold and Edward Gordon Craig, who were the first to claim this practice. Yet even this broad category is not quite adequate, given that Wilson is a remarkable performer and that his singular creative energy also encompasses a writer, a painter, a sculptor and, as well, an installation, video, and landscape artist. More still, Wilson has an unusual facility for trespassing on recognized territories, having established with such early works as *Deafman Glance* (1971) and *Einstein on the Beach* (1976) that theatre and dance, let alone design and other areas of the visual arts, are not confined to generic borders but can coalesce to form what came to be known in the 1980s as 'hybrids' or, soon afterwards, as 'mixed media' and then 'intermedial' performance. His multiple abilities are embodied in Wilson's designs, not least for his Shakespeare productions.

Wilson is a pioneer of cross-overs, and holds his own in the company of younger generations who have grown up with them and for whom Wilson, on a par with composers of mix-and-match, hybridized World Music and video clips, is still a formidable model. He was inspired by Bauhaus experiments with overlaps between visual shapes, movement and music when he was a student of architecture at the Pratt Institute in New York at the beginning of the 1960s. In the years to follow, he recognized his deep affinity with the revolutionary architectural and other spatial projects developed by the Russian Constructivists – 'revolutionary' both artistically and politically speaking. Among them was Aleksandr Rodchenko, the acknowledged theorist of Constructivism, to whom Wilson humorously paid tribute, via a winking video portrait of him, in his 2012 performance of John Cage's solo piece of verbal music, *A Lecture on Nothing*.

Rodchenko was also Wilson's conduit to Constructivism in the theatre and so to Meyerhold. It was with the Constructivist designers and painters of the late 1910s and early 1920s that Meyerhold discovered the power of stage design that was no longer illustrative of something (a room designed to look like a room), but had its own contours, almost as if it were an autonomous entity. Thus Ludmila

Popova, a member of the Constructivist group, built a self-contained outsize object-cum-machine for Meyerhold's 1922 production *The Magnanimous Cuckold* on whose wheels, ladders, bridges and platforms the actors ran, somersaulted and jumped, fully using the contraption as part of their performance: the machinery, with its turning wheels, determined the kind and quality of movement being made and was thus integral to the performance process itself.

Rodechnko's construction-design for Meyerhold's *The Bedbug* in 1929 by their mutual friend Vladimir Mayakovsky displayed a similar awareness of how space was to be active, filling the stage and partnering the actors rather than, like a waiting receptacle, being filled by them.[1] Rodchenko's co-ordination of circles and rectangles was no less ingenious than Popova's, although it was less dynamic. The director's relation to this architectonic structure was one of control. He concentrated scenic action around it, using it to throw the actors' work into relief while foregrounding their cumulative effect not only on the space that they commanded, but also on the spectators who were aware that this particular space and this particular work neither recalled nor repeated anything they had seen previously.

Meyerhold, in his understanding that design was not merely a decorative backdrop but was indispensable for the purpose, sense, and meaning of stage action, set a historic precedent; and it was a radical precedent, notwithstanding innovations regarding space in Bauhaus performances in Germany during the same period (in Oskar Schlemmer's dance pieces, for example), and notwithstanding subsequent imaginative variations, in the 1950s, in the Bauhaus-inspired experiments at Black Mountain College in the United States. It was here that John Cage and Merce Cunningham, who were formative influences on Wilson, combined soundscape, choreography and painting (Robert Rauschenberg was their painter companion) and re-arranged space to discover new potentials for performance.

By a circuitous, but none the less significant route, Wilson's path, although very much his own, leads to Meyerhold and to Meyerhold's initiation of the symbiotic relationship between designer and director. That Wilson is a designer and a director in one is an absolute symbiosis, and it has fostered his belief that spatial organization is the very basis of theatre as such. Wilson has insisted again and again that he always *starts* with the construction of space rather than with a text or script, as happens in 'traditional', literature-based theatre. The designer, then, pre-empts the director, but only in so far as he is immediately reunited with the latter once the spatial structure, or 'architecture', as Wilson calls it, has been secured.

The priority of 'architecture' over any other element required for the making of a production remains constant in Wilson's work, regardless of which type of text he may use. It may be one that he has written himself (*I was sitting on my patio and this guy appeared I thought I was hallucinating*, 1977), or a contemporary play (Heiner Müller's *Hamletmaschine*, which Wilson staged in 1986, the first of a series of Müller productions) or a classic, whether by Shakespeare, Büchner or Ibsen to whom he has returned more than once. Wilson's encounter with canonical authors occurred during the 1990s, two decades into his working life (which suggests reticence towards the classics, if not downright resistance to them), and continues to the present day.

Wilson has staged four Shakespeare productions: *King Lear* (1990), *Hamlet* (1995), *The Winter's Tale* (2005) and *Shakespeare's Sonnets* (2009). All but *Hamlet* were performed in German. *King Lear* was commissioned by the Frankfurt Schauspielhaus, and *The Winter's Tale* and *Shakespeare's Sonnets* by the Berliner Ensemble, the house founded by Brecht serving him as a repertory home for most of the first decade of the twenty-first century; its close connection to Wilson has continued into the century's second decade. *Hamlet* was in English, and was performed by Wilson as a monologue throughout Europe – his only Shakespeare production to have a wide international distribution. *Shakespeare's Sonnets*, although generally highly acclaimed, has toured only to several countries for reasons of expense. It has a cast of fifteen and costly get-up, which includes three days of preparation for the lights alone – lighting design is by Wilson – before the production can be shown.

How Wilson treats Shakespeare is essentially no different from how he treats other playwrights, and this has to do with the fact that he starts with spatial rather than verbal-textual analysis and organization. The latter draws attention to semantic meaning and to how it is to be interpreted. Spatial organization, by contrast, encourages associative meaning, which is not so much a matter of interpretation as of *evocation*. Wilson's is a form-driven theatre interested in what could be called the presence of 'being there' and so in being about nothing but itself. This aesthetics and philosophy of art were caught by Susan Sontag's celebrated 1961 essay 'Against Interpretation' in which Wilson, alongside Cunningham and Cage, among many contemporary artists, saw their aspirations both mirrored and firmly articulated (Sontag 1982). They included such painters as Rauschenberg and Jasper Johns with whom Cage and Cunningham frequently collaborated after their initial Black Mountain experiences.

Form that is centred on form is a principle that Wilson shares with all of the artists cited here, and it pivots, as much for Wilson as for them, on the malleability of space. It is precisely because Wilson sees space as an invitation to form that he settles on his spatial structure before he deals with anything else. Yet his spatially oriented perception requires a design rather than a verbal method. Wilson's solution to the question of how to find such a method for the theatre, where he was, equally, a director, was to devise a counterpart to the hegemony of written texts in the established Western theatre; Eastern theatre differed, in his view – Wilson's main examples are Noh and Balinese dance – because it did not rely on words, written or spoken, but on a gestural, thus visual, 'language'.

The counterpart that Wilson sought to literature or the verbal book (if one may be allowed this pleonasm) was the 'visual book'. Such a book was essential, according to Wilson, because 'Shakespeare, Goethe, Schiller, Molière, Racine, Tennessee Williams are men who wrote words, who wrote literature for the theatre', and their heritage was an exclusively 'intellectual' theatre incapable of producing actors who knew how to sit on a chair or walk on the stage (quoted in Enright 1994: 18). It should be added that Wilson's call for developed techniques of the body to remedy these inadequacies has as much to do with his concern for the visual harmony of scenic space as with his demand that actors show kinaesthetic skill and ease, and fluency of movement in it.

Wilson's 'visual book' is based on the storyboard method of sequences of frames or 'shots' for narrative purposes used in the making of films. What this means is that Wilson draws a series of rapid sketches suggesting how the stage might look at different moments and what might be happening in this or that 'frame'. Occasionally some of the characters involved are also sketched in to see how they would fit into the picture; and they help Wilson to gauge spatial proportions, as well. Objects that are to be part of the design are etched in. They are generally shapes – abstractions rather than life-like representations: a room, in other words, is not drawn to look like a room. A bed, for instance, is roughly outlined by a few horizontal lines; a tree by a column; a mountain by a triangle or a jagged zigzag. Squares or rectangles often suggest where panels, scrims or curtains might appear. Their purpose is to break up the space for specific actions and events while giving it various kinds of depth and changes of perspective. Other details such as dark, heavy shading in charcoal, for example, might indicate that an oppressive mood is to be created for a particular scene. All the storyboard details, irrespective of how they might be expressed, are integral to the design that Wilson envisages for the stage as he draws; and its compact, geometric shaping, together with Wilson's desire to mould or sculpture space rather than merely to decorate it, shows just how deep his affinity is with Constructivism and the Bauhaus.

This work is intensive, although Wilson does not do it alone. He gathers his team about him, some of whom have consistently worked with him for decades – thus Ann-Christin Rommen, his Assistant Director. Others, notably composers, costume designers and dramaturges, join the core team for specific projects, and this alternation of participants is especially marked in the case of those dramaturges who are permanent staff of theatres. Wilson began to work with dramaturges on a regular basis only after his collaboration with Müller, which sparked off his engagement with canonical dramatic texts. Dramaturges vary greatly according to the theatre where a production is to be staged and where, more often than not, Wilson is expected to collaborate with the house dramaturge. His two Shakespeare productions with the Berliner Ensemble are a case in point since they both relied on the input of the company's dramaturge Jutta Ferbers. Ferbers relayed the story, plot and content of *The Winter's Tale*, and teased out the themes of the Sonnets. While doing so, she answered Wilson's questions as he sketched. He asked about the time of day an event occurred, in what circumstances it occurred, where it happened, what happened next, and so on – numerous questions that sought precise information instead of an interpretative account (Shevtsova 2007: 46–52). Questions like these allowed Wilson to focus on the visual effect or 'look' of the production-to-be and on how its 'look' was of a piece with the tone, tenor and atmosphere he intended to have come alive on the stage.

Overall, how a production looks is more important to Wilson than issues to do with its characters' motivations, psychological make-up, emotional states, desires and other concerns intrinsic to mimetic and/or psychological theatre. The choice

Figure 7.1 The Winter's Tale, Berliner Ensemble
Source: Photo Lesley Leslie-Spinks

of dramaturge may not always be free, but the dramaturge's role is of fundamental importance to Wilson's creative process. Not only is the dramaturge a catalyst-informant who opens pathways into whatever text is selected, but this person is also a reader who guides Wilson along these paths. The dramaturge reads aloud as many pages as Wilson needs to see in his imagination or, as he puts it frequently, on his 'interior screen' (Ibid.: 71). Further, he needs to hear the sounds, rhythms, cadences and vocal patterns of the words which he subsequently has his actors stylize to avoid realistic acting. By the same token, the dramaturge discusses the meanings of words and dialogue with him. Wilson's aim, once again, is to by-pass realistic acting and the psycho-emotional characterization that goes with it in favour of clear and accurate exposition. The idea of exposition referred to here involves display – to the way Wilson lays out material, including the speech of his actors, for the eyes and the ears to perceive as sensation, as sensory and sensual experience rather than as an interpretative worldview. Exposition, then, is 'against interpretation' and very much *for* the hedonism of the senses.

The final points necessary for this introductory framework concern light. Light, for Wilson, is integral to design, and it is the element he focuses on next, after having worked out how to construct his space. His visual books occasionally give indications of mood, like the heavy charcoal shading noted above. However, mood, for Wilson, is closely connected to the quality of light to be used. This means that charcoal shading can also be his cue for the kind of light that is to appear at a particular moment in the performance – dark, dense, angled, horizontal, and so on. Increasingly from the later 1980s, Wilson has turned his lighting into an extraordinary palette of colour, and this in itself is a design strategy. Since his productions have virtually no stage sets to speak of, geometry imbued with light-colour replaces the décor of interiors or the 'sets' of exteriors. Washes and walls of light-colour, or only panels, beams or the narrowest slivers of it are part and parcel of Wilson's 'architecture', as of the sense of place that is communicated to spectators. Thus washes of subtly changing hues of light across a cyclorama, which takes up the whole of the stage, conjure up the harbour, sea and sky in *Madama Butterfly* (1993), one of Wilson's most evocative opera productions. Light, in other words, whether coloured or plain, does not solely light up something else, but itself stands for something, or is a surrogate of something. How it works in his productions of Shakespeare, and, at the same time, helps Wilson the director while satisfying Wilson the designer will become evident in the discussion to follow.

Shakespeare

Wilson's adoption of his dual director-designer identity did not come without a price, since uncertainty as to what, exactly, his theatre consisted of generated misgivings as to what, exactly he was doing with such playwrights as Shakespeare: his productions did not add up to the habitual approaches foregrounding themes, issues – historical, socio-political, moral – and narrative and characterization. A world separates *King Lear*, which resounded with the shock of the new, and

124 Maria Shevtsova

Shakespeare's Sonnets, which had benefited from the theatre-going public's growing familiarity with Wilson's idiosyncratic scenic 'language', not least for the classics; and it was perceived as idiosyncratic even in a contemporary theatre rich with diverse idioms, let alone with a history that included the theatres of Constructivism and the Bauhaus.

Acclimatization to Wilson's way of doing involved accepting the predominant role of design in his productions and the fact that it went hand in glove with his direction; and Meyerhold (or, for that matter, Craig) would not necessarily be an immediate reference for performers and spectators faced with the new of Wilson. Nor, indeed, would Cunningham necessarily come to mind for those not acquainted with contemporary dance. Marianne Hoppe, the octogenarian whom Wilson had selected for the title role of *King Lear*, expresses her dissatisfaction with Wilson's shift away from customary procedures. She observed in rehearsals:

> This Wilson can't fool me. I started out at the Deutsches Theater with Max Reinhardt. I know what a director is. Wilson is not a director. He's a lighting designer. A Wilson actor runs here or there only because there's a change in the lights on the Wilson stage. Light pushes the actors around. Light is important, but in Shakespeare, the language is also important. I can speak these lines the way he wants, but I don't believe Shakespeare wrote the part of Lear to be recited by an autistic child.
>
> (Quoted in Holmberg 1996: 137–8)

Hoppe's near-caricature of Wilson as a lighting designer conveys something of his obsessive precision concerning light for all his productions and not exclusively for *King Lear*; and her 'autistic' regarding the delivery of the lines quite eloquently describes the non-emotional style of speaking that Wilson usually prescribes to his actors, but on which he particularly insisted for *King Lear* to avoid the grand rhetoric of tragedy. Furthermore, the actors of *King Lear* have no physical contact with each other and, in any case, are generally at some distance from each other ('autistic' could here also apply).

This pattern is established from the start during Lear's division of his kingdom, when Goneril and Lear are at opposite ends of the large stage. Wilson's preservation of space around his actors is part of his spatial design, as are the horizontal, vertical and diagonal lines marked out by their stylized, posed and slow movement in space. Wilson's spaciousness, which he accentuates by the absence of props, creates a rather severe environment, even an alien one that 'speaks' to the unrecognizable, upside-down consequences of Lear's division of his kingdom. In addition, alienation is reinforced by the fact the actors rarely address each other, let alone look at each other, even in pivotal scenes: Gloucester, for instance, does not look at Edmund at all when he finds the letter that falsely incriminates Edgar. Apart from inducing a sinister atmosphere, this isolation generates the impression that the production is composed of monologues, which, here and there, are interspersed by sudden shrieks and yelps for acoustic punctuation.

Wilson divides Shakespeare's play into sixteen scenes, preceded by a prologue – William Carlos Williams's poem 'The Last Words of My English Grandmother', which, Wilson believed, was a comic parallel to Lear's story. Hoppe recites it in English in the presence of the whole cast, immobile and loosely arranged like statues in a park. Speech in English is unexpected, whereas the rest of the text is in German, and is meant to take the audience aback, to surprise by its incongruity. The monological structure of *King Lear*, introduced boldly by the prologue, is reiterated by the lighting design, which tends to place the characters in separate areas of light, most notably in Act III, Scene vii, when Gloucester is blinded. The blinding scene is worth examining in detail since it demonstrates more fully than any other how Wilson's lighting design both determines and is determined by the design of the stage as a whole.

The scene comes straight after the interval and opens with a black out. A vertical stream of white light goes diagonally from the ceiling to the floor and travels to centre stage, picking up Regan in a red suit. Black velvet covers the entire back wall. Suddenly, a square of brilliant white light appears in the middle of the stage. At its centre is Gloucester around whom a glinting steel coil suddenly drops to the floor, and just as suddenly coils upwards, encasing him in a spiral whose neck faces downwards. Two figures on either side of Gloucester wield long steel rods, pointed like arrows. When one of them – Cornwall – protrudes his rod into the steel cage to pluck out Gloucester's eyes, Gloucester bends forward to meet it. No sooner done than the square turns a blood red. The garish light-colour is intended to be shocking as it indicates, but replaces, a horrifying event.

Regan, in the meanwhile, had been consigned to her own space outside Gloucester's square. As soon as Gloucester is blinded, she has her servant stab Cornwall in the back, after which she and the servant make a full circle and sharply exit. Gloucester, still lit, walks slowly in a straight line towards the front of the stage and, as he walks along this clearly defined vertical, the black velvet of the back wall sharply falls. In its stead appears a cyclorama wall of dazzling white light. The light could well stand for Gloucester's now seeing what he had not seen before. Be that as it may, the conjunction of square, circle and strongly demarcated diagonal, horizontal and vertical lines both of light and of movement is most certainly kin to Constructivist-Bauhaus composition; and this composition, for all its geometric order and precision, stirs unease – not open emotional distress, perhaps, but a sense of discomfort, nevertheless. The light plays a crucial part in this composition and so in the, call it subliminal, inward-driven, discomfort that suffuses the space of the audience.

A similar play of light and line, albeit on a smaller scale, occurs subsequently, when blind Gloucester leads Lear to the cliffs of Dover. Their surrogate is the outline of a triangle in fluorescent light on the floor. The rest of the stage – the heath – is devoid of objects, and only light in deep hues denotes the setting. Perhaps Wilson, here, is making a visual joke with his triangle to take some of the tragic weight away from the scene. Or perhaps he is suggesting that comic contrast brings out tragic import. If so, this may account for the intrusion of the ambigu-

126 Maria Shevtsova

ously humorous poem by William Carlos Williams at the beginning of the production.

Elsewhere, and mostly in the first part of the production (that is, before the interval), the stage design is constructed with what might be called low walls and ledges. Lear's conversation with the Fool in Act II, Scene ii takes place along one such wall, which cuts the space, giving the illusion of split-level action. Kent splayed on a rough wheel (Shakespeare's stocks) is on the second level, closer to the audience and at an angle to, but at a significant distance from, Lear and the Fool. At a certain point, a large frame comes down from the flies, which separates Lear and the Fool from Kent even more. At the same time, it creates greater depth, since, at the forefront of the stage, it throws into relief another frame at the very back within which the lighting changes from blue to red-pink to tawny yellow. Edgar wounds himself at the beginning of the scene, lit up by a narrow but long rectangle of deep blue on the cyclorama back wall. Lear and the Fool are set off against tawny yellow, looking decidedly strange against it, particularly when the second frame, having come down, hides half of their body. All in all, the whole scene appears to be out of kilter, transposing into visual terms the Fool's words to Lear about the absurdity of the situation into which his own actions have led him.

Objects are few, so they are striking when they appear. In Act I, Scene iv, Wilson uses them decisively to divide his space, his showpiece being a long narrow table in the middle of the stage at whose end sits Lear, facing the audience. Behind him is a similarly narrow piece stretching upwards. This piece makes the table look like an unusually high chair, but it is, in fact, a ladder. The Fool's very first appearance is at the top of this ladder. On either side of this table-chair are narrow ledges on thin legs, similar to those of the table. The Fool sings as he walks like an acrobat along one of them until he loses balance and falls. Shortly afterwards, he walks on top of the table as he speaks to Lear behind him. The setting is Goneril's house and, when she enters, she leans against the ledge used by the Fool.

The construction, then, has limited mileage for movement. It serves a spatial-design purpose rather than a functional one; and, from the point of view of effect, it sustains the aura of strangeness that seems to be what Wilson mainly perceives in *King Lear*. The overall effect, for John Rockwell, critic of *The New York Times*, is a negative one of lifelessness, 'icily hysterical, like a frozen scream' (20 June 1990). From the point of view of content – for content there is, irrespective of the 1960s mantra, intoned also by Wilson, that a work need only be about itself – isolation-alienation, as themes emerging from spatial composition, link up with that of random cruelty, locked in a 'frozen scream' throughout.

Hamlet, Wilson's next Shakespeare production, is a veritable monologue in which Wilson showcases Hamlet's soliloquies and not so much plays all the parts himself as changes voice for them. He selected the various speeches himself, aided in the run of scenes – fifteen in all – by his co-dramaturge Wofgang Wiens. The production is extremely compact, one and a half hours long. Wilson chose the essential of a speech to highlight its meaning – verbal meaning being extremely important for him for *Hamlet,* as never before in his oeuvre – possibly because the play has special resonance for him. And he believes that Shakespeare's text is a 'rock', so solid that it can withstand whatever incisions he makes (Kessel 1995: Video). Indeed a rock, or rather slabs of rock, constitute the entire set of his production and can be taken as his central conceit as director-designer *and* performer: indomitable Shakespeare, indomitable *Hamlet*.

What Wilson feels is the quintessence of a speech, or what could even be described as the ellipsis of a speech, places the speech in its performance context, situates a character or an event, connects it to another character or event, connects the meanings that accumulate throughout the performance, and drives forward the narrative being told by Hamlet. The compactness of Wilson's monologue demands swift transitions, which, apart from the vocal changes already noted, involve Wilson's signalling his change of part metonymically. He holds up a white glove on a stake to stand for Polonius; an eye patch – alias a 'mask' – stands for the King Player who recites "Full thirty time has Phoebus' cart gone round", but little else from the players' section of Act III, Scene ii. He holds half of a full-length golden Elizabethan-style dress hanging on a frame against his body to indicate Gertrude, and another for Ophelia. Both dresses come out of a trunk, which appears only briefly and also contains Elizabethan-style shoes that Wilson displays quite ostentatiously to avoid gestural verisimilitude. These are rare signs of historical allusion in the production, sartorial details for Hamlet being confined to relatively narrow trousers, a high-necked jacket in a Chinese rather than Elizabethan style, and an exceedingly high top hat. As always in Wilson's works, costume design blends harmoniously into the scenic design as a whole.

Equally, sound design is indispensable to this whole and so also to Wilson's prompts and instructions as a director, including to himself as a performer. Thus in *Hamlet*, he requests intermittent shattering glass from his sound designer Hans Peter Kuhn, mostly to accompany or to follow Hamlet's words: a sound that, by then, had become Wilson's signature sound, as had, in colour, the deep cornflower blue visible in *King Lear* but whose mysterious, haunting power pervades *Hamlet* completely. However, the sound of most importance in *Hamlet* rather for its associative quality than its aleatory effect (like the glass) is that of the hurdy-gurdy, which connotes the presence of Gertrude. When Wilson's golden dress evokes Gertrude, he also has the hurdy-gurdy invoke the court, reinforcing this invocation with several dance steps and sways to its sound, filtered through a synthesizer to denaturalize it. Sound 'made strange', as Meyerhold and the Russian Constructivists understood the idea, is more stylized than real and, consequently, has a stronger design thrust. Wilson had used a similar ploy with electro-acoustic 'wind' sound for the storm on the heath in *King Lear*. In addition, he had alluded to tempestuous wind by passing streaked dark grey across the top half triangle of light in the cut-out rectangle on the cyclorama at the back, leaving the lower triangle in cold white.

Everything Wilson does in *Hamlet* is centred on his main design feature, the high rock made up of criss-crossed slabs in the middle of the stage. The performance begins with Wilson lying sideways at its summit, with his back to the

Figure 7.2 Hamlet, Berliner Ensemble
Source: Photo T. Charles Erickson

audience. One arm and one leg are slightly raised in a dance-like pose. His silhouette, like the stage, is bathed in blue light. He slowly and very distinctly recites the fragment of Hamlet's penultimate speech, "Had I but time – as this fell sergeant Death/ Is swift in his arrest" (Act V, Scene ii); and its quiet, deliberate enunciation and pace in an aura of solemnity – the pile of stone could be a pyre – sets the tone for the remaining hour until the performance comes full circle, closing with the same speech. There is, however, a minor difference at the end in that the rock is lower and Wilson is now facing the audience. The disappearance of a significant number of slabs suggests physical erosion, as if the construction had measured time; and this image thus understood supports Wilson's claim that the performance is a 'flashback', Hamlet's whole life passing in front of his eyes 'seconds before he dies' (Kessel 1995: Video).

Wilson's construction is the epicentre of all action, not altogether unlike Popova's for *The Magnanimous Cuckold*, even though it is not as thoroughly used as hers, nor as much an extension of the moving body as are her wheels and ladders. Apart from lying sideways on top of it, Wilson, when its form is diminished at the beginning of Hamlet's 'To be' speech (Act III, Scene i), lies on his back on it. A spotlight picks out his hand in both cases, spotlighting it again as he turns on his side for "Ay, there's the rub". Wilson's movement, here, emphasizes the 'concluding' point of Hamlet's thought, and he keeps a good deal of Hamlet's speech intact so as to bring out its many meanings through the meditative approach he had adopted from the very beginning. Elsewhere, Wilson stands on top of the construction, its edges lit to suggest castle battlements ("Frailty, thy name is woman", Act I, Scene ii). Or else he is close to it, or right beside it, or sits at the bottom of the pile when the slabs have been spread closer to the ground; or, again, he walks up the steps formed by the slabs during Hamlet's "O, what a rogue and peasant slave am I!" (Act II, Scene ii). The rearrangement of the construction is facilitated by black outs, some filled with the hurdy-gurdy refrain invoking the court to prevent the audience from losing focus.

On other occasions, such scene changes occur behind a drawn black curtain. Wilson appears in front of it in his top hat, etching out various vaudeville-like numbers that nuance with humour the sombre – indeed, tragic – tone of his performance as a whole. He wears white gloves and a white painted face in which his eyes are heavily made-up to attract attention to their movement. Wilson refers to the inspiration of Peking Opera for his pronounced eye movements, and to the Japanese theatre for his articulated gestures (Kessel 1995: Video); and this is especially true of his hands and fingers. But whatever their sources for *Hamlet* may have been, the upshot of these visual details is that they are integrated in a production whose each and every detail is a scenographic choice *and* a directorial decision at one and the same time. Without exception, Wilson's choices and decisions channel his subjects – time, space, the immediacy of suffering, the ephemeral nature of life, and the shadow of death – showing that they are not solely motivated by purely formal considerations.

Where *Hamlet* is subject-full, *The Winter's Tale* strikes seasoned Wilson spectators as being somewhat insubstantial – a feast for the eyes for the sheer pleasure of the gaze, but nothing much else beyond the gorgeous surface. This impression is aided and abetted by the fact that the production is in the genre of what this writer defines as 'high camp'; and Wilson explores it for his folk-rock music theatre, which includes *Time Rocker* (1996) with counter-cultural icon Lou Reed of the Velvet Underground and, most inventively, *The Black Rider* (1990) with Tom Waits at the Thalia Theatre in Hamburg (Shevtsova 2007: 36–7; Shevtsova 2011: 251–6). Wilson's recent *Peter Pan* (2013) at the Berliner Ensemble is in the same vein, and this whole group of productions can in many ways be best viewed through the lens of Sontag's 1964 essay "Notes on 'Camp'" in which 'camp' is essentially characterized as a matter of 'sensibility' (Sontag's term) or a feeling for artifice and exaggeration (Sontag 1982: 275–92). My additional 'high' is to suggest the ongoing profusion, density, skilful deployment and even manipulation of hyperbolic, theatricalized, over-the-top means that are so fully mastered as to seem a matter of course. There is opportunity here, too, for kitsch. Wilson, tongue in cheek, draws up an animated cartoon as a prelude to Act IV of *The Winter's Tale* in which fluffy sheep gambol across hills … on a starry night!

It is in this full sense of 'high camp' that *The Winter's Tale* accentuates Wilson's delight in space, colour and light, the latter calibrated to the millimetre (Shevtsova: 2005). Space here is governed by pillars evoking Ancient Greece or the Greek columns of Sicily, Shakespeare's setting, and they are grouped variously in parallels of three pillars by three, or two by two, as the case may be. All pillars are well spaced out to let the stage breathe. The seventh, or fifth pillar, as the case may be, is the end point, the perspective to which the eye is drawn. Irrespective of their exact number, or whether the end-point column is elongated so as to look completely unnatural, or is lowered for a sense of intimacy – in which case it is doubled to suggest a portico – the columns elegantly apportion space through which, occasionally, as in a maze, numerous figures either drift by in affected, artificial poses, postures and gestures, or clump their way through, also in an excessively theatrical manner, with their mimicry and limbs over-extended to underscore their artifice.

As in *Hamlet* and *King Lear*, moving bodies incarnate design principles and belong integrally to the design stratagems of the whole; and so Stefan Kurt on Leontes's "Too hot, too hot:/ To mingle friendship farre is mingling bloods" (Act I, Scene ii) almost prances, albeit in slow motion, down the stage on a vertical, thereby tracing a strong line as part of the line pattern established by the columns. The difference in *The Winter's Tale* is that moving bodies are generally super-busy (not the case in its predecessors). Thus Kurt, apart from gesticulating ostentatiously, flaunts a villainous mien. Deliberate, though confident exaggeration of this kind is especially pronounced when figures assemble in Wilson's central space flanked by the columns on either side. These groupings look particularly ornate because of their exquisitely crafted costumes by Jacque Reynaud, Wilson's brilliant, long-term collaborator since after *Hamlet*.

Reynaud's costumes are rich in Elizabethan touches without replicating Elizabethan dress: for the women, there are ruffs, a little away from the neck, tight bodices and sleeves, widened shoulders and hips, the latter supported by heavy wire; for the men, there are freely adapted doublet and hose, some with peaks or bumps added to their bottoms, while Leontes's version of the outfit sports one tail and, on the opposite side of the body, one over-large and over-long sleeve. Velvet in deep, sumptuous hues abounds. Elaborate wigs, and sometimes headdresses, for men as well as women, belong *de rigueur* in this cornucopia.

Design, for Wilson, as is especially evident in *The Winter's Tale*, incorporates costume design, and this totalizing *Gesamtkunstwerk* impetus drives the *auteur* character of Wilson's theatre in general. Yet, where *The Winter's Tale* is specifically concerned, light design is its crowning feature, for, in the ten years that separate it from *Hamlet*, Wilson had become a master light designer capable of the finest gradations of colour. So fine are they now that subtly shifting green, for instance, on the wall of such busy scenes as described above, meets shifting hues of yellow coming from the bottom without any smudge of tone, or any blurring of colour contour. And this extraordinarily refined process immerses whatever scene is at issue, cradling it and everyone in it. The cradling that occurs communicates itself to spectators, and, by some sort of psychological osmosis, it stirs in them the feelings, sensations, images and imaginings that spoken words in the Wilson universe are generally not equipped to do. *Hamlet*, as noted, and, for that matter, a preceding monologue *Orlando*, as performed by Isabelle Huppert in French (1993), are exceptions.

Furthermore, Wilson was now capable of the finest nuances of emotional expression through light design – so much so, moreover, that light speaks the feelings that, quite tyrannically, he forbids his actors to speak. Always fearful of histrionic actors, he enjoins them to dismiss actorly expressivity, and finds, in and through light, the means for having light do the work of conveying feeling for them. Light, then, exteriorizes emotions that could otherwise have been attributed to characters. Kurt, in the scene previously cited, is a useful example. The actor, whose doublet and hose is burgundy red, is enfolded in scorching red light that disfigures even more his exaggerated, vaguely parodied, performance – helped, to boot, by his dissonant, asymmetrical costume. Wilson takes his lighting cue from Shakespeare's 'mingling bloods', and builds on the phrase by projecting one kind of red onto another, figuratively 'mingling bloods'. But, more still, he has the red light speak both Leontes's jealousy and the torments that ensue, and will continue to ensue, from it: this is the fire, it could be said, of hell. Light, in other words, more or less replaces, or at least adjusts, the acting-school-trained actor. Where the abundant richness of Shakespeare's words is concerned, Wilson's approach can only lead him to extrapolate from them, losing, of course, much of their great power as verbal expression.

It remains now to summarize *Shakespeare's Sonnets*, since most of the features already discussed return here. The production belongs to the high-camp music-theatre group identified, even though its extravagances are tempered to some degree by the cool elegance that Wilson prizes – with the exception of cabaret interludes performed by a drag 'queen' in tandem with a 'fall guy'. The music by current celebrity Rufus Wainwright is largely sentimental, but is adjusted to Wilson's playful approach. Wainwright also sings in the production, emerging from the orchestra pit, microphone in hand and lit up, as in a cabaret or vaudeville show. A live orchestra always accompanies Wilson's music theatre.

Wilson, it seems, has gathered Sonnets together by their themes or motifs: eyes, seeing, and false perception; writing poetry to the beloved and the elusiveness of love, youth, age, the passage of time and mortality. Sonnets 43 and 148, whose motifs revolve around the word 'eyes', open the production. Sometimes Wilson groups three or four Sonnets seamlessly, although his design changes, generally rapidly, during the sequence. He also lengthens the duration of Sonnets by first having them sung or in recitative, followed by a spoken version, or the other way around, depending on his spatial construction and who figures in it. Sometimes Sonnets are divided into parts for different voices, but these, too, flow in sequence.

Seamless groupings can include unspoken scenes. A salient example involves a bald, squat and fat Cupid between Sonnets 10 and 121. (The actor's corpulent frame is padded for extra rotundity.) Arrows gently flying towards Elizabeth I, who is asleep on a high chair, coyly announce Cupid. They just stop short of her heart, when Cupid flies in, flapping his short arms. Having landed, he gyrates about the stage to jaunty music, soon joined by another dancer. Elizabeth I had already appeared in the production's wordless opening scene through one of two barely discernible doors flanked by barely visible panels in a pearly grey-acqua room.

Figure 7.3 Shakespeare's Sonnets, Sonnet 148, Berliner Ensemble
Source: Photo Florin Chirea

Wilson's fine demarcation of space here draws attention to a transparent shape echoing the shape of the doors. A seated figure holds this space-within-a-space with his back to the audience. When this elderly man with white bobbed white hair sharply turns his face to the audience, it is clear that he can be none other than Shakespeare. The male actor who plays Elizabeth I appears briefly later as Elizabeth II, who is immediately recognizable by her apparel – not least by her hat and handbag. This is a huge wink at the audience in high-camp fashion.

At other times, instead of tracing an arch, Sonnets are singled out individually; and this reinforces the production's opposing pull towards the fragmentation imposed by the cabaret interludes, by unspoken interludes that stand out against the flow, and by the repeated fall of a black curtain. This curtain is a major scenographic item since it isolates the – generally lewd – cabaret 'improvisations' played in front of it, A variant of it, which falls like a blind, closes scenes within the structure devised from the Sonnets.

All scenes, however, whether in cantilena or in a broken series, are cross-dressed; and all figures, including the Fool, who is performed by a diminutive eighty-five-year-old woman (Ruth Glöss), are played by the opposite sex. Women have small painted moustaches and beards while men have women's hair-dos. Three men, who could well be mock Graces when they appear together, have particularly sophisticated rolls of sleek ginger hair high off the nape of their necks. Roles in *travesti* allow Wilson limitless visual puns on the theme of "the master-mister of my passion" in

Robert Wilson   133

Figure 7.4 Shakespeare's Sonnets, Sonnet 23 – Nozzle, Berliner Ensemble
Source: Photo Florin Chirea

Sonnet 20 throughout the production. His double-gendered images, which, in effect, are androgynous, allude as well, to, the speculations of Shakespeare sleuths on the gender of both the 'only begetter' of the Sonnets and their Dark Lady.

The room cited, or, rather, its rectangular shape is Wilson's basic design element, and he alters it to suit his needs. He adds diagonal panels, for instance, in the scene featuring the flying Cupid so that the arrows may appear, as if by stealth, through its sides. Elsewhere its walls come inwards for perspective. Or else long horizontal lines appear on its back wall, as occurs when a rider on a penny-farthing cycles at a snail's pace against the horizon etched out in light. But, most of all, Wilson favours opening out the rectangular space, either giving his performers freedom to move, or grouping them gracefully to fill out the space without cluttering it up. The variety of configurations he deploys propels the transitions within or between Sonnets referred to earlier. In this way, Wilson prevents the Sonnets from becoming set pieces, whether spoken or sung, and so from falling into the trap of the 'literature for the theatre' countered by his architectonic perception of what the theatre could be.

On several occasions, Wilson dots his extended spaces with props that the performers use, often with surrealistic results. Such is the case for Sonnet 23, for example, where three petrol pumps are placed in a triangular relation to each other. Three women in skin-tight suits of beige-gold, the colour of the pumps, as of the whole space, hold the nozzles forwards, then sideways, as phallic symbols.

134 Maria Shevtsova

Figure 7.5 Shakespeare's Sonnets, Sonnet 66, Berliner Ensemble
Source: Photo Florin Chirea

Meanwhile, they belt out their Sonnet to a blaze of sound – a typical case of Wilsonian juxtaposition between elegant space and burlesque action. Additional juxtaposition is to be had from the fact that Wainwright had sweetened the preceding Sonnet 29 ("When, in disgrace with Fortune and men's eyes/… and curse my fate").

For Sonnet 66, by contrast (preceded by Sonnet 147), a similarly open space is divided by a rounded tree bathed in pearl, blue, orange in swift succession to heighten its artificial appearance. The tree is a focal point for a woman-man who, but for a protruding bit of arm, is hidden behind it. She whips out first an apple and then a snake before she proceeds, singing, down a vertical line from the tree. She sings in a low range, working her way up to a falsetto, swaying her hips as she walks. On either side of the tree, downstage, sit Elizabeth I and Shakespeare, who repeat the Sonnet, singing alternate quatrains and tapping out the beat of the catchy music with their feet. As they sing, the seductive Eve-figure crunches the apple held out on her gloved hand. The position of the three figures cuts the space into what might be called invisible sectors that help to sustain the harmony of the piece. This is the Sonnet that most eloquently captures the high-camp and 'high-society' mix of signs in the production as a whole.

It is also a strong example of how design, in the comprehensive sense of the word demonstrated by this chapter, is not bound by semantic meaning. The Sonnet on the stage is not coordinated to the drift of the words on the page. This is not

Robert Wilson 135

Figure 7.6 Shakespeare's *Sonnets, Sonnet 66,* Berliner Ensemble
Source: Photo Lesley Leslie-Spinks

Figure 7.7 Shakespeare's *Sonnets, Final Scene,* Berliner Ensemble
Source: Photo Lesley Leslie-Spinks

always so in Wilson's work, not least in his work on Shakespeare, as is evident in *Hamlet*. Yet, as Wilson amply shows, words – language – are one component of many in the theatre, and, furthermore, design is a means of exploring possibilities, taking the theatre into the unknown. In this, Wilson fully shares the aspirations of the Constructivist and Bauhaus artists, who, of course, include Meyerhold, one of the most radical innovators in the theatre field; and, although of their lineage, he is very much a man of his own time, who will leave his mark on the future, as they have done. All things considered, in the process of expanding its horizons, Wilson's design fashions the Shakespeare whose essence he seeks, obliquely.

Note

1   The notion of active space discussed here has much in common with Henri Lefevbre's thesis (*La Production de l'espace*, Paris: Anthropos, 1974) that space is never empty but 'produced' through the intervention of social agents – 'producers' – according to their social, ideological and other values. In this way, space is socialized – furthermore, collectively socialized – rather than pre-given or 'natural'. The Russian Constructivists could well be taken as optimal case studies for Levebre's thesis, which he primarily develops theoretically rather than through concrete instances in the artistic field. See, in English, *The Production of Space*, trans, Donald Nicholson-Smith, Oxford: Blackwell, 1991 and especially pp. 68–72.

Bibliography

Enright, Robert (1994) "A Clean, Well-lighted Grace: An Interview with Robert Wilson", *Border Crossings* 13:2, pp. 14–22.

Holmberg, Arthur (1996) *The Theatre of Robert Wilson*, Cambridge: Cambridge University Press.

Kessel, Marion (1995) *The Making of a Monologue. Robert Wilson's* Hamlet. Video. Arts Alive/Caddell and Conwell Foundation for the Arts.

Lefebvre, Henri (1991) *The Production of Space*, trans, Donald Nicholson-Smith, London: Blackwell.

Shakespeare, William (2005) *The Oxford Shakespeare: The Complete Works*, ed. John Jowett. William Montgomery, Gary Taylor, and Stanley Wells, Oxford: Oxford University Press.

Shevtsova, Maria (2005) Unpublished rehearsal notes on *The Winter's Tale*, Berliner Ensemble.

Shevetsova, Maria (2007) *Robert Wilson*, London: Routledge.

Shevetsova, Maria (2011) *White and Black Magic*: Einstein on the Beach and The Black Rider in *Subjekt: Theater. Beiträge zur analyticshen Theatralität. Festschrift für Helga Finter zum 65. Geburstag*, ed. Gerald Siegmund and Petra Bolte-Picker, Frankfurt-am-Main: Peter Lang, pp. 245–57.

Sontag, Susan (1982) *Against Interpretation and Other Essays*, Octagon Books: New York.

Chapter 8

The form of (her) intent

Catherine Zuber's costume design for Nicholas Hytner's *Twelfth Night* (1998)

Brandin Barón-Nusbaum

In this chapter, I will outline conceptual methods for tackling one of Shakespeare's comedies, *Twelfth Night*, as envisioned by critically-acclaimed[1] costume designer Catherine Zuber for Nicholas Hytner's 1998 production at the Vivian Beaumont Theater at Lincoln Center in New York City. Though Ms. Zuber has designed more recent Shakespeare productions—including the 2012 *Richard III* directed by Sam Mendes—this old production stands the test of time and could, with a few minor edits, still be presented as innovative today.

Zuber has a long history of service to Shakespeare, undertaking costume designs for the Shakespeare Theatre in Washington D.C., American Repertory Theatre in Boston, and other national regional theatres during the last 20 years. In 1997, through my inclusion in the NEA/ TCG Career Development Program for Directors and Designers, I was fortunate to spend a month following Zuber as she developed costumes for Chekhov's *Ivanov*[2] at Lincoln Center, a Broadway premiere of *The Triumph of Love*[3] and a Broadway remount of the *Sound of Music*.[4] During this period, I shadowed Zuber and her design assistants through daily sessions at her design studio, in shopping excursions, in fittings with actors, in production design meetings, in consultations with costume professionals at costume shops, and watching dress rehearsals and previews[5] for her ongoing theatrical productions. Though encompassing a relatively short time, the days I observed Ms. Zuber culminated in my greater understanding of how a costume designer can positively shape a production. I would credit her mentorship as more valuable than any of the training that I received throughout my university education. Since that period, I have been an avid fan of her continued design work, and viewed two performances of her 1998 *Twelfth Night* production. In comparing her *Twelfth Night* to her other productions, there are several similarities within her oeuvre of work that lend a better understanding of her talents as a whole: a strong command of art and costume history and how it can shape a concept for costume design; a mastery of color theory; a design sense that prioritizes elegant deconstruction; and a unique and offbeat perspective that creates innovative and unusual design solutions.

Part of Zuber's success at creating successful costume designs comes from an innate (perhaps even subconscious) ability to find visual cues that offer multiple meanings, rather than relying on iconic visual cues that would completely define a character costume. Like *Twelfth Night's* dramatic structure, our memory of visual images bombards us in phases; images of the past are reoccurring, at times forgotten, then remembered again at other moments. The images create meaning in the way that we view other imagery. How much we remember of the entire groups of images is not always relevant as they can be retrieved to fill (again even subconsciously) parts of our visual memory that we have forgotten. In this way, costume imagery can summon different psychological cues from the audience from which to learn more about the performer's role within the play. Zuber is a versatile designer capable of strict, naturalistic, and alternately, totally abstracted styles of concept development, but it is her work at triggering emotional responses through a combination of varied imagery that signal varied reactions in an audience's individual memories that has impacted my own work in the greatest way. For the sake of simplicity, I reduce this kind of concept development as a "multi-visual approach."

Hytner's *Twelfth Night* was produced at Lincoln Center's Vivian Beaumont Theatre and opened July 16, 1998. Catherine Zuber's costume designs were nominated for a Tony in 1999, along with Bob Crowley's for Set Design and Natasha Katz's for Lighting Design. Though Zuber steadfastly credited the success of *Twelfth Night* as a labor of the entire artistic staff and cast of the production, it is clear that her own individual strengths distinguish her from other costume designers in the industry.

In my conversations with Ms. Zuber on how she developed ideas for Shakespeare plays, she stated, "Shakespeare begs for visual solutions without often directly providing them."[6] This quest for finding production concepts begins with the assembling of a design team (set, costumes, light, and sound) that develops design ideas guided by a theatre director. The team is often aided by a dramaturge, who will help introduce theatre history and textual analysis to the discussion. This process, often occurring before performers begin play rehearsal, is called the *pre-production process*. Though preproduction, Zuber develops costume concept research images, and executes costume renderings, both of which will be shown to performers and theatre management to help illustrate how the costumes will look in the production. These important documents are then used by technicians at costume shops who build the costumes, discussed with actors in fittings, and are often altered based on observations of new developments in rehearsal through theatrical previews.

The scenography of *Twelfth Night* as envisioned by Hytner, Crowley, Zuber, and Katz drew on beautifully idealized, exotic settings from Africa and Asia and the post-colonial nostalgia that corresponded such a world of artifice. In viewing the production in 1998, I wrote notes in my program about the production's "familiar disorientation," or the idea that everything was strange and yet somehow accessible. I continued to write: "Haven't I been at this place before, and yet, how could I have been?" In recently asking Zuber how the production had evolved, she answered simply and clearly, "Illyria is a parallel world where layers of pretence are heaped onto dramatic situations obscuring the real."[7]

Twelfth Night is a truly a costume designer's play: clothing, dress, costume, and disguise are the most important devices used in establishing the "layers of pretence"

The form of (her) intent 139

to which Zuber cites. Costumes drive the action of the play; dress establishes the social relationships within it. Shakespeare uses the language of clothing and accessories to tease out recurring themes within the play. The fool Feste compares the Duke Orsino to fashionable textiles and jewels:

> FOOL
> … and the tailor make
> thy doublet of changeable taffeta, for thy mind is a very
> opal.
>
> (Act 2, Scene 4, 70–72)

Clothing and appearance are a means of deception, as commanded by Olivia's maid Maria:

> MARIA
> Nay, I prithee, put on this gown and this beard. Make him
> Believe thou art Sir Topas the curate.
>
> (Act 4, Scene 2, 192)

Shipwrecked Viola deceives through swapping female for male garments:

> VIOLA
> But this my masculine usurped attire,
>
> (Act 5, Scene 1, 241)

Clothing accessories create bonds between characters:

> OLIVIA
> Here, wear this jewel for me. "Tis my picture."
>
> (Act 3, Scene 4, 185)

Clothing allows for romantic attachment, which ultimately leads to the happy end of the play:

> ORSINO
> And let me see thee in woman's weeds.
>
> (Act 5, Scene 1, 265)

> ORSINO
> … Cesario, come,
> For so you shall be, while you are a man.
> But when in other habits you are seen,
> Orsino's mistress and his fancy queen.
>
> (Act 5, Scene 1, 374–5)

Each of these examples provides material for the costume designer to consider a visual world for the actors to inhabit. In addition to textual indicators, there have been some scholarly attempts to define how Shakespeare's costume may have appeared onstage that additionally impact how costume designers place a production within a specific historical or abstracted time period. Douglas A. Russell's *Shakespearean Costume: Contemporary or Fancy Dress* (1958)[8] was introduced to me in graduate school, and also informed the generation of designers who were my college instructors and professional mentors. This article weighed the two theories largely held by scholars: Shakespeare's performers were attired in contemporary (Elizabethan) clothing without an attempt to signal historical costume and/or they were dressed in lavish, abstracted, theatrical finery as developed by designers like Inigo Jones for the court of James I. Though aware of this paradox of common fashion vs. theatrical costumes, I hadn't really seen this concept dually envisioned in production work until I saw Zuber's *Twelfth Night*.

For the generation of costume designers who preceded Zuber—led by Carrie Robbins and Desmond Healy—many of their Shakespearean costumes were presented in naturalistic, historicized productions or highly abstracted productions in the manner of Inigo Jones' theatrical finery, both avoiding gestures to contemporary fashion of their time. Looking critically on their work, the costumes were laden with decoration, often weighing down and over-defining isolated areas of the performer's bodies. This priority on sumptuous décor and an insistence in avoiding a contemporary fashion sensibility distanced the audience in its own understanding of the costumed characters. Characters' garments, though gorgeously decorated, were otherworldly, and therefore did not help to place the characters in any immediate contemporary mindset.

The post-modern movement, in which equal sentiment was directed towards both historical forms and to contemporary trends, profoundly impacted Zuber. Part of her inspiration, paralleling the high fashion designs of Christian Lacroix, Thierry Mugler, Jean-Paul Gaultier, Vivienne Westwood, John Galliano, and Alexander McQueen during the mid-1980s to the late-1990s involves incorporating curated combinations of varied historical garment forms to create innovative designs. These collective designers fused together disparate imagery from scenographic history, fashion, pop culture and fine art trends. Focusing on theatrical form, Zuber's work forged a path that downgraded Robbins' and Healy's dense decoration in favor of simplified historical gesture, reduced isolated surface details in favor of long, elegant silhouettes, and prioritized individual character development to achieve new distinguishing character costume design.

Relating to the combination of past historical silhouettes towards creating new forms, Zuber's frequent use of long, deconstructed garments without needless décor assists the audience to "take-in" the performer's body in a quicker registration. Compared to the traditional idea of a "Broadway Costume Designer" with the implications of layers of decorated trimming, sequins, and feathers of that genre, her work at times could be defined as anti-décor.

As a technically trained fine artist, there are few designers who rival Zuber's mastery of color theory. She is a consummate artist in managing highly specific color palettes that are set well against existing scenic designs, and that work well against lighting designs. One of the great lessons that I learned from her was the use of an evolving color scheme that continues to vary throughout a play's duration based on the dramatic needs of the text. In Zuber's *Twelfth Night*, color unfolds in surprising ways, framed around the dramatic blacks of Olivia's theatrical mourning, Malvolio's severe black uniform, and the folly of stark white tones in Cesario's livery that infect all of the characters by the end of the play.

Among other working costume designers, Zuber's work is often recognizable for its unusual visual cues that could be described as *quirky, offbeat, zany, aggressive, outsider-driven,* and/or *outré*. When a theatre production is comprised totally of elegance, it will eventually become boring. The real magic of costume design happens when the elegance is broken by something surprising. During a visit to New York in 2012, I viewed bus placards with the bizarre image of opera singer Anna Netrebko (usually attired in a diva's sumptuous dresses) photographed in a man's silk top hat for the character of Adina in *L'Elisir d'Amore* as produced by the Metropolitan Opera. The design, another of Zuber's creations, was unusual enough to create an advance buzz for this new and exciting production. Zuber's highly individual style can also be clearly seen in her dynamic costume renderings, such as in the illustration of the swashbuckling Antonio from *Twelfth Night* (Figure 8.1).

It is only through these illustrations, and through response drawings that I made when watching the production, that I may offer visual artifacts of Hytner's *Twelfth Night*; the actual production photos as undertaken by Ken Howard, have vanished. Though this was originally a set-back in my development of this chapter, I now believe it further represents the ephemeral nature of theatre design. Production photos rarely capture the essence of the actual design, and as I frequently impart to my students, the only real way to learn from theatre designers is to view live productions of theatre.

In *Twelfth Night*, Zuber's creativity was focused to reflect the disorienting world of Illyria, the play's mythical setting. As the protagonist of the play, Viola uses clothing and disguise to survive in a hostile country through her own charm and diplomacy.

> *VIOLA*
> Conceal me what I am, and be my aid
> For such disguise as haply shall become
> The form of my intent.
>
> (Act 1, Scene 2, 49–51)

In the case of Zuber's design, additional consideration had to be placed on using the androgynous nature of Viola to inhabit her male disguise, the Duke Orsino's servant, Cesario. Actor Helen Hunt's ease at portraying such an androgyne was an asset to Zuber's costume development, finally realized by clothing her in an abstracted men's white livery costume (Figure 8.3). Zuber's own explanation of the

Figure 8.1 Twelfth Night, final rendering for Antonio, Vivian Beaumont Theater, 1998
Source: Courtesy of Catherine Zuber

costume was linked to history's fascination with livery costume;[9] long past the French Revolution, there was a fashion for the wealthy to have servants attired as eighteenth-century liverymen. Though the costume appeared as an eighteenth-century form, its use beyond that period made it a kind of eternal garment form.

The costume was also linked to the complex visual iconography of travesty costume, culminating in Richard Strauss's Octavian from *der Rosenkavalier*.

Octavian's complicated androgyny—a mezzo-soprano playing a young man who disguises himself as a lady's maid in the first and final act of the opera—mirrored the gender problems of Viola's precarious situation in *Twelfth Night*. In the second act of *der Rosenkavalier*, Octavian is sent on a diplomatic mission to secure the engagement of another man's fiancée and is traditionally arrayed in a spectacular *justacorps* encrusted in silver embroidery, mirror and sequin. It is in this costume that Octavian sings one of the most heartbreakingly beautiful duets in the history of opera. Hunt's resemblance to the iconic form of Octavian reflected the parallel themes that plague Viola: diplomacy in spite of heartache, and an eventual reward of true love for a pure soul.

Figure 8.2 Twelfth Night, author's sketchbook rendering of Viola as Cesario (Helen Hunt), (Act V, Scene 1), Vivian Beaumont Theater, 1998

Source: Courtesy of Brandin Barón-Nusbaum

144   Brandin Barón-Nusbaum

Figure 8.3 Twelfth Night, final rendering for Olivia (Act I, Scene 5), Vivian Beaumont Theater, 1998

Source: Courtesy of Catherine Zuber

Zuber's costume concept for Olivia was modeled after textual references indicating that like Orsino, she was a mutable character who used outward appearances as a reflection of her whims. In a period of mourning for a deceased brother, she uses a mourning veil as a means of feigning extreme mourning in order to gain an advantage to flirting with a handsome visitor. She instructs her maid Maria to:

OLIVIA
Give me my veil. Come; throw it o'er my face.

(Act 1, Scene 5, 150)

The form of (her) intent   145

New York Times reviewer Ben Brantley noted: "our first glimpse of Olivia, in a self-conscious procession of women in exaggerated mourning costumes (the clever work of Catherine Zuber), establishes her as a pose-striker par excellence."[10]

Variety reviewer Charles Isherwood added: "Olivia loses almost with the lifting of her veil the mien of mourning for a lost brother, which should linger as the emotional underpinnings of her sudden, heedless love for Viola (in disguise as Cesario, Orsino's messenger)."[11]

As viewed through the "multi-perspective approach," Zuber's Act I costume for Olivia (Figures 8.4 and 8.5) was a mass of black luxury fabrics, heavily related to a

Figure 8.4 Twelfth Night, final rendering for Olivia (Act III), Vivian Beaumont Theater, 1998
Source: Courtesy of Catherine Zuber

Figure 8.5 Twelfth Night, author's sketchbook rendering of Olivia (Kyra Sedgewick) (Act III, Scene 1), Vivian Beaumont Theater, 1998

Source: Courtesy of Brandin Barón-Nusbaum

history of aristocratic ladies portrayed in all-encompassing black garb, such as in Louis Elle's *Madame de Maintenon and her Niece,* Goya's *Duchess of Alba,* Boldini's *Marchesa Luisa di Casati* and Irving Penn's *Veiled Face*.[12] Olivia's veil had an outrageous Hollywood film scale, highlighting the beautiful angularity of actor Kyra Sedgewick's face and recalling the campy lace headdresses of Marlene Dietrich in *Shanghai Express,* Jane Russell in *Gentlemen Prefer Blondes* and Winona Ryder in *Beetlejuice.*

As the play progresses, Olivia quickly abandons her mourning in favor of a more youthful ensemble. Zuber's design solution for the progression was to feature Olivia's next entrance in a neo-classical gown with pink color accents (Figure 8.7). As observed by reviewer Charles Isherwood: "Spunky, histrionic and sexy in a hot pink midriff, Sedgwick's Olivia is less a countess than a living Barbie doll who suddenly thinks she's found her Ken."[13]

As presented earlier, Feste's description of Duke Orsino as an opal or changeable taffeta presented Zuber with an opportunity to utilize her famed color sense. Orsino, as played by the popular film actor Paul Rudd was swaddled in Eastern-looking robes and sarongs of beautiful fuchsia and violet (Figures 8.8 and 8.9). Rudd's boyish accessibility was masked behind a theatrically foreign, slightly ridiculous haze of purple silk, swarthy skin and black hair that summoned images as varied as Dionysus at Olympus, Jim Morrison, John Paul Getty as photographed with his wife Talitha on the rooftops of Marrakesh by Patrick Lichfield, or a frat brother dressed in 2012 for a (politically incorrect) *1001 Nights* themed party. Charles Isherwood additionally observed:

> Rudd looks spectacular in Catherine Zuber's gorgeous, androgynous harem wear, gold-embroidered purple silks and transparent cottons that fall just so to expose muscled chest or shapely shoulder. With his dark, slightly exotic beauty and leonine mane of curls, he's like Hedy Lamarr with a goatee (or, in the gold boots, tight trousers and jewels of the finale, Adam Ant at the height of his '80s pirate look).[14]

Figure 8.6 Twelfth Night, final rendering for Orsino (Act 1, Scene 1), Vivian Beaumont Theater, 1998

Source: Courtesy of Catherine Zuber

Figure 8.7 Twelfth Night, author's sketchbook rendering of Orsino, (Paul Rudd) (Act I), Vivian Beaumont Theater, 1998

Source: Courtesy of Brandin Barón-Nusbaum

Olivia's haughty servant Malvolio, one of the comic foils of the play, is an important character who visually represents order though he is surrounded by folly. Textually, Shakespeare provided more information regarding his costume, especially related to his chain of office that is worn around his neck.

As Robert L Lublin wrote:

> Beyond the clothes he wears, the primary signifier of Malvolio's social position within the play is his gold chain of office. This item serves the double purpose of highlighting the wearer's importance to Olivia's household as well as his servitude to her nobility.[15] The chain circumscribes the fine apparel Malvolio wears and establishes it as a reference to Olivia's social superiority, not his own. It therefore follows that when he acts in a manner beyond dictates of his visibly inferior position, he renders himself the appropriate butt of comic abuse. Malvolio's efforts to woo his mistress constitute a blatant disregard for the limitations signified by the chain. He is deemed mad for

perpetrating so flagrant a transgression and incarcerated so that the threat he offers to the accepted social hierarchy can be safely contained.[16]

Perhaps because Shakespeare is so present in Malvolio's design, his is frequently the most clearly linked to the Shakespearean/Elizabethan period of fashion. Relating to Lublin's writing, Zuber's design for Malvolio's chain was literal, naturalistic and real. Resembling the heavy, serious and lifelike portraits of the Elizabethan painter Holbein, her Malvolio is a composite of Lord Chamberlains, Ambassadors, Privy Lords and other of Holbein's ilk. Zuber's representations were pieces of several of these portraits, and in such, not attributable to any one portrait. Theatre-goers (who as a demographic have taken more than a few art appreciation courses in their lifetimes) subconsciously remembered the essence of the Chamberlain portrait as a historical emblem of order and establishment. But through Zuber's powerful "multi-perspective approach," their memory did not fixate only on the Chamberlain memory, but rather allowed the audience to fill-in other historical cues related to Zuber's shifting of Malovolio's silhouette, color and line to depart from an exact representation of Chamberlain.

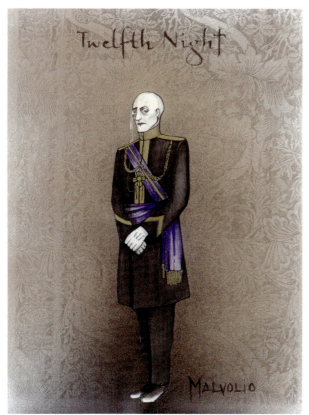

Figure 8.8 *Twelfth Night*, final rendering for entrance costume of Malvolio, Vivian Beaumont Theater, 1998

Source: Courtesy of Catherine Zuber

150   Brandin Barón-Nusbaum

Malvolio's disgrace through the series of tricks played on him by Maria, Feste and Sir Toby manifest in a clownish appearance that is commanded in Shakespeare's text as cross-gartered yellow hose.

MARIA
He will come to her in yellow
stockings, and 'tis a color she abhors, and cross-gartered, a
fashion she detests.

(Act 2, Scene 5, 179–80)

After being trapped in a cellar and left to go mad, Malvolio is finally released and brought back to Olivia, and is shown by Feste his own folly in the play. Zuber downplayed this moment, prioritizing a redressing of all characters to a bleached white palette to reset the order in Illyria.

Dancing with a guitar, Zuber's world-weary Feste summoned shades of Watteau's grainy satin Scaramouches, Harlequins and Mezzetins, the *louche* but loveable Jeff Spicoli from *Fast Times at Ridgemont High,* an over-exuberant server at the Epcot Center themed restaurant, a stunt double to Orsino's Jack Sparrow, and/or a burnout philosophy major at a liberal arts college. Poised behind the ruined Malvolio, arms flailing and legs akimbo, the actor David Patrick Kelly used the ever-evolving visual cues contained in his costume to portray an incredibly poignant portrayal of Shakespeare's great philosopher-clown.

As evidenced by the Tony nomination and the positive reviews, Zuber's work on *Twelfth Night* was largely praised, and has become an important production in the history of that play's history. As of the publication of this chapter, it is still possible to see (pirated) clips of the entire production on YouTube,[17] undoubtedly due to the celebrity cast. As an instructor, I often show this video as a way to demonstrate best practice for costume concept and execution. As stated earlier in this chapter, my own relationship to Catherine Zuber was an essential period in my own development as a theatre artist. This chapter represents a small portion of Zuber's expansive investigation into Shakespeare's oeuvre, but students, scholars and other professional theatre artists would benefit greatly from a more expansive study into her life's work.

Notes

1   Zuber designed critically acclaimed Broadway and Off-Broadway productions of *Julius Caesar* (2003), *Othello* (2001), *King Lear* (1996), *Troilus and Cressida* (1995), *The Merchant of Venice* (1995), and *Two Gentlemen of Verona* (1994). As of the publication of this chapter, Zuber has been nominated eleven times for a Tony Award and has won five times, winning four consecutive times between 2005–8. In addition, she has received the *Henry Hewes Award for Outstanding Costume Design,* the Drama Desk Award, the Lucille Lortel Award, the Ovation Award, and the Obie Award for Sustained Achievement.
2   Gerald Gutierrez directed this production at the Vivian Beaumont Theater.
3   Michael Mayer directed this new musical at the Royale Theatre.
4   Susan H. Schulman directed this production at the Martin Beck Theatre.

The form of (her) intent   151

5   "Previews" are public performances that occur before the official opening of a theatrical production. Tickets for previews are sold for a reduced rate, and the audience is notified that they are watching a performance that is still in development, as the production will be edited based on the audience's reaction to the current state of the production.

6   Phone interview with Catherine Zuber, August 12, 2012.

7   Phone interview with Catherine Zuber, August 12, 2012.

8   Douglas A. Russell. "Shakespearean Costume: Contemporary or Fancy Dress." *Educational Theatre Journal*, Vol. 10, No. 2 (May, 1958), (Baltimore, MD: Johns Hopkins Press), pp.105–112.

9   Phone interview with Catherine Zuber, August 12, 2012.

10   Ben Brantley, "Festival Review; Addled Sailors in Sea of Love." *New York Times* July 17, 1998.

11   Charles Isherwood, *Variety* (July 16, 1998).

12   This portrait of Evelyn Tripp was published in 1949.

13   Charles Isherwood, *Variety* (July 16, 1998).

14   Charles Isherwood, *Variety* (July 16, 1998).

15   Felicity Heal's "Reciprocity and Exchange in the Late Medieval Household" from *Bodies and Disciplines: Intersections of Literature and History in Fifteenth Century England*, ed. Hanahwqlt and Wallace (Minneapolis, MN: University of Minnesota Press, 1993) as treated by Robert L. Lublin, *Costuming the Shakespearean Stage: Visual Codes of Representation in Early Modern Theatre and Culture*, Farnham, UK and Burlington VT: Ashgate, pp. 71.

16   Robert L. Lublin, *Costuming the Shakespearean Stage: Visual Codes of Representation in Early Modern Theatre and Culture* (Farnham: Ashgate, 2011), p. 71.

17   www.youtube.com/watch?v=CpwaTBtlhA0

Chapter 9

Designing sound for Shakespeare
Connecting past and present

Adrian Curtin

What is involved in designing sound for a Shakespeare production? Is there such a thing as 'Shakespearean' sound design – design that accords with aspects of Shakespeare's theatre? One might think designing sound for Shakespeare simply involves supplying the relevant sounds referenced in the plays, or else some mood music to set the scene or lend an atmosphere. This is not so. The growing importance of theatre sound design over the last 30 years has meant that designers typically create distinctive, multi-layered compositional scores, often in collaboration with other members of the design team, including the director, and sometimes the performers too. Sound design for Shakespeare has become increasingly ambitious, adding to the already complex acoustic environment of a Shakespeare play in performance. This acoustic enrichment is informed by cinema, television and radio, concert performance, video games, and the 'sonification' of everyday life via gadgetry, advertising, and soundscaping (the acoustic design of an environment), all of which has led theatre audiences to expect that productions – even productions of centuries-old plays – should be sonically enhanced. Audiences expect not only to be able to hear actors with the same clarity and loudness as speech heard in other media (an unreasonable expectation with regard to loudness, unless stage actors use microphones) but also to have a soundtrack to live performance that accords with contemporary listening habits. Why should theatre be less sonically sophisticated than other forms of entertainment? Hence the rise of the theatre sound designer, who has fashioned brave new (audio) worlds for Shakespeare's plays.

This enhanced sonic 'twangling' (Caliban's descriptor for the musicality of the island in *The Tempest*) is not universally appreciated. If one believes that the most important thing in Shakespeare is the language, then sound design might be deemed ancillary at best. Moreover, even if one recognizes the value of theatre sound design it can still give cause for disgruntlement. Kevin Ewert critiques contemporary theatre lighting and sound design for Shakespeare on account of its perceived excesses and gimmickry:

> Although cinema may have learned it from theatrical melodrama, theatre now copies back the clichés of movie music – the obvious mickey-mousing of

synchronized descriptive music that reproduces, explains and underlines (and often overwhelms) every major moment in order to enhance the audiences' emotional response.

For most directors, myself included, variable lighting and illustrative sound are addictive: we want them even when we don't need them, we use them even when they do no real good for the production. This is a very, very hard habit for us to kick, but it may be even harder for a modern audience to give up. If we 'trust' Shakespeare's language and the powers of our imaginations, then, for example, in 1.6 of *Macbeth* it should be enough that Banquo talks incessantly about birds for us to imagine them as well as the location we are meant to be in. But in a silent theatre [...] wouldn't Banquo's lengthy detour into ornithology, insisting that there are lots and lots of birds nesting here, now seem rather flat or even bizarre without any birdsong to back it up?[1]

Ewert suggests that modern audiences have become accustomed to hearing fully realized, immersive aural environments but this may not be appropriate for Shakespeare's plays, which, after all, primarily create fictional environments through linguistic description and performative utterance. Poorly designed sound for Shakespeare ignores this imaginative world building in favour of generic underscoring and obvious, redundant illustration.

Skilful sound designers know not to overdo the sonic elements of a production by providing sound for the sake of it; furthermore, they are sensitive to the operations of Shakespeare's language. They do not merely reproduce stock sound effects and music cues. Rather, they create a unique aural palette for each production and utilize it judiciously, playing on, but not necessarily fulfilling an audience's acoustic expectations. They find sonic means to match Shakespeare's linguistic savvy, making audiences delight in what they hear, and altering their perceptions as a result. They use sound to engage audiences in the story being told but do not simply tell the story in sound or mask the subtleties of the poetic line. In this chapter, I provide a synoptic overview of sound design for Shakespeare, using input from professional sound designers and composers to locate current practices in a history of theatrical sound-making. My case study is a 2012 production of *A Midsummer Night's Dream* by the British company Filter Theatre. I analyse this production in order to posit some points of contact and continuity between the early modern and the postmodern and to showcase contemporary sonic innovation with regard to Shakespearean scenography.

Sound-designing Shakespeare

The idea that providing sound design for Shakespeare is a relatively new phenomenon is a misconception. Although theatre sound design did not emerge as a named, professionally recognized activity until the latter part of the twentieth century, theatre has always had some form of crafted sound, whether of the musical or 'noises off' variety. Music (a.k.a. organized sound) used in theatrical performances effectively served as sound design *avant la lettre*. Members of the Lord Chamberlain's Men/King's Men, including professional musicians, provided music for Shakespeare's plays at the Globe and Blackfriars theatres. This music took the form of a mixed consort of string, wind, brass, and percussion instruments, positioned in small, makeshift ensembles at different points in the theatres (behind, on, above, and even under the stage).[2] The music was probably conventional and popular and would have been known to the audience. Shakespeare's actors were sometimes tasked with singing songs, and possibly accompanied themselves on the lute.[3] These songs are an integral part of Shakespeare's dramaturgy even if the printed play does not make their affective potential apparent. The same is true of sound-making more generally. The Globe was equipped with means of making thunderous sound (possibly the result of opening the wooden trap door)[4] and had chambers and ordnance to provide battle noise (infamously, a cannon accidentally set fire to the building in 1613). Music and sound effects played vital roles in the theatrical proceedings by engaging those in attendance, denoting place (e.g. hautboys under the stage signalling the underworld) as well as character type and status (the lute and viol indicating nobility) and dramatic action (e.g. magic). Music did not simply support the productions and provide added value. Claire Van Campen, director of music at the reconstructed Shakespeare's Globe in London, comments that it was not until the eighteenth century that theatre music "become about padding and entertainment";[5] music in Shakespeare's theatre was artfully designed and culturally specific. Music performed in productions at the reconstructed Globe and the Sam Wanamaker Playhouse (a neo-Jacobean indoor theatre) in London tends to blend Renaissance and modern musical sources and conventions. This is in keeping with the general ethos of Shakespeare's Globe (i.e. producing work that is informed by early modern staging practices but does not slavishly attempt to reproduce it). However, it is also probably an effect of our relative unfamiliarity with, and distance from, the acoustic world of early modern England. Van Campen states:

> Most modern composers just throw up their hands and go, 'I can't do this, give me a clarinet, that's what I'm used to'. [...] Personally, I feel that if you're going to do a historical production in the Globe, there's so much music from that period that works so well if you arrange it properly for the instruments. But that takes time to understand.[6]

One of the tenets of sound studies (scholarship that investigates auditory aspects of human culture) is that one must account for the historicity of sound and hearing; these phenomena are context specific and should be understood in kind.

Bruce R. Smith (1999) has conducted an acoustical investigation of Shakespearean theatre in the context of early modern England, reconstructing the 'soundscapes' (sonic environments) of city, country, and court, as well as the auditory conditions of the Globe and Blackfriars theatres. Smith undertakes 'historical phenomenology', investigating the sounds people heard and how they made sense of these sounds in a largely oral culture.

The soundscape of early modern London was made up of a number of over-lapping, shifting acoustic communities, centered on different soundmarks [sonic landmarks]: parish bells, the speech of different nationalities, the sounds of trades, open-air markets, the noises of public gathering places. Moving among these soundmarks—indeed, *making* these soundmarks in the process—Londoners in their daily lives followed their own discursive logic.[7]

This logic was predicated on being part of, and able to navigate, a complex sonic environment replete with sociocultural significations. Theatre functioned as a type of echo chamber in this regard. Smith describes the 1599 Globe Theatre in Vitruvian terms as a vintage "instrument to be played upon", a "device for propagating sound" that was "extraordinarily efficient".[8] Shakespeare's plays are composed with sound and hearing in mind, not just in relation to music and sound cues, but on the levels of dramatic action, cultural reference, and philosophical engagement, as numerous scholars have demonstrated through close readings (Folkerth, 2002, Johnson, 2005, Magnus and Cannon, 2012). Sound design is already implicit in Shakespearean drama; it is neither a modern imposition nor a corruption or superfluity. What contemporary theatre sound design may do is creatively respond to the implicit sound of Shakespeare's texts, making them (re)sound for a particular sociocultural context (the time and place in which a performance takes place), audience, historical moment, and artistic matrix (the collaborative production work of actors, designers and director). This process is not without its challenges and complications but such is the nature of artistic enterprise.

Noteworthy sound designs and musical compositions for Shakespeare plays in theatre history include Felix Mendelssohn's music for a private performance of *A Midsummer Night's Dream* at the New Palace in Potsdam in 1843, which features his famous Wedding March. Also notable is Henry Irving's 1888 production of *Macbeth* at the Lyceum Theatre in London, which had music composed by Arthur Sullivan for an orchestra of 46 players and a female chorus of 60 voices. Sullivan's music provided a dramatic counterpart, a "composer's interpretation [...] of the dramatic issues that lay at the heart of Irving's production of Shakespeare's play", and placed emphasis on the supernatural over the psychological elements.[9] In 1908, Herbert Beerbohm Tree devised a sound design for his production of *The Merchant of Venice* at His Majesty's Theatre in London that endeavoured to create an authentic, onstage Jewish community and soundscape, the intended sociological effect of which was to depict Shylock as a representative of an ancient faith rather than a stock stage villain. Tree also wanted to prove that theatre could outdo the competition of the time (e.g. the phonograph, gramophone, and *Phono-Cinéma-Théâtre*) in terms of the audience's auditory experience.[10] Peter Brook's post-1960 Shakespeare productions used subtle sound design, often in the form of single tones, rhythms and unusual percussion to convey the ineffable, "the fundamental metaphysics of the play as Brook [understood] it", its hidden meanings, latent emotions and purportedly universal qualities.[11] The advent of digital sound in theatre in the mid-1980s meant that sound designers could participate more readily in the rehearsal process, responding to ideas and situations developed in the rehearsal room by sampling and playing back sounds. This enhanced flexibility continued into the performance itself, as Ross Brown explains in an interview:

> The National Theatre [of Great Britain]—who [...] were at the vanguard of this in the eighties—and people like Paul Arditti and Scott Myers and Mick Jones who were working in the sound department and sort of playing with samples, and directors like Peter Hall got very interested in using samples in [the] rehearsal room, playing the thunderstorm in *Lear*. [...] [In] *Lear* with Anthony Hopkins [1986, dir. David Hare] [...] it was the first time the sound operator actually was playing the thunderstorm: they actually had thunder claps across a musical keyboard and there was an interaction going on between the actors and the sound operator who was responding, and you know, there was this rhythmic interaction going on there.[12]

Exploration of the possibilities of digital sound continued in postmodern productions of Shakespeare's work, such as The Wooster Group's 2007 production of *Hamlet*, directed by Elizabeth LeCompte at the Public Theater in New York City, which featured the actors' voices mixed live with those from Richard Burton's 1964 'theatrofilm' version of the play. The actors' voices were digitally manipulated and distorted in the process, thereby staging "a more convergent, perhaps conflictual relationship between origin and reproduction, liveness and its remediation",[13] and giving *Hamlet*'s ghosting a newly technological cast.

Despite the manifold opportunities afforded by digital technology, innovative contemporary theatre sound design for Shakespeare does not necessarily entail 'high-tech' doctoring of the actors' voices or the performance soundscape. On the contrary, sound designers may take a relatively 'low-tech' or 'retro-tech' approach to their craft, redeploying previously established methods for making theatrical sound with novel effect. As a case in point, Darron L. West's sound design for SITI Company's 2007 production of *Radio Macbeth*, co-directed by Anne Bogart, was conducted in the manner of a live radio drama, recalling, in particular, Orson Welles' radiophonic and Shakespearean pursuits.

> Just as a radio drama builds its world by manipulating sound, the production created every movement and every sound precisely on the stage: the crack of biting into an apple, a Zippo lighter igniting, a ladder clattering to the ground. Actors used the live microphones to create the play's atmosphere, whispering dialogue, ringing bells, singing, blowing, and gasping into them. They used the available properties to create sounds as well: slapping a board on the table, pulling on the curtains, slamming their scripts shut. During battle sequences they rattled chairs and growled into the microphones. [...] [Stephen] Webber's Macbeth orchestrated the action by controlling the sound effects on stage; in other words, he manipulated the sounds, space, and bodies of the stage to control the total effect heard on the radio.[14]

West's sound design did not disguise its operations; rather, it put them in full view and made them part of the theatrical presentation. Sound design was not relegated to the wings, nor was it broadcast over loudspeakers. It was foregrounded as a dynamic, devised *techne* that had to be experienced by those who saw and heard it – 'noises *on*', to tweak a theatrical trope. If there is such a thing as Shakespearean sound design this overtly theatrical form might be it, or at least some version of it. This is a type of sound design that is not beholden to a model of cinema sound, or indeed theatrical melodrama, in which pervasive musical underscoring and cunning Foley effects delivered from locationally ambiguous, surrounding positions connote an audio-visual illusion to captivate an audience. There is nothing wrong with this approach, and it can be used to great effect, as, for example, in the wordless, physical Shakespeare productions of Synetic Theater (based in Arlington, Virginia), such as their 2002 piece *Hamlet … The Rest is Silence,* and in a multitude of more conventional interpretations of Shakespeare's plays by other companies. The benefit of the *presentational* approach to theatre sound design, however, is that it is arguably more in keeping with the stylistics of early modern theatre since it encourages audiences to be active listeners and contributors to the construction of meaning. Contemporary theatre sound design that is attentive to Shakespeare's language and dramaturgy may find ways of harking back to the dynamics of the Elizabethan stage whilst engaging modern sonorities.

This can take many forms, including homage, as sound designer Steven Brown relates:

> I always try to reference, wherever possible, sound cues which Shakespeare would have used. For instance, a version of *A Midsummer Night's Dream* I designed […] started with the sound of a car chase around the in-the-round auditorium. This finished with both vehicles colliding. Just before this crash, one of the cars tooted its horn three times as a signal the play was about to start, [mirroring] the three notes which would have been blown on a trumpet in Shakespeare's time to signify the same.[15]

Sounds mentioned in the script can also be updated whilst retaining something of their original signification, as designer Lindsay Jones remarks with reference to the courtly trumpet sounds in *Richard III*:

> [I used] a police siren for any time that someone is entering the space, as if they're being escorted by a police escort. It's a very similar concept: both sounds (trumpet and siren) mean the same thing: 'be aware and move out of the way for this very important person', but they both would only exist in their individual contexts.[16]
>
> (2012, pers. comm. 3 July)

158 Adrian Curtin

As a matter of course, sound designers strive to attend to the structural features of a Shakespeare play. This requires sensitivity to Shakespeare's language. Martin Desjardins states:

> In Shakespeare, the verse defines a very specific rhythmic world that must be matched, pushed, held back or countered with intelligence. It's not about having every cue match every line. It's about having the cue align itself with the text in a way that is resonant with the storytelling going on at that particular moment. In Shakespeare, the verse plays a crucial part in defining that rhythmical framework upon which [the sound] design must build and stand, and does so to a degree of primacy that is different from most other forms of drama. As a result, being honest and accurate in my own reading of the verse is critical to building my design.[17]

If the sound designer is substantially involved in the rehearsal process, he or she is able to fashion a sound design/musical score that adds another layer to the sonorous rhythms of Shakespeare's verse, in this way creating a specially crafted acoustic environment or the production.

> By the end of a rehearsal process, quite often the actors are timing their movements and/or speeches to the music they've come to know, and as such the two exist in close sync. This allows me to write music whose dynamics move with a character's speech, as opposed to subsisting underneath or around it.[18]

Rick Thomas concurs:

> The actor's speech is the lead melody and counter-melody to the orchestration. Introducing additional melodic elements [...] is quite commonly a recipe for disaster. I may introduce melodic themes and repeat them around the actors' dialogue, but rarely during. It's the most common mistake beginning composers and sound designers make when doing Shakespeare.[19]

Other common technical concerns and design issues include whether or not actors should be miked (i.e. use microphones) and whether sonic elements should be live or pre-recorded. The sound designers I contacted for my research stated that they generally avoided using microphones, save for actors playing supernatural characters, whose voices could be electronically enhanced with reverberative effects, for example, or for outdoor productions that have high levels of ambient noise. Joe Payne articulates this position:

> I am a firm believer that the difference between theatre and film is the connection between a live performer and an audience. Anything that interrupts that connection, and we ought to be watching a movie. Not to say that

Designing sound for Shakespeare   159

I don't use [microphones]. I just feel I should connect to an actor onstage and not the loudspeaker in front of the audience.[20]

One designer offered a dissenting opinion, however, and advocated for more widespread use:

Miking actors increases their potential dynamic range, particularly in the quiet end, where they can whisper miked and still be heard in the last row. [It] gives the director freedom in staging so that actors no longer need to be down center and pointed at the audience, as Shakespeare did. Finally, miking the actors frees the stage designer to not have to design acoustically, i.e. to put a hard reflective surface behind and around the actors to acoustically amplify their voices. [...] It's not so much about whether the actors sound amplified, it is now about the quality of the amplification, the naturalness, and, most importantly, its ability to make the audience forget about its existence after the exposition of the play.[21]

Likewise, Desjardins weighs up the relative benefits of live versus pre-recorded sound in Shakespeare:

I love the use of live music and the feel it creates by bonding audience, cast, and players. That kind of visceral connection is hard to replace, but it is not always right. Sometimes, for instance, the isolation created by pre-recorded sound is just as moving as the connection created by live music. It's really just a matter of production style. To generalize a bit, [...] I tend to favor live music in contexts where the story is more born of the imagination, something like *Midsummer* or *Tempest*, for instance. By comparison, where the story is more about characters being 'driven', such as in *Macbeth* or *King Lear*, the energy of played-back sound is oftentimes more on the mark.[22]

It would seem there are no rules set in stone for sound-designing Shakespeare, only approaches that may be more or less effective depending upon the production objectives and execution.

Arguably, the most interesting contemporary sound design for Shakespeare makes a virtue of this artistic licence by exploring the conventions and potential of theatre sound, adopting a nimble, improvisational, contingent methodology that captures something of the spirit of the original staging, allowing audience members to 'eke out' the performance with their minds).[23]

Filter Theatre's *A Midsummer Night's Dream*

Filter Theatre's Shakespeare productions exemplify this present-minded, Elizabethan-inspired staging approach. Filter was founded in 2003 by Ollie Dimsdale, Tim Phillips, and Ferdy Roberts, and has quickly built up an impressive reputation, especially in the UK, for imaginative interpretations of classic texts as well as productions of new writing and devised work. A signature element of Filter's style is its virtuosic use of sound, which is typically to the fore, with musicians/sound designers sharing the stage with actors. Filter first adapted its postmodern, non-illusory staging methods to Shakespeare in a production of *Twelfth Night* (2006–2008, 2013–2014), directed by Sean Holmes, created in association with the Royal Shakespeare Company. A reviewer observed:

> As with all Filter's productions, the process was a part of the performance itself. The stage manager sat on stage, all tech was controlled by performers, almost all music and sound effects were created live. This [...] was particularly important in a production that effectively turned *Twelfth Night* into a sound-piece, moving quickly from song to song and turning every set piece into another musical number. Music was used creatively to pitch mood and ideas, as much a part of the narrative as Shakespeare's words. Thus, the play began with a free-form jazz jam semi-conducted by Orsino, out of which he suddenly plucked a single keyboard melody as his strain with a 'dying fall'; and Malvolio's fantasy of being 'Count Malvolio' was conducted to a percussive, bass-led, muddy grunge tune, during which he played air-bass and drums as he got caught up in his own delusions.[24]

Unsurprisingly, Filter's unconventional, non-sacrosanct approach to staging Shakespeare is not to everyone's liking, but they have nonetheless achieved critical and commercial success in revamping his plays for a contemporary audience.

Filter's *A Midsummer Night's Dream*, produced in association with the Lyric Theatre, Hammersmith (London), remixed Shakespeare's play by presenting an edited version intercut with original material and improvisatory or semi-scripted exchanges in modern language. The major elements of the play were mostly intact but were supplemented by compère material, stand-up comedy, improvisatory dialogue, and flights of fancy connected to the staging process. This supplementary material elaborated upon the play's inherent metatheaticality. In the production programme, director Sean Holmes mentions that the company is "respectfully disrespectful" of Shakespeare's work, not afraid to make their own of it or to use it as fodder for theatrical experimentation (2012). Hence Filter's musical approach to adapting *Midsummer*, riffing on the text like a jazz musician or remixing it like a DJ while maintaining a focus on the language, which the actors delivered skilfully. In keeping with Filter's style, the production featured sound as a principal scenographic element, using it not only to set the scene but also to motivate, condition, and in some instances, constitute the action, holding the audience's audio-visual attention throughout.

Tom Haines and Chris Branch created the sound design. Haines and Branch are professional partners, artistic associates of Filter, and members of the London Snorkelling Team (LST), an independent musical outfit that creates quirky electronic and lounge-style music in the vein of Raymond Scott, the American

Designing sound for Shakespeare 161

bandleader and pioneer of electronic music. The LST has the curious distinction of being the official orchestra of the London Institute of Pataphysics, an organization devoted to the pseudo-philosophy of the avant-gardist Alfred Jarry, which gives an indication of the group's offbeat nature and fringe status. According to promotional material, the LST plays "short, sharp tunes that reflect a love of unusual instruments, wonky cartoon music, 1950s sci-fi exotica and cocktail jazz without the solos. Or fairly silly music played very sincerely". This aesthetic informed the sound design for Filter's production of *Midsummer*, though it did not wholly dictate it.

In the performances at the Royal Exchange Theatre in Manchester in July/August 2012, two musicians (joined on occasion by a third), who were cast in the roles of the mechanicals in the play, took up positions at the periphery of the round stage, able to step in and out of the action, and were fully visible to the audience. They had to hand a drum kit, an electric guitar, keyboards (one of which was made to sound like a Mellotron), a glockenspiel, a tuning fork, a small bell, and other sundry sound-making devices, including microphones and laptops. These last items were crucial to the operation, because the sound design was largely achieved by digitally manipulating sounds that were recorded live *in situ*. The musicians would make a sound using one of their instruments (e.g. bowing a glockenspiel key), or take a sound that one of the performers made into a microphone, then filter it (n.b. the company name) through a software programme (Max/MSP) that had been pre-prepared to output sound in a specific way. The musicians began the show with 'empty boxes' in the computer programme (i.e. no pre-recorded sound) and would collect (i.e. record) sounds over the course of the performance, which they used to fashion a variety of sonic environments. This procedure was demonstrated for the audience early on in the show when the actor playing Puck, standing in front of a microphone, rapped on the grooves of a toy wooden tree frog. The action of striking the toy tree frog made a 'ribbit-ing' sound that was then sampled and played back in a variety of pitches on various speakers both inside and outside the auditorium, making it seem as though a whole rainforest of tree frogs was audibly present (see Figure 9.1).

This was a form of sonic conjuring, courtesy of a wooden toy, a microphone, a software programme, and an array of loudspeakers, though this acoustic sleight-of-hand was conducted in full view of the audience. This is integral to Filter's philosophy, as Tom Haines explains:

> Our theory is that if the company (and audience) see and hear the process of sound being created then they have an ownership of the sound, and have to use their imagination in a different way than if they were just piped pre-recorded sound effects.[25]

By seeing Puck create – or at least spark – the sound of the forest, the audience is implicated in its imaginative construction. The theatrical potential of sound in performance is thus matched, or married, with the fantastical nature of

Figure 9.1 A Midsummer Night's Dream, Ferdy Roberts as Puck initiating the sound of the forest, Filter Theatre, Royal Exchange Theatre

Source: Photo Jonathan Keenan

Shakespeare's drama. Filter's sound is not simply ornamentation that furnishes what the text already provides. It provides a meta-text that has to be seen and heard to be 'make-believed'.

Magic, in Filter's production of *Midsummer*, was sonically signified and effected. Titania and Fairyland were associated with chimes, cymbals and various tinkling sounds (digitally sampled and manipulated through the process described above), which signalled magical incursions onto the scene. Minor fairies had a sonic rather than visual presence, their voices created by technologically altering an actor's voice (in full view of the audience) to sound non-human (e.g. 'helium' voice), their movements denoted by a whooshing sound that figuratively flew around the auditorium's multi-speaker system. Oberon demonstrated his power through making a 'zonking' feedback/distortion sound, while the magical flower that he requests of Puck radiated via the throbbing vibration of a single electronic organ note: a tip-of-the-hat to the BBC Radiophonic Workshop, which Haines and Branch count as a creative influence. Similarly, Bottom's transformation into a donkey was achieved through sound, using one of the oldest tricks in the sound designer's book. Standing in front of a microphone, the actor playing Puck clapped two halves of a coconut shell together to make the sound of horses' hooves when the actor playing Bottom moved his feet; likewise, he tinkled a bell whenever Bottom moved his neck. As an audience member within my earshot remarked to a companion, it

Designing sound for Shakespeare 163

was just like Monty Python, as it recalled a similar gag made in the 1975 film *Monty Python and the Holy Grail.*

This is not accidental on Filter's part. The company works to achieve a certain level of 'knowingness' by not disguising scenographical mechanisms: they create illusions, but they also show how the illusions are made. To borrow a line from Brecht, they 'show that [they] are showing'.[26] What this means for their sound design is that it allows audience members to suspend their disbelief, if they so choose, or to revel in pretence and artificiality, in theatrical make-believe. This makes their sound design a dynamic element in the *mise-en-scène*, an element that is also performing, multi-layered, and self-reflexive. As Tom Haines remarks:

> We use the word "like" quite a lot in [describing] this show. The sounds created are "like" sound effects. [...] The sound of the lone toy frog is magically transformed into a sound "like" a rain forest at night. The resulting sound is "like" a sound effect.[27]

By drawing attention to similitude (the condition of one thing being *like*, but not quite the same, as another) over equivalence, Filter's sound designers destabilize supposedly natural operations and draw attention to constructions and conventions, toying with them, staging the unseen Foley artistry of cinema (Haines cites famed Hollywood sound designer Ben Burtt as an influence). In so doing, they invite the audience to reconsider what it thinks it knows, or hears, or sees, just as Shakespeare was wont to do, as in the famous Dover Cliff scene in *King Lear*, when Edgar leads the blind Gloucester – and the audience – to believe, momentarily, that Gloucester has stepped off a cliff while all the time he has been standing on solid ground (the stage).

Filter brought a similar type of cultural knowingness to bear in its musical arrangements for *Midsummer*, some of which were pastiches of musical genres. Just as Shakespeare used songs in his plays, especially popular songs, to evoke shared cultural knowledge, so too did Filter, albeit of a different variety. Shakespeare relied on his audience knowing about the relevant conventions and associations of particular songs. He used this shared understanding to achieve aesthetic shock on occasion, as when Ophelia distractedly sings the 'endearment' song 'Bonny Sweet Robin' to the Danish court in *Hamlet*, thus violating protocol and signalling her derangement as well as the disrepair of the body politic. Bruce Johnson elaborates:

> By playing with an established popular repertoire, disordering and fragmenting it, presenting it in inappropriate settings and juxtapositions, the sense of a known world turned inside out, of poignant ironies, is far more disturbingly achieved than would overtly 'mad' music. [...] Both [Hamlet] and Ophelia are on the edge. The fragmented collage of existing song repertoire emphasises this in the case of Ophelia. [...] Shakespeare's decision to put comic songs at the site of funerary solemnity [in the gravediggers' scene] would in itself have stuck the audience as generically unsettling, rather like the song "Always Look

164   Adrian Curtin

on the Bright Side [of Life]" in the concluding crucifixion scene of the film *The Life of Brian*.[28]

Filter's musical selections played with stylistic collage and audience expectations in a similar manner, except the 'out-of-joint-ness' or aesthetic shock was normalized. One of the conceits of the production was that an audience member (an obvious plant) took the role of Bottom when the scheduled guest star could not perform. This 'audience member' claimed to be a musician, not an actor, and took it upon himself on occasion to launch into various song styles, including 1950s doo-wop when showcasing his ability to play the vein of a tyrant; a Barry White bass groove while observing Lysander's advances on Helena; and a Sid Vicious-style punk rock take on 'The ousel cock so black of hue' – the song Bottom sings to show he is not afraid – after having been 'translated' into an ass. The raucousness of this last effort prompted laughter from the audience when Titania innocently asked "What angel wakes me from my flow'ry bed?".[29] It seemed as though Titania was both deaf to the sound of Bottom as well as figuratively blind to the sight of him, for he sounded like no angel (save a Hell's Angel, perhaps). The pair subsequently performed an impromptu rock duet, latching onto the word 'nay' in the line "And dares not answer 'Nay'"[30] (from Bottom's song) with homonymic ('neigh'), orgiastic fervour.

As the characters in the play moved from one situation to another, so the performers slid between musical styles and sonic registers, depending on shared understanding with the audience for the performance effect to be successful. Thus, the scene in which Puck, under orders from Oberon, leads Demetrius and Lysander to chase after one other fruitlessly in the forest using acoustic misdirection ("Up and down, up and down,/ I will lead them up and down")[31] was reimagined as an arcade video game (think *Pong*), complete with attendant bleeps and bloops, pre-loaded computerized speech, and jingles (including a 'game over' sting that borrowed from Chopin's 'Funeral March' from his Piano Sonata No. 2). The performers triggered these sounds live, using MIDI-enabled joysticks. This was unquestionably a gimmick, but a clever gimmick that substituted computer graphical sprites for the fantastical variety in the mind's eye/ear of audience members familiar with gaming. The performers worked to keep the audience on a constant state of alert (no slumbering in this version of the *Dream*) as the sonic environment continually offered new things to attend to in various decibel ranges and dynamic pockets. Not all of this was achieved digitally. One of the most arresting sonic effects in the production was when actors would leave the auditorium and declaim into the great arches of the Royal Exchange Theatre, which gave their voices remarkable resonance and reverberative power. Not knowing quite what to expect, or knowing that proceedings could be subverted, kept the audience attentive as the sound design *jigged* with the text, alternately leading and following it. While one might have expected the musicians to interpret Oberon's direction to Titania to "rock the ground whereon these sleepers be"[32] as an invitation to grunge, they instead provided a lilting, waltz-like piece (the track 'The Advice' from

Designing sound for Shakespeare   165

the LST's 2010 album *Audio Recording and Map*) to which the couples danced beneath a sparkling discothèque ball, giving rise to soft rocking.

Filter reimagined *A Midsummer Night's Dream* (as they did *Twelfth Night*) as a gig-inspired theatre piece, rounding out the show with the declaration "We have been The Mechanicals – good night!" Their version of Shakespeare's play spoke not only to music festival culture (the show was originally created for the 2010 Latitude Festival in Suffolk) but other aspects of contemporary 'sonification'. Filter's *Dream* seemingly partook of the phenomenon of sonic branding: the association of sounds with products, such as Intel's signature four-note marimba tune, thought to be one of the most recognized sonic tags in the world (Haines and Branch, it is worth noting, also compose music and sound design for commercials and other ventures under the partnership *Brains and Hunch*). Filter's *Dream* presented a world suffused with electronic sounds and jingles, a world in which one's interaction with the environment, objects, and other people is coded, triggered, and soundtracked, recalling Caliban's "the isle is full of noises" speech, with the "thousand twangling instruments" that would hum about his ears.[33] Technological sonification may be more vexatious than dreamy, unlike the "sounds and sweet airs" that give Caliban delight and "hurt not",[34] but it still works to condition our experience and perceptions of the modern world and our roles as consuming/producing subjects within it. The Shakespeare industry is part of this too, so it is not peculiar to have a production of *A Midsummer Night's Dream* inflected by contemporary sonorities and modes of attention; indeed, it would be strange if this were *not* the case given that composition and listening are historically situated activities.

This does not mean that Filter's approach to staging Shakespeare is merely faddish or contrived, overlaying contemporary concerns on a classic text and using it as an excuse to rock and roll. Rather, Filter adopts an early modern sensibility to staging Shakespeare's plays, treating them not as fixed literary texts that are seemingly inviolate due to what W.B. Worthen calls the "ideology of print",[35] but as performance scores that can be creatively amended and improvised upon, to some extent, or cut up and re-spliced, like one of John Cage's collage pieces (another major influence for Haines and Branch).

There is a pleasing and noteworthy terminological coincidence between the language of audio software programming and a name for Renaissance playwriting. Sound designers using a digital software programme like Max/MSP talk about having sample 'patches' with which to create sonic environments – little bits of sonic material that they can re-use for their own ends, fashioning them into new compositions. English early modern playwrights were occasionally referred to (possibly pejoratively) as 'play-patchers' whose job it was to patch together fragmented bits and pieces, including songs, speeches and routines into a semi-cohesive whole. Tiffany Sterne remarks: "There was a sense at the time that plays were not whole art works in the way that poems were. Plays had the bit, the fragment, the patch in their very natures."[36] Conceiving of a Shakespeare play as a patchwork entity, a collection of borrowed bits and pieces, some of which could be re-purposed to circulate in other

166 Adrian Curtin

forms, is consistent with the digital world, and with Filter's sound design for this play, which consisted of a hodgepodge of sources creatively re-patched for every performance. Moreover, on the level of audience engagement, Filter's production of *Midsummer*, staged in the round at the Royal Exchange Theatre, was effectively dialogic. Surrounded on all sides by the audience, the performers – especially, Ed Gaughan in the role of Peter Quince, who functioned as a de facto MC/stand-up/clown – encouraged the audience to break with the modern, bourgeois habit of silent attention at the theatre and become lively contributors to the performance: answering questions, laughing at jokes, talking with neighbours, and clapping along to the music. The resulting hubbub brought to mind the ambient noise and rowdiness of the historical Globe theatres, and activated the spirit of Shakespeare's dramaturgy, which comes to life in a unique way when sounded by performers and re-sounded by an audience: a feedback loop of energy/*energeia* (rhetorical vigour) upon which Shakespeare in performance is founded.

Sound ideas

Theatre sound designers may contribute to the aural efficacy of Shakespeare's verse as well as the complexity of his narratives. Shakespeare, as poet and dramatist, was himself something of a sound designer; contemporary theatre artists working on his plays strive to continue his work by making it newly resonant. Sound designers relish the compositional opportunities that Shakespeare's works affords them. Victoria Delorio notes:

> As sound designers, we [...] get very excited when we are to work on Shakespeare. This is where we get to flex most of our muscles. [For] me it's about the richness of design, the layers you can find, the heightened emotionality, the comic timing of the humor, and the grand theatrical gestures. [...] I have the luxury of being subtle and grand, simple and complicated – all in one production.[37]

The breadth of Shakespeare's dramatic imagining can lead to surprising, novel arrangements, as Martin Desjardins found when working on a production of *Twelfth Night*. In this production, he brought together the compositional worlds of opera, tango and minimalism.

> It was a bizarre combination I never would have thought of outside of being pushed there by the play, and one that bore such wonderful fruit for the production that I had to feel as if its discovery was a gift I was given, rather than something I'd done myself.[38]

Shakespeare's plays can be continually reinterpreted and reimagined; sound design enables and inspires this. Furthermore, it can draw attention to the plays' internal complexity in a way that showcases their meaning. Desjardins again:

Designing sound for Shakespeare 167

I would hope that my designs not only draw out the individual elements of a Shakespearean story, but also help the audience build connections between them. It is in those interconnections that we can really see the brilliance of Shakespeare's work, and as the sound designer, I am uniquely positioned within the design team to both identify and track those connections as they develop over the course of a given play.[39]

Contemporary sound designers, alert to the multifarious ways in which sound, place, action, object and memory can be interconnected, use the tools of their trade to highlight the exquisite patchwork that is Shakespeare's dramaturgy, connecting pieces together that the audience might not otherwise perceive. As theatre sound design becomes increasingly sophisticated in conception and execution, it reveals more about Shakespeare's plays, and what they can mean in changing contexts. Shakespearean sound design is not unitary but multiform, reflecting the diversity of the work itself, though designing in ways that engage with early modern theatre practice is in vogue, and not just at the reconstructed Globe Theatre and the Sam Wanamaker Playhouse in London. Designing sound for Shakespeare can create a connection to the noise of the theatrical past, which, if you listen very carefully, you can sometimes discern in contemporary productions, if only imaginatively or in spirit.

Notes

1   Kevin Ewert, 2011, 'The Thrust Stage is Not Some Direct Link to Shakespeare', *Shakespeare Bulletin*, 29:2 p. 170.
2   David Lindley, 2006, *Shakespeare and Music*, London: Arden Shakespeare, pp. 90–103.
3   Ibid., p. 99.
4   James J. Mainard O'Connell, 2009, 'Hell is Discovered', in Christopher Cobb and M. Thomas Hester (eds.) *Renaissance Papers 2008*. Raleigh, North Carolina: North Carolina State University, p. 79.
5   Quoted in Nick Shave, 2011, 'Shakespeare's Rattle and Roll: Music at the Globe Theatre'. *The Guardian*. [Online]. Available: www.theguardian.com/music/2011/jun/09/shakespeares-globe-music [accessed 30 March 2016].
6   Ibid.
7   Bruce R. Smith, 1999, *The Acoustic World of Early Modern England: Attending to the O-Factor,* Chicago: University of Chicago Press, p. 56.
8   Ibid., p. 208.
9   Kenneth Delong, 2008, 'Arthur Sullivan's Incidental Music to Henry Irving's Production of Macbeth (1888)', in Richard Foulkes (ed.), *Henry Irving: A Re-evaluation of the Pre-eminent Victorian Actor-Manager,* Aldershot: Ashgate, p. 183.
10 John Ripley, 2005, 'Sociology and Soundscape: Herbert Beerbohm Tree's 1908 Merchant of Venice', *Shakespeare Quarterly*, 56:4 pp. 385–410.
11 Helen Cole King, 2008, 'The Echo from Within: The Role of Stage Music in Peter Brook's Performance of Shakespeare', *Contemporary Theatre Review*, 18:4: 412.
12 Emma Johnson, 2004, Interview with Ross Brown [Online]. British Library, p. 15.
13 William B. Worthen, 2010, *Drama: Between Poetry and Performance*, Chichester: Wiley-Blackwell, p. 134.

14 Nicholas John Dekker, 2007, 'Radio Macbeth (Review)', *Theatre Journal*, 59:4 pp. 660–661.
15 2012, Pers. Comm., 18 July.
16 2012, Pers. Comm., 3 July.
17 2012, Pers. Comm., 4 July.
18 2012, Pers. Comm., 4 July.
19 2012, Pers. Comm., 31 July.
20 2012, Pers. Comm., 18 July.
21 2012, Pers. Comm., 31 July.
22 2012, Pers. Comm., 4 July.
23 *Henry V*, 3.1: 35.
24 Peter Kirwan, 2008, The Bardathon: Twelfth Night @ The Courtyard Theatre [Online], n.p.
25 2012, Pers. Comm., 23 July.
26 Bertolt Brecht, Willett, John, Manheim, Ralph and Fried, Erich, 1979, *Bertolt Brecht: Poems 1913–1956*, London: Methuen, p. 341.
27 2012, Pers. Comm., 23 July.
28 Bruce Johnson, 2005, 'Hamlet: Voice, Music, Sound', *Popular Music*, 24:2 p. 263.
29 *A Midsummer Night's Dream*, 3.1: 129.
30 *A Midsummer Night's Dream*, 3.1: 133.
31 Ibid., 3.2: 397–8.
32 Ibid., 4.1: 83.
33 *The Tempest*, 3.2: 150.
34 *The Tempest*, 3.2: 149.
35 William B. Worthen, 2003, *Shakespeare and the Force of Modern Performance*, Cambridge: Cambridge University Press, p. 13.
36 Tiffany Stern, 2004, 'Repatching the Play', in Peter Holland and Stephen Orgel (eds) *From the Script to the Stage in Early Modern England*, Houndmills: Palgrave Macmillan, p. 155.
37 2012, Pers. Comm., 12 August.
38 2012, Pers. Comm., 4 July.
39 2012, Pers. Comm., 4 July.

Bibliography

2012. Programme for Filter Theatre's *A Midsummer Night's Dream*. Manchester: Royal Exchange Theatre.

Brecht, Bertolt, Willett, John, Manheim, Ralph and Fried, Erich 1979. *Bertolt Brecht: Poems 1913–1956,* London: Methuen.

Dekker, Nicholas John 2007. "Radio Macbeth (Review)", *Theatre Journal,* 59:4 pp. 660–661.

Delong, Kenneth 2008. "Arthur Sullivan's Incidental Music to Henry Irving's Production of *Macbeth* (1888)", in Richard Foulkes (ed.), *Henry Irving: A Re-evaluation of the Pre-eminent Victorian Actor-Manager,* Aldershot: Ashgate, pp. 149–184.

Ewert, Kevin 2011. "The Thrust Stage is Not Some Direct Link to Shakespeare", *Shakespeare Bulletin,* 29:2 pp. 165–176.

Folkerth, Wes 2002. *The Sound of Shakespeare,* London: Routledge.

Johnson, Bruce 2005. "*Hamlet:* Voice, Music, Sound", *Popular Music,* 24:2 pp. 257–267.

Designing sound for Shakespeare 169

Johnson, Emma 2004. *Interview with Ross Brown* [Online]. British Library. Available: www.bl.uk/projects/theatrearchive/brown.html [accessed 26 July 2012].

King, Helen Cole 2008. "The Echo from Within: The Role of Stage Music in Peter Brook's Performance of Shakespeare", *Contemporary Theatre Review*, 18:4 pp. 412–424.

Kirwan, Peter 2008. *The Bardathon: Twelfth Night @ The Courtyard Theatre* [Online]. Available: http://blogs.warwick.ac.uk/pkirwan/entry/twelfth_night_the_1_2_3/ [accessed 27 July 2012].

Lindley, David 2006. *Shakespeare and Music*, London: Arden Shakespeare.

Magnus, Laury and Cannon, Walter W. (eds.) 2012. *Who Hears in Shakespeare?: Auditory Worlds on Stage and Screen*, Florham, NJ: Fairleigh Dickinson University Press.

O'Connell, James J. Mainard 2009. "Hell is Discovered", in Christopher Cobb and M. Thomas Hester (eds.), *Renaissance Papers 2008*, Raleigh, NC: North Carolina State University, pp. 65–88.

Ripley, John 2005. "Sociology and Soundscape: Herbert Beerbohm Tree's 1908 *Merchant of Venice*", *Shakespeare Quarterly*, 56:4 pp. 385–410.

Shave, Nick 2011. "Shakespeare's Rattle and Roll: Music at the Globe Theatre". *The Guardian*, June 9. Available: www.theguardian.com/music/2011/jun/09/shakespeares-globe-music [accessed 20 February 2014].

Smith, Bruce R. 1999. *The Acoustic World of Early Modern England: Attending to the O-Factor*, Chicago, IL: University of Chicago Press.

Stern, Tiffany 2004. "Repatching the Play", in Peter Holland and Stephen Orgel (eds.) *From the Script to the Stage in Early Modern England*. Houndmills: Palgrave Macmillan, pp. 151–177.

Worthen, William B. 2003. *Shakespeare and the Force of Modern Performance*, Cambridge: Cambridge University Press.

Worthen, William B. 2010. *Drama: Between Poetry and Performance*, Oxford: Wiley-Blackwell.

Chapter 10

BEYOND LANGUAGE

Performing "true-meant design;"[1] "that risky and dangerous negotiation between a doing ... and a thing done"[2]

Dorita Hannah

> Visual dramaturgy... does not mean an exclusively visually organized drama-
> turgy but rather one that is not subordinated to the text and can therefore freely
> develop its own logic... In this sense the gaze in turn is a reading gaze, the scene
> a writing (graphy), a poem, written without the writing implements of a writer.
> (Hans-Thies Lehmann: Postdramatic Theatre)

Prologue... before the word

Before the word there was a body gesturing in material space, and before that space was scenically written (as sceno-graphy) there was an imagination calling the immaterial (gods and ghosts) into the lived environment. This chapter, acknowl-edging the stage as a liminal space existing both before, through and beyond language, proffers it as a site for designing inter-textual, intercultural and interdis-ciplinary Shakespearean utterances liberated from the burden of an 'original' language.[3] Interlaced with statements contributed by scenographers in Belgium, Brazil, Bulgaria, Canada, Estonia, Finland, Holland, Italy, Mexico, New Zealand, Singapore and Venezuela, the text explores how the spatio-visual dramaturgy of scenography contributes its own language as performative (active and abstract) rather than connotative (descriptive and mimetic) utterances. This furthers J.L. Austin's argument in *How to Do Things With Words*, where 'speech acts' expand beyond language into action itself – saying can be enacting rather than describing.[4] If within the illocutionary act of speaking something is being done, which consti-tutes action itself, then within the illocutionary act of designing something is being done through constructing and crafting thought. Just as statements can be active rather than descriptive, the material, gestural and spatial elements that accompany them also contain a performative force, suggesting *How To Say Things Without Words*, or in the case of this chapter, *How Scenography Does (With and Without Words)*.

But first... some words

Scenography, as an artistic practice, allows us designers to execute our ideas with-out words. However, an essay such as this specifically requires written language to articulate aspects of a lived, communal experience, received via an event. Our role is to design this experience; principally through the skills, materials and artefacts we have as theatre-artists. Words are utilized *before* and *after* the event as *representations* of both an unrealized action and one that has passed. But during the event, design speaks for itself as a *presentation*. Nevertheless what follows unavoidably requires words, especially from those designers for whom English is not necessarily their first language but who fearlessly and joyfully tackle the plays of history's greatest English playwright: claimed as "the favourite playwright and artist of the whole world".[5] In this case words help construct my argument, specifically framed through the lens of performance design as an expanded notion of scenography.

Performance – as an aesthetic, strategic and operational act occurring within and without theatre – tends to be designed. *Design* – as creative undertaking, inventive action and aesthetic artefact – invariably performs. *Performance Design* – a contemporary rethinking of scenography (also referred to as theatre/scenic/stage design) – therefore provides a critical tool for negotiating and critiquing the proliferation of multiple historical, aesthetic and quotidian actions currently played out on the world stage and streamed live to us 24/7 via the screens of smart phones, televisions, computer monitors and architectural façades.

The words that make up the title of this chapter on designing Shakespearean performance beyond the bard's initial language combine his reference to design as a precise and meaningful purpose, and theorist Elin Diamond's reference to performance itself as both reiterative act and discursive object. Performance design is therefore established as simultaneously active and activating: and, as with the many *designs* to which Shakespeare refers (none of which are the visual creative inventions we now associate with the word), something is always at stake. However, what this chapter focuses on is the role design plays when spoken language is no longer central: when Shakespeare's words are translated, truncated or transferred into movement, image, environment, object, sensation, relationship and experience.

Performance text

> *The "visceral" qualities of Shakespearean drama are important to me, because the revelation of the unspeakable and unpredictable truths of human nature and the enigma of the world and the self are a very distant approach to the "heroic" aspect of tragic man and the "cathartic" role of Greek tragedy – my native theatrical culture. However, when producing a Shakespearean play in contemporary Greek, bad or outdated translations tend to "cripple" actors, directors and designers who are held back by a problematic theatrical text, which they cannot fully explore and "exploit". Nevertheless, there are adaptations where the formal language becomes of minor importance. In these cases, theatre creators are freed from the constraints of verse or the play's construction to focus more on its mood, atmosphere and meanings: setting forth a parallelism to actual and local situations and realities. I am interested in going beyond the visual aspects of performance in order for design to speak a "new Shakespearean language": through, for example, aural or olfactory environments, tactile surfaces or by the use of taste. Embracing*

> *the audience in a sensory theatrical experience, and not a purely intellectual process,*
> *contributes to a more in-sightful perception of Shakespearean world theory.*
>
> (Athena Stourna: Scenographer: Greece)

We Anglophone lovers of Shakespearean drama – as spoken poetry and narrative verse – need to recognize that many performances of his work around the world are not presented in its original language: a fact that is highly relevant in relation to the fragmented global reality of our times; dominated as they are by Western-centric discourse and frequently presided over by English as the *lingua franca*. Taking *Performance Design* as a more contemporary practice that moves beyond serving written text and stage direction, I will assert it as the means of harnessing dynamic forces in our lived reality while providing a critical tool for reflecting, confronting and realigning world views. It is the enduring stories and conceptual underpinnings constructed through the poetics of Shakespeare's antiquated language that continue to provide resource material for those who translate him into 'other' languages – spoken and/or gestural – expressing contemporary cultures outside of the English-speaking world. Yet the seminal productions to which I will refer have been presented to, and well received by, Anglophone audiences.

Even for Anglophones Shakespearean is a foreign speech, requiring foreknowledge of the language and narrative or, at very least, a synopsis of the play's events in order for the uninitiated to wade through an archaic vocabulary, which is rhythmically constructed to be ideally pronounced 'trippingly on the tongue'.[6] Yet, despite no longer being in anyone's mother-tongue, Shakespearean performance has tended to focus on the ear rather than the eye, denying the fact that language, not only tongue-based, can be visual. This is in keeping with Peter Holland's observation of "a fundamental anxiety about how Shakespeare's plays are heard rather than watched, about the extent to which the playgoers are audience (hearers) rather than spectators (watchers)."[7] By taking the written word as just one element to be materialized, incorporated, modified or interpreted, I will draw upon Marco De Marinis' reconsideration of the 'theatrical text' as a 'performance text': "a complex network of different types of signs, expressive means, or actions, coming back to the etymology of the word 'text' which implies the idea of texture, of something woven together."[8]

Performance, in its broadest sense – as effective and affective action – could therefore be considered an interweaving of multiple textures in order to be read as a spatiotemporal experience and, ultimately, a woven relationship between elements and among people. De Marinis' definition of dramaturgy as "the set of techniques/theories governing the composition of the performance-as-text" and Hans-Thies Lehmann's assertion of scenography as "visual dramaturgy", makes room for performance design as a fluctuating and ever-emerging interdisciplinary field in which words, images, and other elements form distinctive threads entwined in the unified fabric of the event. This allows for a deconsecration of Shakespeare's written and spoken language in order to affirm the inter-textual possibilities of his work beyond its original wording.

BEYOND LANGUAGE 173

Shakespeare still carries a heavy load on his shoulders: too much respect for his written text tends to extinguish varied kinds of thinking and consequently the opportunity to see his plays differently. Things can go wrong when speaking out his profound stories as literature, because if the theatre tradition is too text-based – even when translated into different languages – artists, directors, performance designers and others can forget the essential question in all art-making: what it is that moves/thrills/interests or speaks to me in this text with respect to the present – in relation to now? In order to interest me as a designer, Shakespeare's written contents should be treated differently: as varying landscapes seen from personal angles. If the creative team is willing to shake it up, to violate and dismember it – to take a risk and add a personal quality to the artwork – I would be keen to go on the journey. This way Shakespeare remains everlasting.

(Reija Hirvikoski: Performance Designer: Finland)

Borderline images beyond language

Shakespeare's stories survive their original spoken texts through reworkings into 'other' texts – orchestrations of music, voice, movement and fragmented language – seen in iconic works such as Giuseppe Verdi's operas (*Macbeth, Otello* and *Falstaff* 1847–93); Prokofiev's ballet (*Romeo and Juliet,* 1935); and Heiner Müller's *Hameltmachine* (1990). Yet there are also interpretive 'Shakespearean-esque' events from which 'a theatre of images' is continually remembered: the collaborations of the two Peters, Zadek and Pabst, in their provocative "travesty versions"[9] (*Merchant of Venice, King Lear, Othello, As You Like It,* 1972–7); Tadashi Suzuki's cultural cross-castings (*The Tale of Lear* and *The Chronicle of Macbeth,* 1988–92); Lindsey Kemp's counter-culture camp caught on video (*Midsummer Night's Dream,* 1984); Heiner Müller's political bricolage (*Hamletmachine/Hamlet,* 1990) as originally designed by Erich Wonder and subsequently staged by USA's Robert Wilson and Argentina's El Periférico de Objetos; Peter Greenaway's mediated vision using cinema, collage and animation (*Prospero's Books,* 1991); Needcompany's multimodal productions (*Julius Caesar, Macbeth, King Lear* and *Storm,* 1991–2001); Societas Rafaello Sanzio's confrontation with the grotesque (Giulio Caesare, 1997), Nigel Charnock's physical onslaught inspired by the Sonnets (*Fever,* 2003); Jürgen Gosch and Johannes Schütz's award-winning abject blood-bath (*Macbeth,* 2005); Toneelgroep Amsterdam's 6-hour production of *The Roman Tragedies* (*Coriolanus, Julius Caesar, Antony and Cleopatra,* 2007–); and, most recently, Punchdrunk Company's mashup of 'that Scottish play' with Hitchcock film noir (*Sleep No More,* 2011).

While Shakespeare's poetry (both original and translated) may ring in our ears long after the event, we can also be left with enduring sensate images and confronting actions: a European Othello in blackface and dreadlock wig smearing his blackness all over the white body and gown of Desdemona; Ariel as Cupid on a swing, creating the tempest by urinating on a model ship tossed about on the surface of a pool; Mark Antony standing on a plinth and delivering his famous address *sotto voce* through a gaping hole in his neck; a dancer feverishly hurling his body off the stage and into the audience while reciting the Sonnets; Macbeth and his bloody clan trapped naked within a black box; Cleopatra slopping champagne onto a beige couch among many beige couches occupied by spectators who gaze at her image on multiple screens; and a broken Lady Macbeth being bathed in a room full of baths surrounded by masked onlookers. In all these impressions – often creating what Dennis Kennedy refers to as "scenic dislocation and visual anarchy"[10] – the very 'real' has infiltrated the theatre through a rejection of mimesis and text analysis, in favour of images presenting what Peter Stein disdainfully referred to as "Shakespeare with his trousers down".[11] This droll remark is echoed in a further enduring image of an empty stage on which a be-suited Lear appears after the storm wearing a magnificent Native American headdress constructed from flowers, and approaches us with his trousers around his ankles. The designer/director of this production is Jan Lauwers of Needcompany who writes:

> *What I am looking for in my theatre work is the moment when form and content make an 'absolute' image that goes beyond all anecdotalism. Moments when time seems to stand still and the image carves itself into the memory. I call them borderline images. King Lear is an image that looks back at the audience, arrogant, provocative and in deathly silence. King Lear does not give any answers. It shows malevolence and suffering without comment. For that reason it is perhaps 'too huge for the stage'.*
> (Jan Lauwers: Director/Designer: Belgium)[12]

Many of the 'borderline images' mentioned above are re-called as signatures of the director: some (like Lauwers) are designers themselves; many utilize designers as instruments to their particular aesthetic; while others have operated in long-term fruitful collaborations with designers as a generally silent partner. Yet what makes all of these images lasting is that design speaks its own language within a multi-layered performance text.

The universal appeal of Shakespeare was played out during the 2012 Olympic Games when all 37 of his plays were performed in almost as many languages in London's Globe Theatre. These performances were generally premised on the long-standing idea that Shakespeare's verbal scenography entails minimal design input and that his universality requires only the standardized Elizabethan stage. However, in order to construct an argument for inter-textuality through perform-ance design, specific to Shakespeare's global significance, this chapter will consider how design performs as a leading element in postdramatic theatre and how non-Anglophone designers approach the task, particularly Dutch scenographer Jan Versweyveld of Toneelgroep Amsterdam whose contribution to *The Roman Tragedies* attends to the complexities of our time. We cannot address contemporary designs of Shakespeare without referring to Punchdrunk's wordless *Sleep No More*, which has extended its reach to those who would never consider attending a Shakespearean play.

Design, liberated from the burden of Shakespearean language, becomes a sensory script for critiquing our contemporary times, saturated with media over-load and ghosts in the machinery as well as the ever-present and problematic threat

BEYOND LANGUAGE 175

of annihilation. The productions mentioned above reconfigure the bard as a theatre artist whose textual thinking remains contemporary when rethought through context as well as scenography (spatial inscription): demonstrating what William B. Worthen advocates as *interpretive participation rather than interpretation.*[13] Although the focus here is on high-profile European productions, many of the statements peppering the text (indented and italicized) come from a range of fellow scenographers who responded to my query: "What is the importance of Shakespeare's work to you and how can design speak a new Shakespearean language?"

> *Shakespeare provides a foundation for poetic language in the English-speaking world. As such his texts are more than just theatrical scripts, but exist as a common vocabulary of archetypal characters, dramatic devices and poetic strategies that a wide range of creative practices make use of. Performance design expands on the limits of spoken language using the holistic treatment of performance through design and fine art strategies to engage with the underlying spatial constructions in Shakespearean text and his intricate poetic worlds. Thus, the equally 'multivocal' and poetic languages of design practice can make use of vocabularies that are visual, aural, material, experiential, and social to construct alternative languages for performance beyond the didactic and logocentric worlds of traditional dramatic performance.*
>
> (Sam Trubridge: Performance Designer: New Zealand)

Performance design

> As an interdisciplinary model *performance design* considers how design artefacts – whether objects, materials, images, gestures, garments or environments – are inextricably bound to performance through notions of embodiment, action and the event in which stories are told, forces are harnessed and roles are played out. In considering the participatory role of a co-creative audience, this fluid and emerging field provides a critical tool for reflecting and challenging worldviews.
>
> (Hannah/Harsløf: Introduction to *Performance Design*)

While the *Routledge Companion to Directors' Shakespeare* focused on platforming the singular heroic director, we know that designers in theatrical productions are multiple, playing with various materialities and media. We are also mindful that, since this 2008 directors' cut, a proliferation of artistic ensembles (avoiding the word theatre) have confounded a clear definition of creative roles. The conventional hierarchy of the theatre company has been troubled by more horizontal playing fields in which the players mix it up: swapping the various parts to complicate authorship and keep the live action fresh and in-the-moment. Designers (who variously orchestrate sound, light, costumes, setting and image) now have greater opportunities to move beyond the traditionally staged theatrical scene emerging from the shadows that bound them to serving director and script, and into the light where they can be actively present theatre-artists; instigators of and collaborators in

176 Dorita Hannah

the event. This new role is more appropriate in a world that, as theorist Jon McKenzie states, "has become a designed environment in which an array of global performances unfold".[14] McKenzie proposes that the complexity of our contemporary condition, in which grand narratives, theatricality and the everyday fold into each other, could be understood through the discursive tool of 'performance design'.[15]

In order to advocate an expanded approach to scenography or theatre design – in which theatre-artists design performance (rather than *for* performance) and design itself performs alongside live actors – it is necessary to further elucidate what design is and does.

Design today is broadly understood as the conception, development and execution of a plan or convention for generating objects, environments, materials and systems. As a relatively recent, cultural and professional practice encompassing many fields – from fashion to architecture, from installation to communication – design tends to focus on the creative process undertaken towards a constructed product by utilizing aesthetic and technological principles. It also involves a tactical approach, conscious decisions and multiple varying philosophies through an integration of the scientific (rational) and the artistic (intuitive): the pragmatic and the poetic; matter and thought. However, going back to the fourteenth century, the term design (from *designare:* de+signare) enters the lexicon as an act of marking, signing or distinguishing, in which actions and things are contrived, devised and appointed; binding artistic thinking with tactical strategies through invention.

For Shakespeare, design – as a scheme, plot, plan and enterprise – tends to be political and strategic, and therefore far from an aesthetic creation. Lucio's claim in *Measure for Measure* that Duke Vincentio's "givings out were an infinite distance from his true-meant design" reveals the ever-present gap between the saying and the doing: between language and its reception; between idea and its ultimate realization. We now speak of designing campaigns, curricula, crimes and even war. As a form of invention, design is a carefully conceived strategy that, not always achieved, is capable of falling short of affect and effect. Both verb (a doing) and noun (a thing done), it is a potentially energetic and galvanizing force. In conventional theatre, design is a *projective strategy* – initially represented through descriptions, drawings and models – and a *complex artefact* that orchestrates the material and immaterial elements comprising what Arnold Aronson calls "the all-encompassing and transformative visio-spatial field of the stage".[16] However, Performance Studies, with its interdisciplinary focus – or even its claim to be a "post-discipline of inclusions"[17] – has provided a more open discursive field that works between theatricality's overtly orchestrated artifice and the dynamic, fluctuating forces of performativity, whereby the lived world is regarded as a complex construction of manifold macro – and micro-performances capable of being isolated, framed and manipulated. This opens up a new interdisciplinary design field within which to practise and theorize aesthetic, cultural and everyday experiences, where cultural artefacts are recognized for their performative charge.

Scenography has its roots in ancient Greek drama and, by the Renaissance, Continental theatre integrated perspectival stage scenery and performers with the existing architecture occupied by an audience arranged before an ideal view. As 'spatial scripting' it strongly influenced urban, rural and domestic planning, rendering the designed world theatrical as exemplified in Sebastiano Serlio's *Architecttura* (1545) where *scenografia* incorporated the spectators, scenery and building in perspectival constructions, influencing architectural constructions outside the theatre. However, over the centuries, this 'Italianate model' tended to focus on a constructed scene created solely within the controlled environment of a prescribed (and therefore pre-scripted) stage, burdened by regulations and expectations for which scenographers design. This pervasive proscenium stage continues to dominate, despite radical spatial revolutions from last century's avant-garde. Nevertheless, through continuing developments from representation to presentation – from the mimetic to the authentic, from stagecraft to artistry – the most interesting and relevant contemporary scenography has become interdisciplinary, intercultural and interactive: thereby occupying a productive place *in-between* the conventional theatre and life's multiple stages where perceptual and imaginative shifts can occur.

Over the past century theatre design discourse has broken through the traditional conception of 'scenography', as the framed perspectival scene, in order to proffer a more contemporary notion of 'performance design' as the interplay of shifting perceptual dynamisms in which the designer takes on a more constructive, dramaturgical and directorial role. As previously mentioned, rather than design things – sets, costumes, lighting, sound and projection – the role is to orchestrate material and immaterial elements at play within the performance field in order to design the event itself as a shared spatiotemporal experience. This addresses Marvin Carlson's bracketed remark in *Performance: A Critical Introduction:* "(even in the theatre we do not speak of how well the scenery or costumes performed)".[18] As I have written elsewhere, this exclusion of designed elements reinforces a general denial of the performativity of places and things, and their ability not only actively to extend the performing body, but also to perform without and in spite of the human body. Jiři Veltrusky counters this bias when he writes, "even a lifeless object may be perceived as the performing subject, and a live human being may be perceived as an element completely without will".[19]

Rather than standing in for scenography, performance design expands its definition and reach. By adopting a performative approach, scenographers are aware of the dynamic role their work plays within the event: transforming 'scenery' into an environment that expands beyond any physical or virtual frame. Operating as a *performance field* this environment is a symbiosis between the varying onstage elements (including performers and spectators) that fluctuate in their powers but unite in their effect. Through an aesthetic 'acting out', performance design recognizes that space precedes action – as action – and is therefore culturally and politically loaded. I am consequently positing performance designers as active agents: artists, provocateurs, collaborators, activists and socio-political commentators, whose 'designs' – as marks and a marking out – are inter-textual orchestrations in time and space.

178 Dorita Hannah

Having explicated the historic trajectory of scenography, it could be said that this legacy bears little relevance to the Elizabethan stage, since English theatre stood apart from the baroque exemplar that developed into the enduring Italianate stage. And yet, if we were to ignore the perspectival construction of the image and look at Serlio's *scenografia* principally as the amalgamation of architecture, stage and audience, then the Shakespearean model, which wraps its vertically layered public around the universal landscape of a raised platform, provides an ideal (and idealized) model.

Working with Shakespeare is an artistic privilege in every way. I have been blasted by the power and beauty of his poetry and the profoundness of his language, which I am able to enjoy in English but have also worked and experienced it through translations into other languages. Having designed seven Shakespeare plays so far – Midsummer Night's Dream, Twelfth Night, (twice), The Tempest (twice), Othello, and Lear – I consider him to be one of the finest architects of words. However I deeply believe that his unique power is more about action, emotion and space-time fluidity. Since I was a student I became aware of the relationship between the Elizabethan stage and the structure of its plays. I apprehended how Elizabethan playwrights understood the potentiality of that stage and wrote for peculiar spatial conventions. The action works malleably through doors and traps, entrances and exits. Simultaneous events in different locations may be easily staged without worrying about the audience de-coding fluctuations in space and time. Shakespearean texts work, even in translation, because they are not only about words and diction but mainly concern the perfect combination of human actions and emotions in a spatiotemporal journey. They therefore flow well in foreign languages, with characters becoming real and present even if they are dressed in silk kimonos or saris. Shakespeare is not about words; he is about the World.

(Monica Raya: Scenographer: Mexico)

Going global

Perhaps Shakespeare is treated with more artistic freedom in non-Anglo cultures because the translation to another language becomes the first stage of textual interpretation. So often a rather loose artistic interpretation is the only way to convey the true essence and spirit of the original text. Some English-speaking Bulgarian directors intermingle Shakespeare's original text and its translation, while others create postmodern collages from several of his plays. As far as design is concerned, realistic and illustrative approaches are long forgotten. I have therefore never perceived Shakespearean language as a burden or a limitation in my practice. On the contrary – it is a most powerful and delightful source of inspiration and much more important than the plot itself. Since Shakespeare's stories focus on human nature they still move people deeply and allow for design to constantly reinvent itself and speak a language that is true to its time – contemporary, sincere and live.

(Marina Raytchinova: Scenographer: Bulgaria)

BEYOND LANGUAGE 179

Elizabethan theatre is *indigenous* to England along with its wooden O – the iconic Globe Theatre – fittingly described in the prologue to *Henry V* as capable of cramming many worlds within its embrace.[20] This concept of a universal realm has been notably outlined by Francis Yates who referred to the Globe as 'a cosmic theatre' for acting out "the drama of life within the theatre of the world... the pattern of the universe, the idea of a Macrocosm, the world stage on which the microcosm acted its parts".[21] However, rather than the simplistic notion of a simple stage, relying solely on "imaginary forces" to conjure up manifold worlds through words, this architectural model established a complex spatiality for horizontal and vertical movement and three-dimensional placement during the performance, this was afforded by multiple entrances onto a platform with floor trap and posts supporting a roof with a descent machine, as well as the overlooking balconies that extended the audience's galleries into the stage fabric. As Nicholas Till maintains in his essay 'Oh to make boardes to speak!', "we are deceiving ourselves if we believe that minimalist performances of this kind lack a scenographic dimension".[22]

The Globe is what Edward Gordon Craig would have referred to as a 'simplified stage',[23] something the English designer sought to create throughout his career. Rather than the representational *Pictorial Scene,* Craig focused on the presentational *Architectonic Scene,* which was more fixed in form with shifts of location and atmosphere defined by discretely moving constructed elements, large iconic properties, groupings of performers and coloured lighting.[24] Emphasizing 'place' Craig wished to render scenography a "*genuine* thing. A work of architecture. Unalterable except for trifling pieces here and there."[25] Searching for essential form he distilled common and persisting features in historic and international architecture into theatrical archetypes, which were later cohered into his proposal for *St Matthew Passion* (1918) – represented in a large wooden model archived in London's Victoria and Albert Museum. Like the Globe, Craig's monumental architecture, with its levels, stairs, bridges and receding arches, suggested a complex performative setting constructed of multiple spatialities that worked with an audience's imagination to complete the places it evoked. This abstract, performative environment is akin to that which Fabrizio Crisafulli calls for when eschewing historic reconstructions of the Globe in favour of more contemporary "non-referential" settings:

> *Trying to reconstruct the original architectural conditions of the Elizabethan theatre to perform Shakespeare's plays, as with the various "reconstructions" of the Globe Theatre, doesn't make sense. The social context and public expectations in which such theatres were conceived and operated no longer exist and cannot be rebuilt. Rebuilding the physical structures only creates simulacra: just empty forms. In representations of Shakespeare's plays now, we should work on the universal characters and themes that continue to survive in our time, which we must necessarily face with a contemporary look. Regarding design, places in Elizabethan plays were evoked primarily through the word (the so-called "verbal scenography"). It would therefore be consistent now to translate the evocative power of the word into that of a non-referential setting with*

abstract character: enabling free associations and avoiding connotative elements with respect to place and time. Abstract scenic elements, motivated by our present world, are capable of giving space to the fantasy and allowing the spectator a wide range for imagination, as with Shakespeare's "verbal scenography", but in a new way.

(Fabrizio Crisafulli: Theatre Director and Visual Artist: Italy)

Before the late twentieth-century project to create literal reconstructions of the Globe around the world, its universal landscape became the architectonic scene of the symbolist avant-garde and eventually influenced later scenographers as an abstracted performance landscape. What is most valuable about the original Shakespearean stage is its intention to provide a utopian global model, which is not only spatial but also conceptual: a phenomenon that speaks across boundaries, languages and epochs. For over 500 years, academia has tended to focus on Shakespeare as a literary dramatist rather than a commentator who captured the breadth and details of the human condition and its multiple, on-going performances: in war, in love, in play and in power. As Henry Turner points out, Shakespeare's plays provide the means to explore and question contemporary humanity, through their manifold historical, social, political and ethical circumstances.[26]

The notion of the playhouse as the site where Shakespeare explored identity through difference – allowing us to question 'outsiders' in modern society – was taken up through the *Globe to Globe* project during London's Cultural Olympiad in 2012. Running concurrently with the Olympic Games, the World Shakespeare Festival co-opted England's indigenous stage as a universal landscape for universal issues by staging "37 plays in 37 languages" – including Maori, Italian, Arabic, Lithuanian, Greek and British Sign Language – all in the reconstructed Globe Theatre on the banks of the Thames. Michael Boyd, artistic director of England's Royal Shakespeare Company, claimed, "Shakespeare is no longer English property. He is the favourite playwright and artist of the whole world, and studied at school by half the world's children", while the Globe's director, Dominic Dromgoole asserted, "Shakespeare is the language which brings us together better than any other." Although proclaiming the bard as 'the world's playwright' may have played into the ubiquitous nationalism of Olympiad hosts, the event also sought to celebrate the "vast array of ethnic communities that make up London's vibrant multicultural landscape" with each of Shakespeare's plays performed in the language of varying companies from around the world.[27] Having significantly contributed to the gentrification and tourism within its neighbourhood of Southwark, the Globe Theatre has come to represent a cosmic universality and the myth of a united world. This is in keeping with Lehmann's description of Shakespeare's theatre as giving the "impression of an open world without borders", reaching across varied spaces and genres, realities, and fictions. The *Globe to Globe* project was unique in globalizing the local and localizing the global, all within that 'girdle' of its wooden walls.

Designing for Shakespeare is like drawing a continent anchored to a territory situated between the firmness of literary excellence and the exasperating fragility of the civilization that produced it, which remains fragile today. The tenuousness of human relations in their power struggles – the main theme of so many historical dramas, tragedies and even some comedies – was materialized, as a metaphor, in the economic poverty that I always faced when I embraced the dream of young theatre groups in Brazil, constantly eager for "new things". Thus, the Merry Wives of Windsor, The Two Gentlemen of Verona *and* Othello, *produced by "Centro de Demolição e Construção do Espetáculo" ("Centre of Demolition and Construction of the scene"), were staged in a small architectural structure of Elizabethan inspiration, which I constructed out of fruit crate boards obtained at street market grounds in Rio de Janeiro – the same material used to build the poorest houses of the favelas at that time. Despite being so fragile, this modest theatre setting was able to travel, withstand rain and storms, and survived. Shakespeare has never frightened or overwhelmed me and I have never intended to produce any "new" image through my various experiences with his work. What I did was take advantage of his spirit of poetic adventure in order to find a poetic language in tune with the world around me, organically, based on what he offers as symbolic material, with total creative freedom and without any embarrassment.*

(Lidia Kosovski: Theatre Design: Brazil)

Corrupt images

Chiara Guidi of Societas Raffaello Sanzio maintains in today's theatre it is absurd to take a piece of Shakespeare and put it on stage... If the text is the fulcrum of the production, it is not possible to invent upon this text and stay true to the text at the same time.[28]

As Guidi's Italian company has also shown, truth to text is no longer relevant because the real has become stranger than fiction: witnessed in productions where the stage fiction is constantly interrupted by an "alien reality" that disturbs the clarity of the spectator's vision by summoning the *real* into reality.[29] In Societas Raffaello Sanzio's 1997 production of *Giulio Cesare* (Julius Caesar), Shakespeare's text was hacked apart and performed in Italian while bodies that do not comply with any 'true-meant design' confront the spectator. Mighty Caesar is a feeble geriatric, Cicero morbidly obese and both Brutus and Cassius are played by anorexics. Live and stuffed animals provide an unsettling stage presence, as do the projected vocal cords of an actor with an endoscope inserted in his throat. Some speeches are made in squeals after inhaling helium and Mark Antony's celebrated "Friends, Romans, countrymen" is croaked out by a man lacking vocal cords, baring the hole from a laryngectomy in his neck (Figure 10.1). Here the field of symbolically constructed representations is exceeded, exposing the *Real*, which Lacan described as an impossible condition associated with the preverbal and thereby transcending language. The power of words is deliberately withheld in this production that focused on the manipulation and misuse of rhetoric inherent to Shakespeare's play.

Figure 10.1 Giulio Cesare, Dalmazio Masini as Marco Antonio, Societas Raffaello Sanzio
Source: Photo courtesy of Societas Raffaello Sanzio

As Lehmann articulates in *Postdramatic Theatre*, our contemporary theatre no longer constructs a "purely fictive cosmos", having lost faith in the dramatic "formation of illusion" when faced with the very 'real'.[30] The dystopic environment that folds audience into an inter-textual scene has replaced Modernism's vision, which prescribed the poetics of a universal spatiality. The revolutions of the avant-garde have finally led to a 'theatre of images' in which visuals, freed from serving the text, develop their own logic as presentation rather than representation. Karen Jürs-Munby states in the introduction to her English translation of Lehmann's book that the world is no longer represented as a surveyable whole and the text has "become just one element in the scenography and general 'performance writing' of theatre".[31] Although the fractured visual landscape of contemporary scenography – withholding a dramatic unification of time, place and action – becomes another form of writing and the performance a text(ile): the philosophical and political become foregrounded in productions that talk about living in the contested and corrupted realities of our own times.

> *For the imaginative practice of scenography, Shakespeare's plays always already contain corrupt images that undermine the unified structure of their narrative universe. This is relevant to his tragedies and his comedies alike. In these corrupt images, the corrupt figures inhabit corrupt scenes in corrupt sites of action, structuring the spectator's*

*consciousness by evoking new images that are equally corrupt. For a scenographer work-
ing with images, these corrupt imaginings become central while generating the
scenographic concept.*

(Lilja Blumenfeld:, Scenographer: Estonia)

Streaming multiple texts

While Lehmann was composing his influential treatise, director-designers such as
Robert Wilson, Jan Fabre, Romeo Castellucci, Jan Lauwers and Robert Le Page
created universally celebrated Shakespearean adaptations coming out of North
America and Europe. However, this section focuses on a long-standing collaboration between Netherlands-based Belgian director, Ivo Van Hove, and Dutch
designer, Jan Versweyveld, who have tackled many of the bard's classics since the
founding of Toneelgroep Amsterdam in 1987. Their production of *The Roman
Tragedies* (Shakespeare's *Coriolanus, Julius Caesar* and *Antony and Cleopatra*), which
has been playing since 2007, situates the audience in the middle of a theatrical,
political, and mediated arena where a continual flow of virtual and visceral
performances is played out for almost six hours.

> *Why Shakespeare? You can only answer with clichés. For instance, in the* Roman
> Tragedies *I am struck time and time again by how contemporary it is, how it's about
> us, right now! It's very mirroring and universal. Other than the dramatic power of the
> language I cannot see the world without Shakespeare. He has been translated into
> Dutch by numerous great writers and we can compare translations and see the richness
> of the language which is fantastic in contemporary Dutch. In the* Roman Tragedies
> *we used a spare translation which still retained a sense of verse. However, the show is
> full of text not only spoken in Dutch, but also subtitles on the monitors and projections
> of the performance with newsreels, and information streamed above the stage with live
> newsfeed as well as the spectators' SMS messages, tweets, and comments taken from
> Facebook and the show's blog. The production is still playing and being adapted around
> the world. It's a living organism that is still very much alive with our company. Over
> the last eight years media has changed and the public themselves are modernizing it.*

(Jan Versweyveld: Scenographer: Holland)

As a demanding touring show, which requires the entire company of 55 performers and technicians, *Roman Tragedies* is staged in a classical proscenium theatre
(Figures 10.2–10.8). However, the audience is invited to move around the auditorium and to occupy the stage, which has a bar for purchasing food and drinks, and
an accessible internet station, as well as makeup and props tables situated in its
wings.

Scattered throughout is a proliferation of beige couches, potted plants, and
video monitors showing live action subtitled in the language of the host country.
Technicians hover and camera operators move discreetly about, following the
action of performers embedded within the onstage audience who eat, drink, and

Figure 10.2 Roman Tragedies, Toneelgroep Amsterdam
Source: Photo Jan Versweyveld

Figure 10.3 Roman Tragedies, Toneelgroep Amsterdam
Source: Photo Jan Versweyveld

BEYOND LANGUAGE 185

use their phones to record the show or communicate to friends and social media (some of their texts returning as streaming data on the *news ticker* above). While a series of clocks shows the current time in various world centres, cameras and microphones are being constantly mobilized to record the highs and lows of politics and romance being played out by the leaders, politicians and lovers whose actions are as relevant today as they were in ancient Rome or Elizabethan London. Pre-recorded footage and streaming LED texts intermix with dramatic action while real-time world events enter the auditorium. The intermedial stage then spills out onto the street when Caesar is chased from the theatre pursued by his rivals and cameramen: exposing an unsuspecting public to violent action, which is difficult to differentiate as real or staged.

Evoking a featureless lobby co-opted for a political convention, the stage setting is deliberately and excessively bland, resembling the predictable décor of a globally distributed hotel chain that can be found in any of the cities where the show is performed. Implanted centrally are two glass walls – war room screens written and overwritten in white marker with battle strategies until completely smeared – between which a platform moves like a mortuary slab carrying the body of each dead character photographed from above and projected to the audience like a crime victim from a tabloid newspaper (their names and dates blazoned above in red LED diodes). The fragmented, multimodal production refers directly to ubiquitous live-streamed news channels – such as BBC, CNN and Al Jazeera – that beam political conventions, global politics, neoliberal agendas and celebrity affairs into our homes, hotel rooms, airport waiting rooms and urban sites.

Here design 'acts out' on an ever-shifting trajectory between conventionally staged scenography and provocative events in public space. Versweyveld, who designed setting, costumes and lighting, states:

> What interests me is to create a new stage reality that is not an illusion or illustration... I am trying to make whatever happens on stage real and for its own purpose. Everything you see on stage is real and present... you see bars, TVs, cables and the technology. We use light to create a dynamic and to subtly lead the public around, but never to make you believe you are somewhere else. We are here together, now, not in Rome or Alexandria.
>
> (Jan Versweyveld)

As a "living organism" the streaming text from world news and social media is absolutely specific to the time and place of each performance. Interweaving the play's events with current affairs and audience responses, the harsh reality of continual conflict and political struggles is brought directly into the theatre. Over its eight-year run (and still counting) geopolitical clashes have come and gone in the world, while some are still being played out on the global stage in the never-ending theatre of war. The spectators who move on and off the stage are as at home as one would be in the anonymous space of a hotel conference centre: in-transit they become part of the performance and therefore complicit as history's bystanders.

Figure 10.4 Roman Tragedies, Toneelgroep Amsterdam
Source: Photo Jan Versweyveld

The inclusion of social media commentary was initiated by the audience itself during the London run (2009) and became an incorporated feature. Versweyveld – acknowledging his collaborative role in the core creative team of director, designer, dramaturge and video-artist (incorporated within a larger team of composers, translators and technicians) – successfully established "a universal forum and a space for debate where the public could share experiences with the players/politicians". He has co-created a performance landscape in which many intersecting texts (visual, aural, written and spoken) combine to emphasize Shakespeare's proposition that the most critical and complex stage is the global one we occupy here and now.

As a framed scene viewed from the auditorium, *Roman Tragedies* includes a constantly shifting onstage audience within its unstable borders. It therefore operates between conventional and immersive theatre practices. The vanguard of contemporary immersive theatre is the UK-based Punchdrunk Theatre, which has been creating celebrated productions in disused buildings since 2000, the most renowned being *Sleep No More*: a 1930s riff on *Macbeth* staged within a highly atmospheric and labyrinthine environment. In the McKittrick Hotel (established in London 2003, Boston 2009 and New York City 2011), words have been replaced by choreographed movement and a warren of gloomy spaces filled with objects that we are invited to explore and touch.[32]

Figures 10.5 Roman Tragedies, Toneelgroep Amsterdam
Source: Photos Jan Versweyveld

Figures 10.6 Roman Tragedies, Toneelgroep Amsterdam
Source: Photos Jan Versweyveld

Figures 10.7 Roman Tragedies, Toneelgroep Amsterdam
Source: Photos Jan Versweyveld

Figures 10.8 Roman Tragedies, Toneelgroep Amsterdam
Source: Photos Jan Versweyveld

Designing experience

While text is, of course, pivotal and central to Shakespeare and its adaptation, there are other ways of underscoring narrative, and poetry that can be as potent or more potent, compelling, and affective. Dance and physical theatre spring to mind here. The physical narrative of these métiers can be devastatingly powerful in reaching out to spectators who are not born to Shakespearean iambic pentameter but who can understand when the right gesture, the right spatial relationship grabs their gut and turns it.

(Kathleen Irwin: Scenographer: Canada)

The design of *Sleep No More*, as a complex spatiotemporal strategy rather than a standalone scenography, advances my earlier claim that space precedes action – as action. Focusing on the third and longest running iteration, housed in an abandoned warehouse within NYC's Chelsea neighbourhood, this section articulates the work of 'artistic director' Felix Barrett and his 'design associates', Livi Vaughan and Bea Minns, who led a design team of over 200 people to create and furnish 93 rooms that lie in wait for a disparate and mobile audience. Meticulously detailed, each installation (Figures 10.9–10.10) enacts its own characters and texts, even before spectators engage with them through their particular actions and inter-actions. Describing the environment as a "cinematic wonderland", Barrett explains that all of Shakespeare's lines were taken apart "with a fine tooth comb... and woven back into the space".[33]

From 7:30–8:30pm every night audience members arrive at 15-minute intervals, leaving the contemporary city behind to walk a dark and winding passage that leads to a noisy speakeasy bar before moving beyond the heavy red velvet drapes to don a hollow-eyed carnival mask and step inside an elevator operated by a cheerful bellhop (he whispered in my ear "I think you will be lucky tonight"). They disembark on any one of five floors and experience an unfurling vertical and horizontal labyrinth of evocative locations tinged with the patina of a bygone era. These include a hospital ward, asylum cell, apothecary's chamber, detective's office, taxidermist's shop, a maze of ruined brick walls and one of wintry trees as well as a forested ballroom – all discovered in the haze of flickering candle light, accompanied by varying aromas and moody music from Hitchcock films. Wandering randomly through the seemingly endless sites spectators can tangibly explore the macabre details (piles of ceramic bedpans, hanging wet clothes, animal bones and false teeth, faded books with sliced pages, jars of dusty curios and baths with blood-stained water). For three hours this community of masked observers drifts, lingers, or races from room to room following unmasked enigmatic characters who occasionally inhabit the shadowy spaces, performing ambiguous actions, snatches of dramatic intrigue and wistful dances. Occasionally a performer unmasks a spectator in an intimate yet uncomfortable private moment (a nurse pulled me into a small room, wrapped me in a blanket on a medical table and stared into my face before inaudibly whispering in my ear).

Anonymized spectators become random phantasmatic elements of the scenes as

Figure 10.9 Sleep No More, Punchdrunk and Emursive
Source: Photo Sarah Krulwich/The New York Times/Redux

Figure 10.10 Sleep No More, Punchdrunk and Emursive
Source: Photo Sarah Krulwich/The New York Times/Redux

they watch from couches and corners or lean over the shoulders of performers. This sensorial design-led production evokes the spatial *emballage* of Tadeusz Kantor where ordinary rooms and objects are rendered dynamic by the multiple meanings in which they are wrapped. Yet Shakespeare's *Macbeth* can only be recognized by the cognoscenti: principally referenced in its obsession with "superstition, and witchcraft and folklore"[34] as well as the more referential appearances of the lead character and his wife who have separate scenes of bathing the blood off their bodies, a banquet scene of repeated gestures visited by a bloody Banquo, and in the final assembly within the ballroom when the forest of rolling trees gathers and disperses leaving a man hanging above the parting audience as it returns to the reality of New York's night-time city.

Of *Sleep No More*'s wordlessness, the *New Yorker* critic wrote:

> Because language is abandoned ... we're forced to imagine it, or to make narrative cohesion of events that are unfolding right before our eyes ... We cannot connect with the characters through the thing that we share: language. We can only watch as the performers reduce theatre to its rudiments: bodies moving in space ... Stripped of what we usually expect of a theatrical performance, we're drawn more and more to the panic the piece incites, and the anxiety that keeps us moving from floor to floor and from room to room, like shuddering inmates.[35]

This sense of entrapment and powerlessness counters the company's claim of freedom, a point emphasized by Worthen who refers to the "depoliticized" masked spectators as "constructed within the spectacle as realist voyeurs, watchers and *readers*, not agents". While *Roman Tragedies'* onstage audience (always aware of being on a stage) are present as individuals, capable of moving around and contributing to the performance through their smart phones, the masked spectators in *Sleep No More* who are instructed to switch their phones off are presided over by black-masked stewards in the shadows, reducing a so-called free choice "of what to watch and where to go".

Combining promenade, environmental, site-specific, and interactive characteristics, works such as *Sleep No More* prompt us to consider the active forces inherent to the natural, constructed and virtual world in relation to scenography. Its cinematic qualities extend the audience reach: appealing to a generation brought up on reality television, film, and gaming who are much more proficient with visual texts and simulacra than the archaic language of Shakespeare. However, the more mediatized approach of Toneelgroep Amsterdam allows the lived world to cohere with that of *The Roman Tragedies*, encouraging us to immerse ourselves while remaining cognizant of the political dimension and continuing relevance of 500-year-old texts.

Epilogue... to say more

> *José Ignacio Cabrujas' interpretation of Othello* — Sonny, Diferencias sobre Otelo, El Moro de Venecia — *poeticized colloquial Venezuelan language while sustaining the*

192 Dorita Hannah

tragic dimension of Shakespeare's characters. Cabrujas used the same language in his stage directions to describe places and actions: atmospheres suggested with poetic turns that had to be interpreted to create in both actors and spectators the perception of a passionate coastal town imprisoned between mountain and sea; light's radiance on the beach, sweating stevedores and a salty stickiness on the skin. I felt plastic on my skin, and I married it. Freed from the constraints of Elizabethan language, I created stairs and levels, small pathways and labyrinths, which I later lined with wrinkled plastic stained with rust; labyrinths that allowed one to be seen and to hide. The result was a rough masculine set – where the feminine felt out of place – in which design, as an essential part of the total experience, contributed to a different understanding of the play without betraying Shakespeare's original intent.

(Fernando Calzadilla: Set/Lighting/Costume Designer: Venezuela)

While postdramatic theatre abjures slavish attention to a single text and purely mimetic representation, it retrieves theatricality in relation to Barthe's notion of "theatre-minus-text", in which the original script becomes submerged in an external language of "sensuous artifice – gesture, time, distance, substance, light". Referring to Shakespeare among others, Barthes advocates "a devouring theatricality" in which "the written text is from the first carried along by the externality of bodies, of objects, of situations; the utterance immediately explodes into substances".[36] The designers to which this chapter refers are aware of how we perform in our daily lives and how their design practices perform as a bridge between onstage scenography and the reality of socio-political strategies in the lived world. Their borderline images exceed the text just as the devouring theatricality of our lived world exceeds the stage. Therefore if we were to consider a designers' Shakespeare then the true-meant designer is Shakespeare himself – the strategist behind the work: devising his multiple and enduring texts for our conscience and imaginations: as generals do war, as presidents do their own campaigns, as terrorists do the perfect attack, leading us into new territories beyond language.

Shakespeare-inspired productions that I have designed for Theatreworks in Singapore (directed by Ong Keng Sen) have used only the bones of the original Shakespearean plot as a framework, replanting them in South Asian scenarios and more contemporary spaces. Spoken word was simplified and re-written, sometimes into the indigenous languages of the cast, and traditional Asian performance cultures were introduced into the mix: Noh, Beijing Opera, Thai classical dance and Indonesian Gamelan as well as contemporary indie rock. This extensive re-thinking allowed me great freedom in design, concocting an almost arbitrary locale for the stage settings. To work on new Shakespearean-inspired productions was a great privilege and the original story's quality remained beguiling, intriguing, and surprisingly accurate when applied with skill to another place, time, or culture. And what fun I had going on these epic design journeys, no longer constrained by an enclosing European architecture or landscape, but free to devise and be liberated in the process. This led me into new territories where oblique cultural references inspired elements to support the main spaces; in Lear *enormous faded*

Indonesian batik curtains and Burmese carpets hinted at a decay in court, and a giant crushed paper screen became a distant and elusive wall of cloud; while in Desdemona *(derived from Othello) a hidden gold-leafed bed within the rough Indian stage served as a kind of gleaming throne of precious metal, and also as a place for madness to unfold.*

(Justin Hill: Scenographer: Singapore)

Notes

1   William Shakespeare. *Measure for Measure.* Lucio: Act 1, Scene 4, line 59.
2   Elin Diamond, *Performance and Cultural Politics* (London; New York: Routledge, 1996), 5.
3   I am indebted to Christopher Balme, who at the ADSA (Australasian Drama Studies Association) conference in 2004 (Wellington, New Zealand) suggested that perhaps more discursive and critical performances eventuate when stagings of Shakespeare are not performed in the original written and spoken language.
4   J.L. Austin: *How to Do Things with Words* (Cambridge, MA: Harvard University Press, 1975), 5–8.
5   www.rsc.org.uk/about-us/updates/world-shakespeare-festival-launch.aspx (accessed 17 April 2014, but since removed from the RSC website). This statement by Michael Boyd, Director of the Royal Shakespeare Company, proliferated in the publicity and press for the World Shakespeare Festival discussed later in this chapter.
6   William Shakespeare, *Hamlet* Act 3, Scene 2, 1–4.
7   Peter Holland: "Shakespeare in the Twentieth-Century Theatre", in *The Cambridge Companion to Shakespeare* (Cambridge: Cambridge University Press, 2001), 208.
8   'Dramaturgy of the Spectator', in *Performance: Critical Concepts in Literary and Cultural Studies*, ed. Philip Auslander (London: Routledge, 2003), 219–35, 209).
9   Dennis Kennedy, *Looking at Shakespeare: A Visual History of 20th Century Performance*, 2nd edition (Cambridge University Press, 2001), 267.
10 Ibid., 270.
11 Ibid. Stein cited by Kennedy.
12 www.needcompany.org/EN/king-lear (accessed 11 February 2016).
13 William B. Worthen, "Intoxicating Rhythms: Or, Shakespeare, Literary Drama and Performance Studies", *Shakespeare Quarterly* 62 (3), Fall 2011, 309–39, 333.
14 Jon McKenzie, "Global Feeling", in *Performance Design* (Copenhagen: Museum Tusculanum Press, 2008), 128.
15 Jon McKenzie, *Perform or Else: From Discipline to Performance* (London: Routledge, 2001), 176.
16 Arnold Aronson, *Looking into the Abyss: Essays on Scenography* (Ann Arbor, MI: University of Michigan Press, 2005), 7. Note that I refer, myself to the *spatio-visual* field, placing the spatial first and thereby privileging a more immersive and sensory approach.
17 Barbara Kirshenblatt-Gimblett, "Performance Studies", in *The Performance Studies Reader*, ed. Henry Bial (London and New York: Routledge, 2004), 43.
18 Marvin Carlson, *Performance: A Critical Introduction* (London: Routledge, 1996), 3.
19 Jiri Veltrusky, "Man and Object in the Theatre", 84.
20 William Shakespeare, *Henry V* (Act 1, Prologue, l 10–15).
21 Frances Yates, *Theatre of the World*, London, 1987, 189.
22 Nicholas Till, "Oh to Make Boards to Speak!" in *Theatre and Performance Design: A Reader in Scenography*, eds., Jane Collins and Andrew Nesbitt (London: Routledge, 2010), 154–161, 160.
23 Craig, Scene (New York: B. Blom, 2006), 15. Craig wrote of "Place" and "Scene": "It is a Place if it Seem Real – it is a Scene if it Seem False", 1n.1.

24 Ibid., 22.
25 Ibid., 5.
26 Henry S. Turner, "Generalization", in *Early Modern Theatricality*, Oxford Twenty-First Century Approaches to Literature (Oxford: Oxford University Press, 2013), 9.
27 www.bbc.co.uk/news/entertainment-arts-14790154 (accessed 11 February 2016).
28 From "A Conversation about the Future", in *The Theatre of Societas Raffaello Sanzio*, Joe Kelleher, Nicholas Ridout, Claudia Castellucci, Chiara Guidi (Taormina: Comitato Taormina Arte, Romeo Castellucci), 25.
29 Alenka Zupančič, "A Perfect Place to Die: Theater in Hitchcock's films," in *Everything You Always Wanted to Know about Lacan (But Were Afraid to Ask Hitchcock)*, Slavoj Žižek (London and New York: Verso, 1992), 79.
30 Hans-Thies Lehmann, *Postdramatic* Theatre (Abingdon: Routledge, 2006), 22.
31 Ibid.,12 and 4.
32 The production is a collaboration between Punchdrunk and Emursive.
33 Video for *Interior Design: Designers' Interviews*, 10 November 2011, www.interiordesign.net/idtv/detail/571/ (accessed 17 April 2014).
34 Ibid.
35 "Shadow and Act: Shakespeare without Words", Hilton Als, *The New Yorker*, 2 May 2011, 86–87, 87.
36 Roland Barthes, from "Baudelaire's Theatre", in *Critical Essays* (Evanston, IL: Northwestern University Press, 1972), 26.

Afterword

Understanding the ways in which designers work to build the settings, costumes, lighting, and sound for productions is akin to understanding the playwright's process. Once we begin to get a sense of the grammar of composition then we can begin to consider the shape of the dramaturgy. The contributors in this volume applied a range of lenses to analyze the ways in which designers created settings, costumes, lighting and sound as a mode of making Shakespeare comprehensible to audiences.

While each demonstrated modes of design analysis, they also reveal through process analysis the methods by which designers parse out meaning and experiment with the potential effectiveness of the choices they make for audiences in their storyboarding or in their collaborative exchanges with the other members of the production network. Ultimately, it is through experiences of performance or the artifacts of performance that capture the visual world of the play that visual analysis begins. They considered the choices of staging, costumes, lighting and sounds in relationship to the plays and to the contemporary circumstances of the audiences present at the performances. Through their methodologies we can better understand how to use the archival remnants of production to color our readings of Shakespearean text. Design history, theory and analysis rely on the interpretation of sketches, renderings and production photos. Each of the contributors made use of these resources to understand the circumstances in which productions were created and made to share a particular interpretation of a range of Shakespearian works.

These scholars considered the interrelations of the designers alongside the collaborative team with whom they worked to build the visual and aural worlds. Both the social and political context of the contemporary period and the social and political worlds of the plays converge in the physical manifestation of the design. For example, as many times as I have heard *Julius Caesar* recited or read its text, it was not until I saw Societas Rafaello Sanzio's *Julio Cesare* that I was able to understand the devastation of civil war and its effects upon the plebian populations of Rome. Both through the use of atypical bodies whose mastectomies and tracheotomies demonstrate the atrocities of war, the burnt out aspects of the stage setting showed these characters in the context of the devastation of the ruins left

196 Afterword

by war. These images stick with me in a more visceral way that the speeches we learned by rote growing up ever did. "Friends, Romans, Countrymen" seems far different when intoned by an actor with the visible markings of war. Color, shape, movement and line created mood and evoked the atmosphere and socio-political climate of the plot. Designers search for the indications within a text for the information that will feed the images that they create. What are the clothes worn to evoke this feeling? Where do the characters need to be? How are locations made clear in the organization of stage space? Further to that we as audience members are given tools to understand how that organization can reveal further nuances about the actions performed.

Designers have a history of practice and style to contend with when collaborating with other members of the production team. The designers showcased in this volume have been particularly adept at finding distinctive solutions in creating their designs. Each has had a significant influence or is typical of dominant trends of a particular period for time. Whether we are speaking of Ming Cho Lee or Alison Chitty who have taught as many designers as designs they have wrought, or of Svoboda or Herrmann whose techniques have influenced a generation of other designers from their sheer innovation or performance designers such as Robert Wilson or Romeo Castellucci their conceptions of Shakespeare have become influential watersheds that have set audience expectations of what Shakespeare should look like in the twenty-first century.

Designs help us gain access to Shakespeare's words and help us understand why the characters behave in the manner that they do. In many of our novice students' minds these productions should be filled with characters dressed in Renaissance garb, wielding swords and golden goblets. Designers analyze Shakespeare to find the clothing, the familiar settings, and sounds that will make tangible equivalent worlds for a contemporary audience. Each of these seminal designers has found a way to make use of the open Elizabethan staging in a manner that allows an imaginative depiction of long lost worlds. While some designers make spare choices to suggest a local or suggest a personality trait, others use broad, bold strokes to challenge audiences to see the plays as they are rather than what they expect them to be.

It is these challenges that reimagine each play in a world that makes sense to its audience, a challenge to find a language or a style to bring out the choices of a director, scenographer or performance designer. Most interesting are the choices that defy expectation and use the familiar in unfamiliar ways opening the words and actions to the experience of live bodies watching actors on a stage carrying out dramatic actions. Designers make actions and words make sense and help audiences to understand what they see and hear. Without the visual and aural environments the plays ought to be poems or radio plays. Live bodies in the presence of an audience are necessary, but also the designed environments to give context to the words and actions performed by actors.

The beauty of Shakespeare is that the plays can be performed with little or no visual and aural embellishment, leaving the audience the space to watch the actors

Afterword 197

move through space and the listen to the text. On the other hand, not necessitating much visual or spatial embellishment opens up the possibilities for whatever can be imagined. As Ninagawa combined Japanese and Chinese styles in his visual display or Orson Welles a pseudo-Caribbean aesthetic, the plays are versatile. Dorita Hannah's final chapter suggests a fashion of a non-language based experience of the plays rooted in the evocation of emotions and feelings within audiences. This post-cultural configuring of culture speaks across cultures to some innate understanding of what it means to be human. As artists explore the ways that new technologies can augment performance the plays bring us back to quintessentially humanistic concerns of what it means to interact with others in tempestuous political and social times. Designers have a skill in organizing and making ineligible experience.

Designers take the unfamiliar and help guide audiences through and experience creating a context and a set of intelligible rules to dictate how to understand and how to begin to interrelate all that is being depicted. Designers see different things in Shakespeare because they are showing us how to pay attention to the social and political attributes that help make a character's action intelligible. Whether a designer unpacks language to find out what a characters wears and why or whether the designer determines how, where and when a character enters a room, their analytical tools foreground different qualities of the play from a director's vision or an actor's interpretation. Theirs is a form of interpretation grounded in providing a framework for others and grounded in the assumption that those present need help to make sense of what is going on. As a result they can discover the visual and aural worlds beneath the explicitly articulated settings of the play. They can discover the way a high status character can be preoccupied with clothes and show how that preoccupation can help an audience member understand why they must behave. They unpack the elements that make the plays more intelligible in performance.

Index

Adorno, Theodor 58, 59, 79
Aldredge, Theoni 85, 93
American Shakespeare Festival 82, 83
Antoon, A.J. 89, 91, 92, 100
Appia, Aldolphe 1, 39, 82
Arditti, Paul 156
Aronson, Boris 81, 87

Bahaus 7, 118, 119, 121, 124, 125, 136
Bailey, James 39–41
Benjamin, Walter xvi, 5, 55, 58, 59, 68, 74,
 78, 79, 80
Berlin Schaubuhne 58, 66
Berliner Ensemble x, 31, 39, 43, 45, 57, 58,
 120, 121, 122, 128, 129, 132, 133, 134,
 135, 136
Blackfriar's Theatre 154
Blumenfeld, Lilja 183
Boyd, Michael 180, 193
Branch, Chris 160, 162, 165
Brecht, Bertolt 5–6, 31, 46, 48, 56, 57, 61,
 76, 79, 81, 84, 89, 92, 120, 163, 168
Brook, Peter 1, 4, 22, 38–53, 155, 167, 169
Burton, Richard 156
Bury, John i, 38, 39, 41, 43, 45–52, 109

Cage, John 7, 48, 118, 119, 120, 125, 165
Calzadilla, Fernando 192
Castellucci, Romeo 183, 194, 196
Charnock, Nigel 173
Chitty, Alison i, vii, x, 6, 102–17, 196
Ciulei, Liviu 95–6, 100
Constructivism 7, 40, 81, 88, 118, 119, 121,
 124, 125, 127, 136, 177
costume design xii, xiv, 1–11, 40–1, 45–51,
 68, 71, 73, 85, 93, 102–17, 127, 130,
 137–51, 175, 177, 185, 195
Craig, Edward Gordon 1, 4, 16, 40, 82,
 118, 124, 179, 193

Crisafulli, Fabrizio 179–80
Cunningham, Merce 7, 119–20, 124
Czech National Theatre 12, 17

De Nobli, Lilia 39, 44
Delacorte Theatre 81–101
Delorio, Victoria 166
Desjardins, Martin 158, 159, 166–8
Divadlo J. K. Tyla 13, 36
Dowling, Joe x, 96, 98, 99
Dromgoole, Dominic 180

Eisenstein, Sergei 68
Electra 87, 92
Ewert, Kevin 152–3, 167, 168

Farrah, Abdel 39, 48
Filter Theatre 9, 153, 159–66
Freedman, Gerald 83–7, 93

Gielgud, John 4
Gill, Peter 103, 105–9, 115, 117
Globe Theatre 154, 155, 166, 167, 174,
 179, 180
von Goethe, Johann Wolfgang 54, 120
Gosch, Jürgen 173
Graham, Martha 81, 87
Greenaway, Peter 173
Guthrie, Tyrone 82, 83, 101

Haines, Tom 160, 161, 162, 163, 165
Hall, Peter 38–53, 109–16
Heeley, Desmond 39, 43
Herbert, Jocelyn 39, 49
Herrmann, Karl-Ernst i, vii, ix, x, 5, 54–80,
 196
Hill, Justin 193
Hill, Loudon Saint
Hirvikoski, Reija 173

Index   199

Holmes, Sean 160
Hurry, Leslie 39–45

Irving, Henry 155, 165, 168
Irwin, Kathleen 189

Jacobs, Sally 39, 43, 50
Jessner, Leopold 16, 40, 54, 82
Johnson, Bruce 163
Jones, Lindsay 157
Jones, Mick 156
Jones, Robert Edmond 4, 40, 82, 105
Jory, Jon 96–8

Kahn, Michael x, 88, 89, 96, 98, 99, 100
Kemp, Lindsey 173
Kennedy, Dennis 1, 11, 36, 54, 78, 80, 82, 101, 174, 193
Kenny, Sean i, 43, 47
Koltai, Ralph i, 39, 43, 47, 48, 50, 107, 113, 117
Kosovski, Lidia 181
Kott, Jan 39, 41, 42, 48, 51, 52, 65, 79

Laterna Magika 12
Lauwers, Jan 174, 183; *The Roman Tragedies* xi, 173–4, 183–91
Lee, Ming Cho i, vii, xii, 5, 6, 81–101, 196
Lepage, Robert 55
lighting design i, ix, xviii, 3, 7, 9, 11, 16, 22–6, 29–30, 35, 40, 46, 49, 83, 85, 105–6, 111, 123–31, 138, 141, 152–3, 177, 179, 185, 191–2, 195
Littlewood, Joan 39, 45–6
London Snorkelling Team 160–1, 164–5
Loquasto, Santo 95
Lord Chamberlain's Men/King's Men 154
de Loutherbourg, Philippe 41
Lyric Theatre Hammersmith 160

Macháček, Miroslav 30, 32, 33
Messel, Oliver 40
Metropolitan Opera 81, 100, 141
Meyerhold, Vsevolod 118–19, 124, 127, 128, 136
Mielziner, Jo 81, 87, 88, 93
Morley, Christopher i, 39, 50, 51 70, 71
Moseiwitch, Tanya 40, 43
Motley 40, 41, 112, 113, 115, 116, 117
Müller, Heiner 57, 78, 79, 119, 119, 121, 173; *Hamletmachine* 57, 173
Myers, Scott 156

Národní divadlo 13, 14, 16, 17, 18, 26, 29, 30, 32
National Theatre [of Great Britain] 92, 102, 108, 109, 110, 112, 115, 116, 156
Neher, Caspar 31, 45, 56, 58
New York Shakespeare Festival x, xii, 83, 85, 88, 89, 90, 91, 92

Old Vic Theatre 46, 82, 113
Olivier, Laurence 33, 102, 109, 110, 117

Papp, Joseph 83, 84, 86, 93
Peer Gynt 56, 60–1, 62, 69, 74–5
performance design 3, 8, 171–93
El Periférico de Objetos 173
Peymann, Claus 55, 56, 59, 76–7, 80
Pleskot, Jaromír 14, 17, 26, 29, 32
Popova, Ludmila 119, 128
Public Theater xii, 90, 156
Punchdrunk xi, 173–4, 186, 190, 194; *Sleep No More* xi, 173–4, 186, 189–91

Quayle, Anthony 40, 52

Radok, Alfréd 12
Rauschenberg, Robert 7, 119–20, 124
Reinhardt, Max 34, 54,124
Riverside Studios x, xiii, 102–3, 104, 106, 107, 108
Rodchenko, Aleksandr 118–19
Royal Exchange Theatre, Manchester xi, 8, 17, 51, 151, 160, 161 162, 164, 166, 168, 195
Royal Shakespeare Company xii, vii, 4, 11, 22, 38–53, 102, 130, 157, 160, 180, 189, 193

scenography 3, 12–37, 38–54, 74, 170–94
Schütz, Johannes 173
Scott, Raymond 160
set design 12–37, 38–54, 81–101, 118–36
Shakespeare, William; *Anthony and Cleopatra* x, 28, 81, 86, 96, 109, 110–12, 115, 116, 173, 174, 183; *As You Like It* 5, 29–30, 55, 56, 57, 60, 61, 62, 65–75, 77, 78, 80, 87, 173; *Comedy Of Errors* 40, 96; *Coriolanus* 57, 173, 183; *Cymbeline* 89; *Hamlet* 14, 15, 16, 17, 20, 23–5, 32, 33, 47, 49, 51, 57, 82, 89, 95, 120, 126–8, 129, 130, 156, 163–4; *Henry IV* 35, 47, 57, 93–5; *Henry V* ix, x, 30, 31, 47, 168, 179; *Henry VI* 47; *Julius Caesar* x, 57, 82, 101, 103–6, 109, 115, 150, 181, 183,

185, 195; *King John* x, 96, 98–9; *King Lear* ix, x, xiv, 10, 22, 23, 25, 40–2, 43, 44, 52, 57, 93, 94, 120, 123–7, 130, 150, 156, 159, 163, 173, 174, 178, 192–3; *Othello* x, xix, 10, 44, 56, 57, 75–6, 77, 79, 96, 97–8, 150, 173, 178, 181, 191–2, 193; *Richard II* 11, 46; *Richard III* x, 16, 47, 49, 56, 59, 79, 82, 87, 88, 94, 137, 157; *Romeo and Juliet* ix, x, 20–1, 23, 41, 52, 89, 96, 97, 101, 173; *Macbeth* ix, x, 25, 26–9, 32, 40, 52, 57, 82, 96, 98, 99, 153, 156, 159, 167, 168, 174, 186, 191; *Midsummer Night's Dream* xi, 1, 18–19, 39, 41, 153, 154, 157, 159–66, 168, 173, 178; *Measure for Measure* x, 52, 57, 78, 88, 89, 105–7, 110, 176, 193; *Merchant of Venice* x, 13, 40, 57, 84–6, 96, 100, 57, 150, 155, 167, 169, 173; *The Merry Wives of Windsor* 13, 181; *Much Ado About Nothing* x, 81, 91–3; *The Tempest* 41, 48, 52, 56, 57, 65, 83, 84, 96, 152, 159, 168, 173, 178; *Timon of Athens* 57, 89; *Titus Andronicus* 40–1, 52, 57, 78; *Troilus and Cressida* 44–5, 150; *Twelfth Night* x, xi, 17, 18, 19, 34–5, 55, 137–51, 160, 165–9, 178; *Two Gentlemen of Verona* x, 91, 150, 181; *Winter's Tale* x, 56, 57, 120, 121, 122, 129, 130, 136
Shakespeare's Memory 55, 56, 60, 62–5, 69–70
SITI; *Radio Macbeth* 156–7
Societas Raffaello Sanzio i, xi, 10, 173, 181, 182, 194, 195; *Gulio Cesare* xi, 181–2, 195
Sontag, Susan 120, 129, 136
sound design 9, 127, 152–69
St Denis, Michael 38, 43
Stein, Peter 55, 56, 57, 61, 62, 68, 70, 71, 73, 76, 77, 80, 174
storyboard x, 6, 7, 102, 103, 104, 105, 121, 195

Stratford Shakespeare Festival 82, 83, 97, 100, 101
Suzuki, Tadashi; *The Tale of Lear* and *The Chronicle of Macbeth* 173
Svoboda, Josef i, vii, ix, 4, 12–53, 55, 196
Synetic Theater; *Hamlet … The Rest is Silence* 157

Tabori, George xvi, 55, 56, 57, 75–7, 80
Ter-Arutunian, Rouben 83–4
Theatre Workshop 39, 45–6
Thomas, Rick 158
Tippet, Michael 102, 114
Tree, Herbert Beerbohm 155, 167, 169
Tröster, František 30, 35

Wainwright, Rufus 131, 134
Wanamaker, Sam 154, 167
War of the Roses 47–8
Weiss, Peter 50
Welles, Orson 5, 82, 89, 156, 197
West, Darron L. 156–7
Whistler, Rex 40
Wilson, Robert i, vii, xv, xvi, 6, 7, 10, 55, 118–36, 173, 183, 196; *The Black Rider* 129; *Deafman Glance* 118; *Einstein on the Beach* 118, 136; *I was sitting on my patio and this guy appeared I thought I was hallucinating* 119; *Orlando* 130; *Shakespeare's Sonnets* x, 120, 124, 131–5
Wonder, Erich 173
Wooster Group 156

Verdi, Giuseppe 97, 173
Versweyveld, Jan 174, 183–7

Zadek, Peter 57, 62, 78, 79, 173
Zeffirelli, Franco 44

Theatre design involves everything seen on stage: not only scenery but costumes, wigs, makeup, properties, lighting, sound, even the shape and material of the stage itself. *Designers' Shakespeare* presents and analyses the work of a half-dozen leading practitioners of this specialist art. By focusing specifically on their Shakespearean work, it also offers a fresh, exciting perspective on some of the best-known drama of all time.

Shakespeare's plays offer an unusual range of opportunities to designers. As they were written for a theatre which gave no opportunity for scenic support or embellishment, designers are freed from any compulsion to imitate original practices. This has resulted in the extraordinarily diverse range of works presented in this volume, which considers among others the work of Josef Svoboda, Karl-Ernst Herrmann, Ming Cho Lee, Alison Chitty, Robert Wilson, Societas Raffaello Sanzio, Filter Theatre, Catherine Zuber, John Bury, Christopher Morley, Ralph Koltai and Sean Kenny.

Designers' Shakespeare joins *The Routledge Companion to Actors' Shakespeare* and *The Routledge Companion to Directors' Shakespeare* as essential reading for lovers of Shakespeare from theatre-goers and students to directors and theatre designers.

John Russell Brown directed plays in England, the USA and around the world. He was an Associate Director of the Royal National Theatre for fifteen years and chaired the Drama Panel of the Arts Council of Great Britain. He authored numerous works on Shakespeare and contemporary theatre, including *New Sites for Shakespeare* (Routledge, 1999) and was editor of *The Routledge Companion to Actors' Shakespeare* (2011) and *The Routledge Companion to Directors' Shakespeare* (2010).

Stephen Di Benedetto is currently Chair and Associate of Theatre in the Department of Theatre Arts at the University of Miami. He is Associate Editor (Drama) for *ASAP/Journal*, Associate Editor for *Scene*, and Treasurer of the Association for the Study of the Arts of the Present. He authored *The Provocation of the Senses in Performance* (Routledge, 2010) and *An Introduction to Theatre Design* (Routledge 2012).

DRAMA AND THEATRE STUDIES / DESIGN

Cover image: Final scene of *Shakespeare's Sonnets*, Berliner Ensemble. Photo: Lesley Leslie-Spinks

www.routledge.com

ISBN 978-0-415-52507-7

Routledge titles are available as eBook editions in a range of digital formats